ROSES

AND HOW TO GROW THEM

by

R. Barton-West

Editor of the "Indian Gardener",
Horticultural Correspondent to the "Asian", "The Statesman"
and Indian Correspondent to the Principal English,
Continental, and American Horticultural Journals

2004

BIOTECH BOOKS

DELHI-110 035

ISBN 81-7622-096-5

Published by : **Biotech Books**
1123/74, Tri Nagar,
Delhi-110035
Ph.: 27382765
e-mail : biotechbooks@yahoo.co.in

Showroom : 4762-63/23, Ansari Road
New Delhi - 110 002
Ph.: 23245578, 23244987

Laser Composed by : **Vaishnav Graphics & Systems**
New Delhi - 110 055

Printed at : **Chawla Offset Printers**
Delhi-110 052

PRINTED IN INDIA

PREFACE

Established custom authorizes and in fact almost demands a preface, the object of which presumably is that the writer may apologise for his own short-comings, if he has discovered them, rectify any errors, and induce the reader by gentle persuasion to wade through his pages. In the present work the writer is conscious of many deficiencies, the subject being not only a large, but a very varied one; this assertion at first sight may appear strange seeing that it only deals with one genus, but then it must be borne in mind that this family embraces upwards of eighty distinct species and thousands of varieties; besides this the subject presents additional difficulties in this country from the great variations in temperature and rainfall in different districts. A book dwelling on the various operations of the garden could be followed with almost mathematical exactness were our seasons equable, but no book ever written or that ever can be written will save the Amateur from the necessity of exercising his own judgement so as to adapt his garden operations not only to the climate but also the weather and the state of the soil.

The principal portion of the matter comprising the present volume has already appeared in serial form either in "The Asian" or "The Indian Gardener." As these papers appeared, the author was gratified by reports from many quarters that the instructions they conveyed were appreciated by, and proved useful to, their readers, and especially from many amateurs, of whom he had never heard before, the request, or rather the suggestion came to collect and extend the papers into the form of a book. Such a reason as "being requested to publish" is not, however, regarded as sufficient for the appearance of this volume. The best apology the author can offer is the conviction that such a publication is needed by many. In the following pages will be found descriptions of upward of one thousand varieties; this list could have been extended almost indefinitely, but it has been considered preferable to include only those kinds that can be thoroughly relied on rather than to tire the reader with a host of names, many of which would be merely synonyms of those now given, or of worthless varieties not deserving of a place in any good Rosarium.

To be practically useful to all classes of readers has been the object throughout the whole work, and every endeavour has been made to make it as plain as possible, presuming that it may fall into the hands of many about to commence the culture of the "Queen of Flowers," and it is hoped that the directions given will be sufficiently intelligible to enable them to successfully prosecute their object, and at the same time prove instructive and useful to those further advanced in the art.

Contents

Introduction

"How much of memory dwells amidst thy bloom,
Rose! ever wearing beauty for thy dower;
The bridal day, the festival, the tomb,
Thou hast thy part in each, thou stateliest flower;
Therefore with thy sweet breath come floating by
A thousand images of love and grief;
Dreams filled with images of mortality,
Deep thoughts of all things beautiful and brief.
Not such thy spells o'er those that hailed thee first,
In the clear light of Eden's golden day,
There thy rich leaves to crimson glory burst,
Linked with no dim remembrance of decay."

Mrs. Hemans

Although we can scarcely follow the imagination of the poetess and trace the history of the Rose as far back as "the clear light of Eden's golden day," still there is abundant evidence to prove, that from time immemorial it has been *par excellence* the flower of flowers. Take for instance the many times the Rose is mentioned in Scripture. The Rev. S. Reynolds Hole, who is undoubtedly the best living authority on the Rose, in his "Book about Roses" (8th edition) writes as follows :-

"When in sacred history, a chief prophet of the Older Covenant foretold the grace and glory which were to be revealed in the New, - when Isaiah would select, and was inspired to select, the most beautiful image by which to tell mankind of their exodus from the Law to the Gospel, slavery to freedom, fear to love, - these were the words that came to him from heaven : 'The wilderness shall blossom as a Rose.' In the Song of Songs the Church compares itself unto the 'Rose of Sharon,' and in the apocryphal scriptures the son of Sirach likens wisdom to a Rose plant in Jericho, and holiness to a Rose growing by the brook of the field."

Much controversy, however, exists as to whether these references are actually regarding the Rose or not, many believing that the first has reference to the 'Oleander,' and the 'Rose of Sharon' is generally believed to be a species of Narcissus. This is borne out by the fact that the Jewish Commentaries so explain the word, the modern name *Buseil* used by the inhabitants being identical with the Hebrew title in the Bible.

Leaving, however, all Biblical references aside, there is the undoubted fact that more than 2,000 years ago Sappho wrote : "If Jupiter wished to give to the flowers a Queen, the Rose would be their Queen;" and, strange to say, this proud title of the "Queen of Flowers" has adhered to it up to the present day. Another ancient writer, Anacreon, in his 54th ode, gives the following fabulous origin to the Rose :-

"When Cytheraea, naked to the light
Waked from her Neptunian birth!
To fill with love the circling earth,
Then, then, in strange eventful hour,
The earth produced an infant flower
By chance, upon a blooming thorn,
Such as the heavenly halls adorn.
Some nectar drops in ruby tide,
Its sweetly Orient buds had dyed;
The gods beheld the brilliant birth,
And hailed the Rose,- the boon of earth!
They bade them bloom, the flowers divine
Of him who shed the teeming vine,
And bade them on the spangled thorn
Expose their bosoms to the morn."

It is generally believed that the Rose is entirely of Eastern origin. Such, however, is not actually the case, its various species being in fact scattered over almost the whole world, several being found in the Himalayas, though none in the plains of India. In China and

Japan at least twelve or fifteen distinct species are found, and it is from some of these, notably *Rosa indica* and *Rosa odorata,* that many of our best families of garden Roses have sprung. America is the home of many diverse forms, extending from Tennessee in the south to the shores of Hudson's Bay, where *Rosa rapa,* a double-flowered variety, is found. In Africa, on the borders of the Great Desert of Sahara, *Rosa moschata,* the parent of all the musk roses, grows abundantly. This is also found in Egypt, Morocco and Madeira.

In Iceland, a country where there are less than a hundred species of plants, *Rosa spinosissima* (known also as the Scotch Rose) grows luxuriantly. In Great Britain there are supposed to be ten distinct indigenous species, France claiming to have seventeen. The Swiss mountains, and the whose of the Alps, contain many varieties, notably *Rosa Alpina,* the parent of many choice kinds. *Rosa hispanica* is confined exclusively to Spain. Germany is the poorest of all the European countries, having only three indigenous species, namely, *R. turbinata, R. arvensis* and *R. lutea.*

Many persons who have taken so prominent a part in public life as to have attracted the attention of history, share, according to the *Pall Mall Gazette,* with the black-beetle a positive distaste for the Rose. The famous Chevalier de Guise could not smell a Rose without feeling uncomfortable; and Venier, one of the Doges of Venice, suffered under the same disqualification for the pursuits of gardening. Anne of Austria, wife of Louis XIII, could not even look at a Rose in a painting without being seized with tantrums. Nevertheless, many people who are willing as a rule to take examples from the great, have persisted in entertaining friendly sentiments towards this flower, and every time that the spring and early summer bring back its flowering season they fall to telling one another all they know about it. In the East there is still a belief that the first Rose was formed by a tear of the prophet Mahomet, but nations of more cool and disciplined imagination have sometimes admitted that its origin is lost in obscurity. Roses were used very early in history among the most potent ingredients of love philters. They seem to have been imported by the Romans from Egypt until the reign of Domitian, Antiochus slept upon a bed of Rose-leaves. Mark Antony begged that Cleopatra would cover his tomb with these flowers, and "mea rosa" was a favourite term of endearment among Roman lovers, as one would say "mon chou" (my Cabbage) nowadays in France. Homer has adorned the shield of Achilles and the helmet of Hector with Roses. Among the Greeks it was the custom to leave bequests for the maintenance of sepulchral Rose-gardens over the grave of the testator; and at Torcallo, near Venice, an inscription may still be seen that shows that this fashion was adopted in Italy. In Stock's collection of engravings on stone there is a beautiful design cut in garnet. It represents a butterfly settling on a Rose, and it is supposed to commemorate the death of a young girl. In Turkey a stone Rose is often sculptured above the graves of unmarried women. A charming bas-relief on the tomb of Mdme. De la Live, who died at the age of twenty, represents Time mowing a Rose with his scythe. According to Indian mythology, Pagodasiri, one of the wives of Vishnu, was found in a Rose. Zoroaster is said to have made a Rose-tree spring out of the earth and bud and blossom in the presence of Darius, who had called upon him to perform a miracle. In Babylon a preparation of shoe-leather was much esteemed when it had been impregnated with the scent of Roses; and Abdulkari, an eminent Turk, who wanted to live there, being made aware of this fact, discovered an ingenious way to profit by it. In reply to a demand which he had made for the freedom of the city, the Babylonians sent him a bowl brimful of water, to signify that there was no room among them for an intruder. Abdulkari placed a Rose-leaf on the surface of the water without spilling a drop of it, and having thus indicated that he might be received without making a mess, he obtained the object of his desire.

In one of the books attributed to Solomon, eternal wisdom is compared to the plantations of Rose-trees at Jericho. Princess Nourmahal, the most lovely lady in the harem of a Great Mogul, had a canal filled with Rose-water and rowed about on it with her august consort. The heat of the sun disengaged the essential oil from the water, and their Majesties having observed the fact, invented otto of Roses. The Emperor Heliogabalius filled a fish-pond with Rose-water – it is nowehere said whether the fishes approved of this proceeding. When the Soldan Saladin, who had so much trouble with the hard-fisted English King Richard and his turbulent Christian friends, took Jerusalem in 1188, he would not enter the Temple, which he profanely called a mosque, till he had its walls washed with Rose-water, and Sanut assures us that 500 camels were no more than sufficient to carry the purifying liquid. Also after the taking of Constantinople by Mahomet II. in 1455, the church of St. Sophia was solemnly purified with Rose-water before it was converted into a mosque. The high priest of the Hebrews wore a crown of Roses when he offered up certain sacrifices under the Mosaic dispensation; and it was perhaps in remembrance of this fact that the Synod of Nismes, which was held in the third century, enjoined every Jew to wear a Rose on his breast as a distinguishing mark of inferiority. In many countries the Jews still celebrate the festival of Easter Flowers, during which they ornament their lamps, chandeliers, and beds with Roses. Thus it happened that these flowers were hateful to the early Christians, and are often condemned in the writings of the Fathers, who professed that they could not understand that pious people could think with equanimity of Roses when they remembered the crown of thorns; afterwards this hostile feeling seems to have died out. When Marie Autoinette passed through Nancy on her way to be married to Louis XVI., the ladies of Lorraine prepared her a bed strewed with Roses. In the Middle Ages, Roses were held so precious in France that a royal license was necessary to grow them. Charlemagne recommended the cultivation of the Rose in his "Capitulation". The Persians of Shiraz stop their wine-bottles with Roses, which gives the wine a pleasing smell; and during the festival of Abrizan, which takes place during the equinox, Persian ladies throw roses at each other when they pay visits. At Rome it was the practice of the Church to bless the Rose on a special day set apart, which was called Rose Sunday. The custom of blessing the Golden Rose seems to have begun in the eleventh or twelfth century. The benediction was pronounced with particular solemnity on the fourth Sunday in Lent, and the Golden Rose thus consecrated was given as a mark of the Sovereign Pontiff's favour to some prince or princess. Alexander III, who had been received with great honour during a journey which he made in France, sent the Golden Rose to Louis the Young as a sort of graceful compliment. Subsequently the giving of the Golden Rose became an authoritative act by which the Pope officially recognised the rights of Christian sovereigns. Thus Urban Vgave the Golden Rose to Joan, Queen of Sicily, in 1368, thereby preferring her to the King of Cyprus. Henry VIII of England received a Golden Rose both from Julius II and from Leo X. Towards the close of the last century the Golden Rose appears to have been given almost indiscriminately to any travelling prince who would pay a sum equivalent to about £400 in fees for it.

There are an infinite variety of stories about Roses. When Milton was blind the Duke of Buckingham, who visited him, observed that his wife was a Rose. The lady had a fine high temper, and so Milton answered that doubtless she was, for he could feel her thorns. Frederick the Great was walking in the gardens of Potsdam with Voltaire, and asked the amazing Frenchman for a Rose. He picked one and presented it to the King with the remark that it had grown beneath his majesty's laurels. Luther had a Rose graven on his seal. A Rose-tree in the park of Roxburgh marks the place where James II of Scotland died. At Santiago, in Chili, whenever a stranger is received in a house each of the ladies of the family offers him a Rose. To show the preference which Madame de-Genlis entertained for old men above old women, she was fond of saying that Oaks improved with time, but Roses faded. It may be mentioned in passing that Madame de-Genlis has the credit, if we have been rightly informed, of having introduced the first Moss Rose ever seen, into France.

Among the incredible number of names given to Roses there is the Rose of Scotland (R. Spinosissima); it is a very prickly flower. The Rose of York and Lancaster (Rosa damascena versicolor), a red and white Rose, recalls the ending of the greatest English civil war. There is quite a nobility of Roses, nearly all the heroes and heroines of history being identified with some flowers of this type. It is as good a nobility as any other. There is even a Brown Rose (*R. Brownii*) in Nepaul, which will transmit that gentleman's name to posterity with the Lawrence Rose, but the Brown Rose will not survive a frost, says the perfect gardener.

Among the Greeks, the Romans, and the Gauls, Parsley, Ivy, Myrtle, and Roses were looked upon as valuable remedies for people who had drunk more wine than was good for them. In Capua Roses were employed by the local medical men as tonics good for stomachs fatigued by over-eating. A decoction of Roses was supposed to have excellent astringent properties. Hoffman recommends it in pleurisy; Paraclesus thinks that when mixed with honey it will lengthen life. A long list of authorities may be produced to show that Rose leaves discreetly used are a perfect cure for hydrophobia. A spirit made or flavoured with Roses was the favourite cordial of Philip the Handsome, and was considered by Charlemagne as a specific against fainting from loss of blood in battle.

A poultice of Roses was long employed for flesh wounds, and Roses preserved are still believed in many places to cure consumption and all diseases of the throat and lungs, a welcome statement if supported by fact, but that is not the case. The best preparation is said to be made from Rosebuds and sugar in equal parts.

The Families of Garden Roses

The following are the principal types or sections into which the Rose family is divided, and also the species from which they have originated :-

Provence or Cabbage	(= Rosa Centifolia)
Moss	(= Rosa Centifolia muscosa)
Scotch	(= Rosa Spinosissima)
Damask	(= Rosa Damascena)
French	(= Rosa Gallica)
Austrian Briar	(= Rosa lutea)
Sweet Briar	(= Rosa rubiginosa)
Bourbon	(= Rosa Bourbonica)
Hybrid China	(= Rosa Indica hybrida)

Hybrid Bourbon. The Roses in this class are obtained by intercrossing *R. Gallica* or *centifolia* with the Bourbon Rose.

Hybrid perpetual. The first vareities of this class were obtained by crossing the Hybrid China and the Hybrid Bourbon and tea-scented varieties. By this means perpetual blooming Roses were obtained; the first of this race was our well-known old friend *Princess Helene;* this was introduced in 1837.

Tea-scented. These all originated from *Rosa odorata* crossed with *Rosa indica,* and were first introduced into Europe from China in 1793.

Noisettes. The parent variety of this family was the result of a cross between *Rosa Indica* or *Rosa odorata* with *Rosa moschata.* This was raised in America and sent to France in 1814.

Climbing Roses

Ayrshire	(= Rosa arvensis)
Multiflora	(= Rosa multiflora)
Evergreen	(= Rosa sempervirens)
Boursault	(= Rosa Alpina)
Banksian	(= Rosa Banksia)
Macartney	(= Rosa bracteata)
Musk	(= Rosa moschata)

Chapter I
Propagation and Cultivation of the Rose

There is probably no plant in cultivation that better appreciates good treatment, or, on the other hand, sooner rejects anything prejudicial to its well-being than the Rose. The high state of perfection to which it has been brought has also given it such a sensitive organisation, that it seems instantly to comprehend when it receives the care and attention due to sterling merit, and rewards us accordingly, and equally as soon repudiates any attempts on our part, either by unskilfulness or neglect, to bring it down to the level from which it sprung. And yet Roses will survive bad treatment, as is so frequently seen in this country, but instead of being a "thing of beauty", are but a continuous source of disappointment to all concerned. Those who wish to grow Roses properly must have plenty of time to attend to them. They must also have a knowledge of the individual varieties, their peculiarities and characters, and must be prepared to meet with failures and losses in spite of appliances, experience and materials, for there are many misfortunes that are beyond the best control, and cannot be helped. To proceed, however, to the propagation of the Rose, we come first to that of seedlings – a mode but few would care to attempt, considering that the seeds generally take four to six months to germinate, and after that from two to three years to flower, and perhaps in a batch of a hundred seedlings not more than one or two would be worth preserving, and yet, to the enthusiast, there could hardly be a more interesting experiment, especially if he has gone to the root of the matter, and carefully hybridised any good distinct varieties. In this country, this could be much more easily accomplished than in Europe, where only a very few kinds can be induced to ripen seed at all; whereas here, provided the flowers were properly fertilised, there would be no difficulty on that score. As for the tedious delay in having to wait two or three years for results, look at the patience exercised by that prince of hybridisers, "Dominy," who waited for upwards of ten years to see the flower of the first hybrid Orchid raised by him - a delay well rewarded, for this was such a grand success that it has completely revolutionized Orchid-growing in England. In a recent article in the *Gardeners' Chronicle,* the following interesting remarks appear on this subject :

"All who write upon and love the Rose have their dreams of the future in regard to it, a hybrid perpetual as yellow as Marechal Niel, or as white as Niphetos, or a dark crimson as large and fine in build as Marie Baumann, while some long for dark teas with strength and vigour, that shall always be as floriferous as the teas are, but with the vigour and strength of the hybrid-perpetuals. All who express these hopes look to the artificial fertilisation of the flower to attain their object; and yet, strange to say, the Rose has not hitherto proved itself so amenable to the efforts of the hybridiser. The very finest Roses that we have up to this time, have been the result of chance hybridisation, not of artificial impregnation. Pradel's great find of Marechal Niel was a chance find, probably from Cloth of Gold, and the grand old Gloire de Dijon came up in a walk in Jacotot's garden at Dijon. Marie Baumann was the result of chance fertiliasation, and it would be hard to name any Roses which can equal them in their respective classes.

"I know not how far English raisers have adopted artificial crossing. Mr. Laxton certainly has done so; but then his Roses though good are not to be compared with foreign-raised flowers."

"We know of some instances where this has been done, but the results have not equalled the expectations of those who attempted it."

Many years ago Old Margottin, of Bourge la Reine, near Paris, who was the raiser of that grand old Rose Jules Margottin (a result of natural cross breeding) felt that Rose-growers were getting too much into the strain of General Jacqueminot, and so he determined on trying what could be done by going back to those of his own strain crossed by others. He has not, however, since then raised a Rose at all comparable to his first production. In 1867 Guillot obtained the Rose La France, which has ever since been so highly thought of, and, despite the adverse opinions of a few Rosarians, it takes one of the very first places among hybrid perpetuals. When Guillot obtained it he used to say that he hoped it would be the parent of a new race. This it certainly has not been; it still stands alone in its glory.

Whatever may be the modern practice among French growers, it certainly was not formerly the habit amongst them to artificially hybridise, and yet all the grandest Roses we have, date back to long periods.

Thus in one of the elections of Roses which took place a few years ago, and to which nearly fifty Rose-growers contributed their opinions, we find amongst the first twelve, Charles Lefevre raised in 1861, Alfred Colomb, in 1865; Marie Rady, 1865; Madame Victor Verdier, 1868; Marie Baumann, 1863; Baroness Rothschild, 1867; Louis Van Houtte, 1869; Marquis de Castellane, 1869; Francois Michelon, 1871; while coming next to them are Dr. Andry, 1864; Comtesse de Oxford, 1869; Duke of Edinburgh, 1868; Senateur Vaisse, 1859; and even now there are only one or two Roses of the last two or three years that are likely to displace these older varieties, namely A.K. Williams, and it may be Abel Carriere.

Let us now turn to English raisers. The grandest Tea Rose almost that we have - Devoniensis - was a stray seedling of forty years ago, and no Tea Rose has ever been raised in "Merrie England" since that time, for Letty Coles was only a sport, and it is to the French, and especially the Lyons' growers, that we are indebted for the lovely flowers belonging to this class. In 1862 Mr. Ward of Ipswich brought out that grand old fellow John Hopper; and although other Roses have perhaps superseded him, and he is not so often seen in the post of honour as he used to be, yet no Rose-grower, however small his collection, would consider it complete unless it included John Hopper.

Now Mr. Ward is a careful hybridiser, but he has not since that time raised any Rose that is worth naming; he did send out two, but their life was a very short one, and they are probably unknown, even by name, to most Rose-growers. Cheshunt hybrid, a Rose that has been generally admired, and which is grown in every garden, has a very doubtful origin. That it was not the result of artificial hybridisation is, however, clear. Mr. George Paul believes it to be a cross between Madame de Tartas (Tea) and Prince Camille de

Rohan (hybrid-perpetual), and his idea is that it is a seedling by insect fertilisation between the two. As a garden Rose it is very fine, standing apparently all climates and vigorous enough in growth to prove a good climber; but it has not proved the forerunner of anything of the same class. We now come to the latest and best known of all the attempts of artificial hybridisation which have been made with the Rose - that of Mr. Henry Bennett, late of Stapleford near Salisbury, who some three or four years ago startled the Rose world with his statements regarding the success that had attended his efforts in hybridising the tea and hybrid perpetual; he announced nine as worthy of being sent out. It was stated that some of them at that time were less than two years old from the seed-pod; a great deal was written in their favour. One of his plants, covered with seed-pods, was exhibited before the Royal Horticultural Society, and he was complimented on his success. There were some doubtful and some adverse criticisms, but these were put down either to trade jealousy or to prejudice. What, however, has been the result? Instead of their being the great success that an enthusiastic raiser imagined, they have, in England, turned out almost a failure. There is one great fault they all seem to possess – they grow well, come freely into bud, and there they stop. We are told, however, that in the hot climate of America they open better. Mr. Bennett seems to have been on the right track; perhaps one of the parents he selected, *alba rosea*, was too full, but it and President and Madam de St. Joseph were the mother plants of the nine he sent out, and these were crossed with Comtesse d' Oxford, Louis Van Houtte, Lord Macaulay, Madam Victor Verdier, &c.

It will be seen from the above remarks that much more has been accomplished by nature than by art in the raising of new varieties of the Rose from seed, up to the present time, and we may, therefore, be content to commence our experiments from self-fertilised seed of any good varieties that we may find available. Many of the older kinds here seed very freely, and amongst a number of seed-pods the probability is that some of them will have been fertilised by pollen from other varieties through insect agency, for the Rose, like most other plants, displays a partiality to being crossed by pollen from a distinct variety in preference to its own. Having secured our seeds they should be sown as soon as ripe in light rich soil, and in shady situation, keeping them carefully watered. Do not be in a hurry to imagine they will not germinate, for as a rule, they will not commence to do so for at least three months, and then only at intervals extending over perhaps nearly a year. As soon as the plants are three or four inches high, they should be either transplanted into beds of good rich heavily-manured soil, or put singly in pots filled with the same compost as recommended for pot roses. Treat them liberally, encourage them to grow as vigorously as possible till the first flowers appear, then reject only those with actual single flowers, retaining all doubles and semi-doubles, noting carefully the peculiar characteristics of each seedling. Grow them for another year under the same liberal treatment till they flower a second time, when you will be able to tell the success that has attended your efforts. Be not discouraged if you do not find a *Paul Neron* or *Marechal Niet* amongst them, or even if you have to discard them all. Let it only encourage to future exertion; the next batch may be more successful. It well remember my first attempt at raising a hybrid Croton, a cross between C. Weismanni and C. Pictum. Out of five flowers fertilised, I only managed to secure one perfect seed. How anxiously this was tended and watched through the period of infancy till it gradually developed, not into a "thing of beauty" oh! no, but into one of the most nondescript varieties ever seen, not even equal to the worst named variety in cultivation, and yet at the time I was more proud of that plant than of any other in my possession, for it was *the first hybrid Croton raised in India,* and conclusively proved that what had been done in Europe in raising seminal varieties of this genus, could be done equally well, if not better, in this country. Encouraged by this I have since raised, and am now raising, a large number of seedlings, and among them there are several that probably will eventually rank high in public estimation.

CHAPTER II
PROPAGATING BY CUTTINGS

We now come to what may be termed the natural method of propagating the Rose, and one which, taking all in all, is perhaps the best; until the last few years, however, it had almost fallen into abeyance, having been completely superseded by budding or grafting. Now, again, it seems to be coming to the fore, and probably in a few years we shall once more find it the most popular system, for it has advantages that no other can claim. In the first place when a plant is on its own roots we are not troubled with suckers of worthless brier – a source of much annoyance, and if not properly looked after, of much loss among grafted or budded plants; secondly, from cuttings, plants are generally far stronger and better bloomers than worked ones, owing probably to the fact that they are not dependent on foreign blood for their support.

It is too generally believed that to strike Rose cuttings successfully is a work of considerable difficulty, and undoubtedly it is when carried out in the manner that we frequently see attempted in this country, that is, at the annual pruning season to take the wood that has been pruned out, cut all into suitable lengths, plant under the shade of some friendly tree, and leave the rest to chance – and a very poor chance too. No wonder we hear so many laments about the difficulties in striking Rose-cuttings. Why don't we treat our Crotons, Draceanas and other foliage plants in the same way? Surely the Rose is worthy of as much consideration as any of them. No; "the truth is just this, these parrot-like cries" regarding the difficulty of striking Rose-cuttings have been handed down from generation to generation of gardeners till it has eventually become a fixed belief that it is almost an impossibility, and where cuttings are inserted at all it is only on the off chance of one or two stray waifs rooting. Having said so much regarding what we have not done, let us now to turn to what we should do to insure a successful result. I am not going to attempt to prove that the Rose can be made to root just as easily and as certainly as the Croton or Eranthemum, for such is not the case; but with intelligent care and management it is possible to obtain as large a percentage of plants as from almost any other method of propagation. First, as to the best season for making cuttings. As a rule Tea Roses and Noisettes root best during the rainy season, and Hybrid Perpetuals and Bourbons in October or November, or again in February and March. However, with proper appliances available in the shape of good close frames or large bell-glasses, cuttings of most varieties may be struck nearly all the year round.

The principal point to attend to is to get the wood in a condition most favourable to the emission of roots; immediately after blooming, when the wood is about three-fourths ripe, is the best, if taken before that they are too succulent, and afterwards the wood becomes too hard. Practice alone will soon teach us the proper stage when the roots seem most willing to bring forth when placed under genial conditions. Insert them at any time when they reach the proper state, and surround them with sufficient nourishment, and they are sure to grow.

Avoid all strong overgrown shoots as much as possible. These never root so freely as the small sized side shoots. Where possible, take these off with a heel, and leave three or four eyes above it. If plenty of these heeled cuttings are available, never trouble to insert any of the top part of the shoots; the latter may possibly root, the former are certain to do so.

The best soil in which to root them in is a compost of one-third each of leaf mould, good rich loam and silver sand. If they are to be struck in a frame, this compost should be filled in to at least a depth of six inches, having first placed a layer of four or five inches of broken crocks for drainage. This is a very important item, as the slightest degree of stagnation would be fatal. Another important point also is to have everything ready, so as to do your work off hand as quickly as possible from the moment the cuttings are taken off until they are inserted, for, if allowed to lie about and flag, it take them a long time to recover.

Where heeled cuttings are not available in sufficient quantity, moderate sized shoots should be selected, cutting them into lengths of four, or at the most five joints each, and the base of each cutting should be cut cleanly through a joint. At least one leaf must be left entire on each cutting, and where possible, two are advisable, but one is imperatively necessary to sustain the cutting until it is properly rooted. And one of the principal points in the after treatment is to keep these leaves fresh and green for at least a fortnight after they are put in, and better still, if possible, till they are actually rooted. The base of the cutting must rest firmly in the soil, and this should be pressed down as hard as possible. For the first three or four days they should be kept entirely dark and all air excluded, giving them a slight sprinkling of water morning and evening. Gradually more air and light may be admitted, but only in the evening and early morning, closing and shading them carefully during the day. The soil about the cuttings must at all times be kept moist, and a fairly moist soil means a genial growing atmosphere, which will promote the formation of root as well as top growth. As a rule, about the end of the fourth week both air and water may be safely increased, assuming always that the grower takes into consideration the state of the weather, for, as a matter of course, in dry parching weather more water will be required than in dull weather when the air is heavily charged with moisture. Another system of growing Roses from cuttings consists in heeling off young buds when about an inch in length, at any time when they can be had in that state. These should be inserted in pure sand and covered with bell-glasses; these require very careful treatment both as regards shading and any excess of damp, which would immediately prove fatal. Roses can be rooted very quickly in this way. There is, however, so much more risk of failure owing to the exceeding delicacy and tenderness of the cuttings, that this method had better be left to the more skilful cultivator. Shirley Hibberd, in his "Amateur's Rose Book", gives the following interesting method of striking cuttings from a single eye or bud :-

Eyes or Wood Buds - The next practice will be to make one leaf and one eye suffice for a cutting with an inch of wood attached, and this is easily done, and ought to be done to prepare the practitioner for a skilful handling of eyes which makes better plants than cuttings, and, in fact, the best plants that can be had; they have the vigour of seedlings, with the advantage of being true to the kinds from which the buds were taken. Once more cut from the tree a nice stout rod of this year. If the buds are pushing good, but if pushed, they will not do. In other words if you see the buds and they look as if they meant to grow this season you are safe; if they have already begun to grow, and have perhaps pushed to the extent of a sixteenth of an inch, reject them, for you will probably fail in all your efforts to persuade them to make roots. Having your nice plump, green rod half ripe, yet in a condition to peel easily, in fact, just such a rod as you would cut if your were intending to bud briers, you are in a fair way to proceed safely. Instead of preparing cuttings, take out each bud with its leaf by a crescent-shaped cut, the same, in fact, as cut for budding briers, but the leaf is not to be removed, and the wood is not to be removed, so you escape all the "niggling" that is the stumbling-block of nine out of every ten amateur rosarians. Have your pans and glasses ready; the pans with a layer of leaf mould at the bottom and at least an inch and a half of silver sand at top. Plant the bud with the

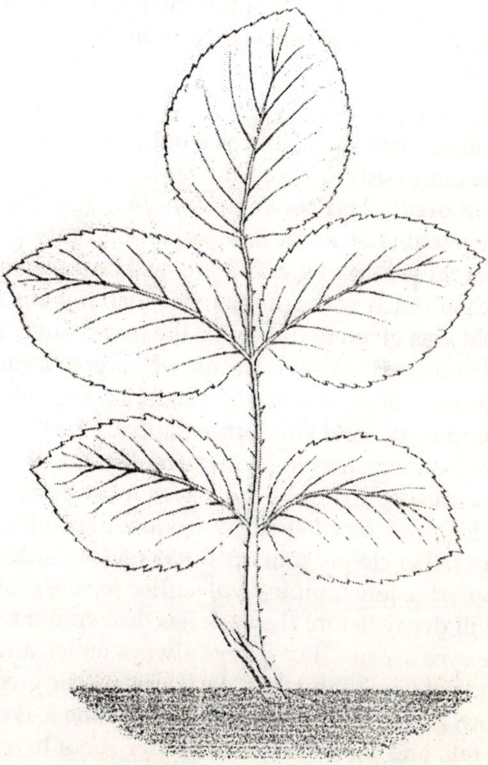

Plate 3 : Single Leaf or Bud Cutting

leaf upright, keep it moist and shaded, and in due time it will throw out roots from the edges of the bark all round, and then the leaf will fall and the bud will start and grow. Having succeeded in preparing the buds properly, perhaps the principal difficulty will be to get them nicely dibbled in so as to stand firm with all their leaves up above the soil. We always take the bud in the left hand, press a hole in the sand with a bit of stick held in the right hand, place the bud in the hole as deep as just to cover the point of the bud with the sand, and then press it firmly with the thumb placed on one side of it. They may be placed very close together in the pans, and if the leaves are very large and when wetted fall over, clip off the top leaflet; the two leaflets then left will suffice to keep the bark healthy till it emits roots for its own keeping.

"When a pan is filled sprinkle the leaves; never mind wetting the sand, if that is just damp it is sufficient; put on you bell-glasses, place them in a frame and take satisfaction to yourself that you have done something."

It is about thirty-five years since we were taught this plan of propagating Roses, and remember as if but yesterday we were told "all you have got to do is to keep the leaves alive, if the buds are dry it don't matter". And so we always found it. There will be hundreds of persons at work this season on buds through the appearance of these remarks, and there will be thousands of eyes lost through too much water. Remember then not our lesson but the lesson that was given to us : "keep the leaves alive; if the buds are dry it don't matter". What is the use of water to a chip of wood that has no roots? Of no use at all; it must be kept plump, but a very little damp in the sand will suffice for that. One the other hand, to keep the sap moving and to preserve the vitality of what is now dependent on absorption only, the leaves must be always moist, and that is to be accomplished by frequent sprinkling and by keeping them rather closely shut up. But herein lies another danger, if not daily aired, a few minutes will suffice for the first fortnight, the leaves will decay before the bark has thrown out roots. If this happens the eyes are lost. But if kept always moist, always warm and close and yet never saturated, the leaves will be green till roots begin to grow, and at the first start of the bud the leaves will turn yellow and fall, and up will rise the tender shoot to tell you that your work was ably done. Of course the process of potting off must then commence, and the little plants must have thereafter all the care needful to make big ones of them. They must be carefully potted in the smallest pots in light sandy soil, and be kept close and warm until they being to grow more fully, and must then have more air and light by degrees.

"If in the dibbling of the buds into the pans it is found difficult to make the leaves stand up, take some fine twigs and stick in to support the leaves, or put a few light stakes round the sides of the pans and draw a few lengths of twine across against which the leaves may rest. But all such small difficulties will shortly vanish; the few manipulations needed are so simple that any one with a will is sure soon to discover a way."

Landolicus in his "Indian Amateur Gardener" gives a description of an American system of striking cuttings of hard-wooded plants or trees. Having tried it with Roses and met with great success, I can hardly do better than give his instruction *in extenso.*

A new method of rearing cuttings of hard-wooded plants is now in vogue, and I have found Roses succeed well when treated as follows :- Make cuttings in the ordinary way, about six inches long (cut close over a bud straight across the stem at the top of the cuttings and obliquely under a bud at the foot of the cuttings, tie them in bundles of fifty, and dip the bottom ends in a mixture of cowdung and water of the consistency of thick cream, take a box about a foot deep, put three inches of ordinary soil into it and press it down firmly. On this put your bundles of cuttings, with the bottom ends of the cuttings upwards. Sprinkle in more ordinary earth between the cuttings and press it down firmly, as you go on adding it, until it is within half an inch from covering the cuttings. Then take soil three parts and sand one part; mix it and fill the box with it, thus completely burying the cuttings. The cuttings should be lightly watered daily, or every two days, as necessary or requisite to keep up a regular moisture for three or four inches of the surface soil only, and the cuttings will, in about eight weeks, or nine at the most, have sent out roots into the surface soil, and most of the buds will have swollen while others have already started into growth. The cuttings may then be taken out by inverting the box bodily, and each one planted as ordinary rooted plants, but with only one, or at the most two buds, above the ground. In the cold season the box may be placed in the garden in the sun, but in the hot weather it is best placed in the shade.

The above are the best methods of propagating from cuttings where proper appliances, such as frames or glasses, are available for the purpose, and while strongly advocating the use of these, we certainly do not wish to discourage those who are compelled by circumstances to grow their cuttings in the open air, for with careful attention a very fair percentage may be obtained.

Perhaps the easiest, and at the same time the most successful method of propagating Hybrid Perpetual and other Roses from the old wood is this : - As soon as the leaves fall, cut the slips into pieces of about four or five eyes each, using of course a sharp knife, so as to make a clean cut - not a pair of shears, which bruises the end of the slip. It does not matter where the cut is made, provided it is a clean cut. The slips may then be planted pretty closely in boxes 3 in. or 4 in. deep, leaving one or two good eyes above the surface, in a soil composed principally of good clean sand free from salt, to which a small quantity, say one-fourth, of loam and leaf-mould may be added. Water well to settle the soil close round the base of the slip, and then place in a cool shady position, watering very sparingly, giving just sufficient to keep the soil moist and friable. When the cuttings are to be grown in the open ground, a position exposed to the early morning sun, but shaded during the rest of the day, should be selected; avoid, however, the too common practice of planting under the shadow of trees. If the soil naturally is not of a free, open nature, enough sand should be added to make it sufficiently light, more so considerably than that which Roses succeed best in when planted permanently. The advantage of this is, that when the plants have become well rooted, they can be taken up for removal with very little loss or mutilation of the roots, as compared with that which is inevitable out of soil that is heavy and adhesive. With a view to still further adapting it for the purpose, it should be thoroughly broken and pulverised, so as to reduce all the hard lumps and fully incorporate the sand with the whole. A good deal of the success, too, depends on the way in which the cuttings are planted after making the soil firm. The best plan is to make a cut with a spade, then let each cutting rest on a firm bottom, treading them in so firmly that a moderate pull with the hand will not remove them. If any commence to grow before the base of the slip has formed a good callus, farewell to all hope of its over making a plant; it may grow as long as the sap stored in the slip keeps it alive, but will then die. The amateur need not get discouraged if success does not attend his efforts the first time. I have seen 99 per cent grow one year, while not over 25 per cents. would reward our efforts at another; but the cause was traceable to neglect, not to the system.

I am informed that the system of growing Roses from cuttings has now almost entirely superseded every other means of propagation at the Royal Botanical Gardens at Saharunpore. Under the method adopted there, Hybrid Perpetuals average 70 to 80 per cent of plants, and the glorious old Marechal frequently produces a plant from every cutting.

CHAPTER III
BUDDING

We now come to what may be termed the "modern" method of propagation. Scarcely more than a century ago it was almost entirely unknown, and only practised by a very few scientific horticulturists who certainly lived ahead of their time, and whose "strange doings" were frequently looked upon as something akin to witchcraft. It is only, however, during the last thirty years that its practice has developed so enormously, having now almost entirely superseded the many systems of grafting, inarching, layering and other means of increasing a vast number of species of plants; but it is principally in the propagation of the Rose that it has become so universally popular, and for this purpose, in Europe and America, it has almost entirely superseded every other means.

In this country, and especially in Bengal, it has, however, been but very little practised. This is probably owing to the difficulty experienced in finding a suitable stock that can be worked easily. Firminger, in his Manual of Gardening, gives the following method of raising stocks suitable for working :

"Lay down in an open piece of ground, at the end of the rains, a good supply of cuttings of Rose Edouard, about a foot long, having first removed all buds but the lowermost one at the base of the cutting and the two uppermost. Lay the cuttings as slopingwise as possible, burying as much as two-thirds of them, so as to leave only the topmost bud exposed, and press the earth down firmly upon them. When they have struck and become thoroughly established, they will be ready for budding upon, but they must be left just as they are till required for that pupose, at which time the earth must be removed, the upper part of the cutting laid bare, and the bud inserted in the usual way as low down on the stock as can be conveniently got at. The bark of the stock will be found always to part readily so long as kept moist by being let remain beneath the soil."

The above remarks apply equally well to *Rosa gigantea,* and this will be found a better stock than the preceding for hybrid-perpetuals and other strong growing roses, but for tea roses it is preferable to substitute the old China rose *Duc de Berri* or *Archduke Charles,* both of which root very readily, and they have the additional advantage that the bark separates much more freely from the wood than either Rose Edouard or *Rosa gigantea.*

The best time for budding is during July and August, as at this time both stock and scion are in a vigorous state of growth, and besides, at this period the bark of both yield more freely than at any other time. Budding in England has now been reduced to such a science, that a really experienced hand will rarely lose more than three to five per cent of the stocks budded. In this country, with its many disadvantages, we can scarcely hope to attain the same measure of success, but still budding, when properly carried out, is much more certain in its results than the style of grafting that is generally adopted here. I remember last season being anxious to get up a good stock of *A.K. Williams,* and had only one old plant of it. By grafting I might have got six or seven plants, but by budding managed to work on about 60 stocks, upwards of 50 of which were successful. Many people imagine that grafting, or rather inarching, is much more expeditious than budding, whereas the contrary is the case. Admitted that you may get a comparatively large plant to start with, the fact of removing it from the parent plant frequently gives it such a shock as to keep it at a standstill for months. A bud, on the contrary, is like a helpless infant made over to the care of a foster-mother, who does not recognise the change of diet till he has become thoroughly accustomed to it, thrives accordingly from the first, rushes along at a glorious pace, and soon overtakes his big brother, who had been rudely torn from the parent stem after having arrived at an age when it had learnt to appreciate the comforts of a maternal home.

Budding is one of those operations that is much more easily practised than described; and, although extremely simple to the initiated, it is far from easy to the beginner, the slightest clumsiness or carelessness marring every prospect of success. The following, which lately appeared in the columns of the *Garden,* gives a very graphic description of the whole process, and we feel assured will prove of much assistance to any of our readers who wish to practise budding for the first time :

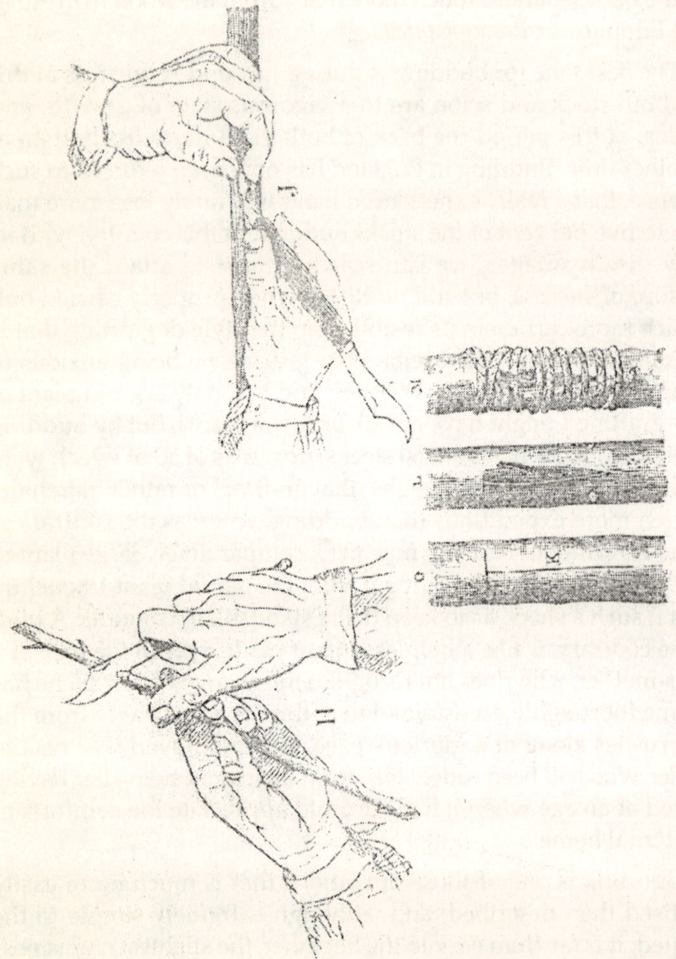

Plate 4 : Propagation by Budding

"The practice of stopping before budding is always of doubtful utility. It is positively wholly mischievous when the stocks are far ahead of the rose buds. So long as the extremities of the roots continue in vigorous growth, the mere ruch of the sap keeps the bark in a running condition. Once the sap is fairly arrested by drought, heat, stopping, completion of growth, or any other cause, the bark gets fixed for the season, and budding from that moment becomes difficult and precarious, if not absolutely impracticable. By cutting Roses early, and even when necessary, sacrificing buds, a powerful influence is given to the plumping up of the woodbuds. Plumping up is essential to success in budding for three reasons. The first is, it gives the bud sufficient viality or selfsustaining power to enable it to support itself until the stock takes it on, or in so closely as to feed it from its own larder - the roots, - and enables it to breathe through its own lungs and heart - the brier leaves-until it is furnished with these vital organs for itself. Further, plump, well filled buds become active agents in promoting the union desiderated between the stock and the Rose. Weakly, imperfectly developed leaf buds, are at best only passive. Should they survive removal from the parent rose, and live long enough in their novel position, the brier may or may not take them on or into its system. The chances are strong that the brier will not. But the first bud rushes half way or more to meet, unite, and become one with the brier, and consequently a union thus promoted from both sides, like marriages based on affection, are sure to prove attractive, successful and happy to all concerned.

The last reason for plumping up buds for budding is that only such can be properly prepared and inserted with all their growable properties intact. It is not till buds are fairly and fully developed that they can be detached from the parent Rose with base, bark and sap in a growing condition. With all these qualities in perfection, the rose-bud takes to the brier as a matter of course. Writing figuratively, its new home is so like its old one, that probably the bud never knows the difference, not at least till it has advanced too fast and too far to retreat. All this, however, assumes not only that stocks and buds are in the most perfect condition, but also that the transference is skilfully and rapidly accomplished, that no clumsy wounds or bruises of bud or bark are made, and that no sap is dried up or mixed with separating water in the process. It would be hard to say whether water or air is the more fatal to a perfect and rapid union.

The wise budder will, as far as possible, avoid both, and make the passage of the buds into the stock as short and swift as possible. The more quickly, the wounds are laid bare both of the Rose bark and brier rind, and the sooner the buds are housed and finally fixed by secure tying into the stock, the higher the ratio of successful budding, and the longer lived and more healthy the roses will prove.

"Some stop the shoots on the stocks a week or two before budding. It gives freer access to the brier and renders the work of budding easier, but the shoots are better left intact. The stopping dams back the sap, and forces the buds off the stock, and also the rose-buds to break into growth. This precocious development is looked upon as an evil to be avoided by the experienced Rosarian. The free flow of the sap along the shoots of the stock helps the foreign buds to take more perfectly, facilitates the healing of the double wounds in the bud and the stock, and keeps the bud from breaking, while enabling it to be filled up plumply with the best that the roots can supply.

Having prepared the stocks, the next operation is putting on the buds. Are they to be picked out singly or cut off in the mass? Must they be kept dry or plunged in water ? May they be exposed to the sun or closely shaded? And should they be taken at morning, noon or night? Such are samples of questions that all who grow Roses have to answer.

"It may, therefore, be useful to answer them once more as briefly as possible. Where the supply is limited, and the Rose buds are near the stock, it may be well to take off each bud singly. Buds may thus be removed from shoots without injuring them much, or arresting their growth. One-third of the section of wood is mostly deep enough for the removal of its shield or section of the bark. This leaves the pith intact, and the shoots will continue to extend as if no buds had been removed from its sides or base. But generally shoots from six to nine inches long are the most convenient from which to obtain a supply of buds. The latter must be plump and well formed, though by no means in a growing state. It is seldom that more than six such buds will be found on a single shoot; the base may be too far advanced, the top too immature for buds.

Cutting the shoots where the useful buds begin, the upper and useless portion is removed as well as all the leaves, except a small portion of the petiole or stalk. The spines are then to be rubbed off sideways with a quick action of the finger and thumb. Shall we plunge them in water till wanted? No, by no means ! Each drop of water that reaches the fresh bark of the bud is a hinderance to its union with the stock. Nor must the buds be dried. Sun or air-dried buds are hindered seriously from growing. If the drying goes far, growth becomes hopeless. Therefore the shoots, with their supply of buds, should be shaded from the sun and sheltered from the air. As to the time to take the buds off and put them on again, morning and night are preferable to noon, and dull days to light ones, though, for reasons already stated, wet days should not be chosen for budding. Having proceeded so far with the buds the next point is to insert them. Dash off the spines on the place selected for the buds; the best spot is about the centre of the space betwen the sets of leaves. Here the bark runs freely. Choose a space as near the base as possible, and this, not because it is always or often the very best possible for the taking of the bud, but to avoid the pest of suckers after the rose is established. Make a slit with the knife about one inch long in the centre of the shoot, and on its upper surface for convenience. A cross cut may also be made at the top or bottom of the slit about one-third round the circumference of the trunk. This facilitates the insertion of the bud with the shield of bark, otherwise it is not essential, and may often be injurious. Great care must be taken not to penetrate the wood in the slightest degree in making either slit or cut. To prevent the possibility of this, the ivory handle of the budding knife is to be preferred for making the vertical slit.

The knife, if sharp, must be lightly handled in making the vertical one. Hundreds of stocks are broken off short by the buds, through the knife slightly penetrating the wood in the making of this cross cut. Slightly raise the bark on one side to see that it runs freely. Then turning to the stock of buds on the branch cut one off, always from the bottom upwards, beginning from a quarter to half an inch below the bud, and penetrating to from a quarter to a third of the diameter of the wood. The section of the wood and bark should average about one inch in length, the thickness depending on the size of the rose wood and the diameter of the stock. The amount of bark is of less moment than that it should be clean cut, unbruised, and that the wood should be abstracted from it without drawing out the base of the bud. Seizing the section of wood and bark in the left hand, between the thumb and middle finger, using the base of the petiole and the bark on either side of the bud as a hold fast, the point of the forefinger is used as a slight lever to separate the bark at the base of the section from the wood. No sooner is this done than the point of the budding knife and the thumb of the right hand are used to grip hold of the wood and give it a sudden jerk out. The moment the bud is freed from the section of wood, it should be plunged into its new home. Raising the edge of the stock already separated, the edge of the shield is slipped under the budding knife, which at the same moment should be brought down under the other edge of the stock, the bud following it home. Not an instant should be lost between the removal of the woody section and the sending the bud home among the healing uniting forces of the stock; once safely home, with no more wounds and bruises than is incident to the operation, leave well alone. The tying should be done at once, and every budder should tie his or her own buds. Various time-saving ties have been suggested, such as those of flexible metal, India rubber, elastic or adhesive felt or paper, &c. But there are no ties in fact equal to wool, matting, or grass. The ties must be tight to render the buds immoveable, for there can be no union apart from immobility at first. Tightness is also needful to get the edges of the bark as close together as possible. The wounds are thus speedily healed, and the bud made part and parcel of the stock as far as its health and supplies of food go. There are different modes of tying, some proceeding from the top downwards, and others from the base upwards; the latter is to be perferred. Either way care must be taken to leave the bud room to swell. In a fortnight or three weeks, or at the latest a month, it is well to go over the plants and remove or renew the ties. Where the buds have taken and the wounds healed, the ties should be taken off. But where the uniting process is not quite completed, a new and looser tie should be substituted for the older one. In all cases, too, where there is any doubt about the union being complete, a fresh tie should be given. As the sudden exposure to the sun of only partially healed wounds often causes them to open afresh and renders them very difficult to heal, this untying is really all that should be done, except in special cases, such as when the stock seems to be taking away most of the strength from the rose, or when the bud has already burst into a shoot. In the former case, the point or a portion of the brier should be pinched out or cut off; in the latter, it is better that the end of the shoot is pinched off after it has made three or four leaves. The pinching in of the rose shoots prevents their being blown out by the wind in cases in which they have not been properly tied to the stakes attached to the stock. The weight of the rose shoot alone is frequently sufficient to wrench it from the stock when the union betwen the two can hardly be said to have grown into solidity. The stopping of course reduces the weight to very small proportions, the three or four leaves left affording but slight purchase for the wind. But this practice has other and more permanent advantages. Started buds, left unstopped, mostly throw their strength into the crowns of the shoots. Their vital force is not seldom thrown away in flowers, which amateur budders are proud of pointing to as triumphs of skilful budding, but the production of which experienced budders discourage. And if these premature shoots do not flower, their best buds are almost sure to be found on their growing extremities. The result is that, when cut back, they break weakly from thin and undeveloped buds at their base; whereas by stopping the shoots the bottom buds are well developed. Consequently these are ready to produce a good shoot each, and thus lay the foundation of a healthy symmetrical plant the first season. On the whole, there is no doubt that dormant buds, as a rule, yield the best results. But some roses are so excitable that almost before they have taken to their new quarters they begin to grow, and wherever such is the case, the pinching plan is far better for the future plant than letting them run."

After the buds are well established and growing freely the stock should be headed back to within three inches of the rose-bud, so as to throw the whole of the sap into the rose. If this is done too soon, or cut too close to the Rose bud, the latter does not grow well. The Rose when in active growth, will soon heal the wound, and absorb all the sap from the stock, and thoroughly takes possession of the brier – in a word becomes in fact a Rose only; but never is the proverb "More haste less speed," more true than in regard to the rapid conversion of the brier or stock into a flowering rose within three months or so of the time of budding.

CHAPTER IV
GRAFTING

You see, sweet maid, we marry
A gentle scion to the wildest stock;
And make concieve a bark of baser kind
By bud of nobler race; this is an art
Which does mend nature; change it rather, but
The art itself is nature."

- Shakespeare

Grafting is one of the most ancient of all the arts or practices in gardening. Till within the present century it was almost exclusively employed for the propagation of every description of plant that would not root readily, or that required stronger blood than its own to support it. With the Rose, this has been almost entirely superseded by budding, which, however, after all, is but a system of grafting with buds instead of wood in a more fully developed state. In Europe many experienced Rosarians still retain grafting proper for the propagation of many varieties, especially of Tea-roses; in this country, however, I believe it has but very rarely or ever been attempted, nor in the plains could it ever be practised with any measure of success, owing to the fact that the Rose with us is always more or less in an excited state of growth; whereas for the successful performance of the operation it is essentially necessary that the scion at least should be practically in a dormant state. Any attempt to graft with wood in which the sap is flowing freely must invariably end in failure, owing to the fact that it loses all its vital forces by evaporation long before it can become sufficiently accustomed to its new home to enable it to draw nourishment from it.

Inarching

Inarching, or more properly speaking "grafting by approach," is the method generally adopted in this country for the propagation of the Rose, and I am sure that any of my readers who have had any practical experience in Rose-growing will readily admit that at best it is a most unsatisfactory system. All that is necessary to perform the operation successfully is to select stock and scion which are not only of the same diameter, but also in the same stage of growth. The most convenient part of each should then be selected, and about one-third of the diameter of both cut away with a sharp knife for a length of two to three inches. The two should then be tied carefully together, taking care, as in grafting, that the inner sides of the bark meet exactly. The union is greatly facilitated if the junction is covered with grafting wax. As soon as the graft has become established, it may be severed from the parent plant, at which time the stock should be headed down to about two inches above the union, so that all its sap may go to feed the young plant established thereon. A mistake frequently made by the uninitiated is to graft the largest and longest branches possible, imagining that they threreby get large plants at once. Occasionally such may be the case, but they quite overlook the large percentage of plants that are lost entirely; the smaller the graft the more certain the union, and the less it suffers when disconnected from the parent plant.

Layering

The best time to layer Roses is during February and March after the plants have done flowering. Roses vary considerably as to the time they take to root, but if put down at the time stated, most of them will be found to be well rooted by the commencement of the rains. Layers are generally made of wood from one to two years old, though a better plan is to take wood of the present season's growth, provided it is sufficiently firm for the purpose. One of the leading English Rosarians, Fish, gives the following instructions on this subject: – " If pieces with a heel can be chosen, and part of the heel be cut off so as to form a portion of the base of the layer, rooting will be all the sooner effected. But any part of a shoot will answer for a layer, provided it is sufficiently matured. Many also layer not only old wood but branches; the larger the layer the larger the plant formed by it. But it should also be added that the longer, as a rule, will it be in rooting, and the greater also the risk that it

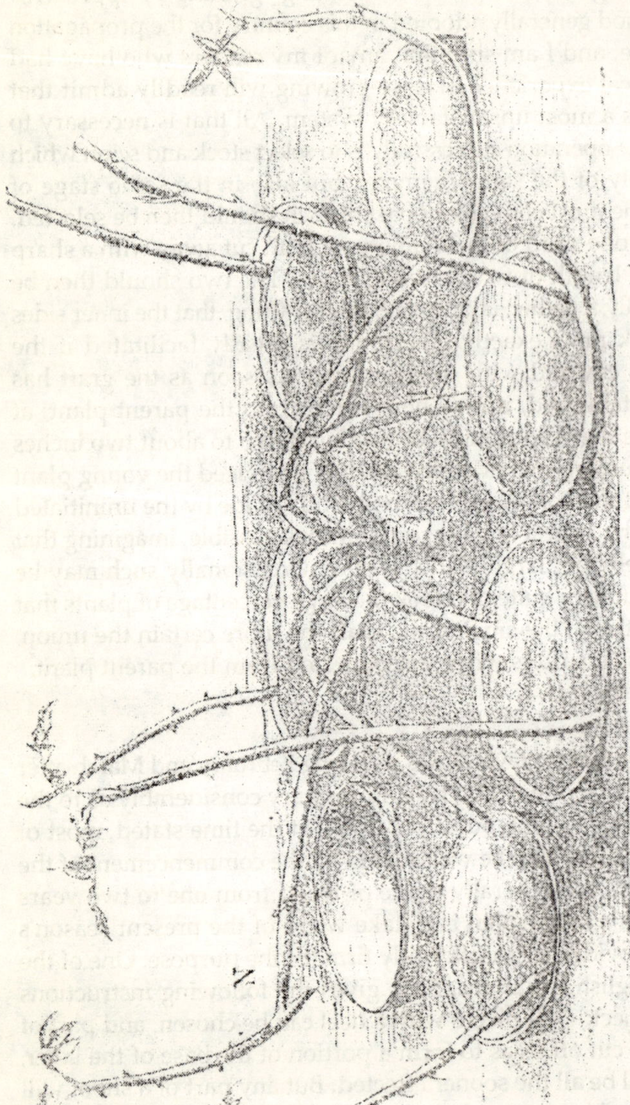

Plate 5 : Layering in Pots

may not root at all. However, layers with from 6 inches to 1 foot of wood beyond the portion buried in the earth are on the whole the best. Any of the more common modes of making the layer may be adopted, such as slitting or tonguing, on the removal of a ring of bark from the layer immediately below a bud. Very few Roses will root by being simply laid in the earth. But by cutting the shoot half through, immediately under a bud, and running a knife up the pith for an inch or two, thus dividing the shoot in half, a very good layer is formed. A small peg of wood or a pebble should be placed in the slit to keep the two sides asunder. The removal of a cylinder of bark, or the tying of a tight ligature round the part layered, answers a similar purpose, though the result is not quite so good a layer. The object is to arrest sufficient sap at the point operated upon to form root, while permitting sufficeint to pass into the layer to support it until it is furnished with sufficient roots to support itself.

The mode of burying the layer. A good deal depends on this; the soil should be dug or forked over, so as to be light and porous. A slit should be made with a spade or trowel, and unless the soil is sufficiently light, place a little sand or light compost on the bottom of the slit. Then place the tongued or barked part of the layer into the slit, twisting or bending it, so that the detached portion shall penetrate the soil as much as possible, and be nearly separated from the growing stem. Press the earth down firmly upon it, and, if necessary, make the whole immoveable with a strong peg near the rose or root end of the layer, and a stake at the growing points. In filling in see that every part of the wound made in layering is closely compacted around with soil, so that everywhere a hard suface may be presented for the layers to strike roots into. It will be well, however, to make sure that they are well rooted before cutting the branch through that connects them with the parent plant. Planted in rich soil, and cut back to four or five eyes, layers make capital dwarf roses. They have rather a greater tendency to produce suckers than roses raised from cuttings, but the suckers being all rose this matters little. Some of the latter, in fact, come so strong and vigorous that it is a good plan to allow them to take the place of the original layers. So sure and certain is this primitive mode of propagation, that to all who have had difficulties in increasing their Roses sufficiently fast by other methods, we would give this advice with confidence–try layers."

In this country care must be taken to keep the layer well supplied with water. To insure this in dry weather, a very good plan is to keep a flower pot half filled with soil over the layered part. The pot should be filled up with water daily. This gradually percolating through the soil supplies all the moisture that will be required.

CHAPTER V
SOILS

There is certainly no subject that is so generally neglected by the majority of amateur gardeners as the proper selection of soils in which to grow Roses. The too prevalent idea seems to be that we must take a soil as we find it, no matter whether it is light or heavy, rich or poor, wet or dry–in whatever state nature has left it, we must be therewith content. And herein lies the secret of half the failures and consequent grumblings as to the impossibility of growing good Roses that we so frequently hear about. But is the soil found in most of our Indian Gardens (that is where it has been well cultivated) unsuited for Rose culture? We certainly think not; on the contrary, we are inclined to believe that it is generally better adapted for the purpose than the majority of soils found even in the most favored districts of England. But there is no soil in the world that would grow Roses–that is Roses perfect in shape and form, and of good size–under the treatment that is too generally meted out to them by our native gardeneres, especially where their employers do not take sufficient interest to personally superintend the management of their gardens. I remember an incident that came under my notice a year or two since. A very enthusiastic amateur, (one of Flora's butterfly acquaintances, who commence at a furious pace and almost invariably break down before they are half through the race) determined to form a Rosarium, and for this purpose a piece of ground was selected that had formerly been used as a vegetable garden, but had remained entirely untilled for nearly three years. This was levelled, dug up to the depth of about six inches only, and the plants put in early in February. These consisted of a really fine collection of young plants in about one hundred and fifty varieties; they were planted three feet apart each way, and a small quantity of half rotten cow manure was given at the time of planting. They were watered freely for the first month or so, and allowed to grow as they liked, without being cut back at all. After the first two months they were left almost entirely to themselves, the owner's ardour even then having commenced to cool down, being in all probability disappointed that he had not reaped the enormous crops of flowers that he had drawn such vivid pictures of is his imagiration. All through the rainy season they were left to take care of themselves. In October an attempt was made to prune them, and while this operation was in progress they happened to attract the notice of an old Rosarian, whose curiosity was excited at what at a distance appeared a wonderfully vigorous growth, considering the short time the ground had been planted. On nearer examination, however, those rampant shoots, which had been the pride and admiration of their owner, proved to be simply suckers from the stocks of *Rosa Gigantea* on which the Roses had been grafted. On going carefully through the plants, it was found that more than half the number of Roses planted had succumbed, and the remainder were in such a weakly state as to render their resuscitation almost an impossibility. When this fact was explained to the unfortunate owner, he was at first incredulous. Could it be possible that those glorious shoots which he had so frequently pictured as being laden with Marie Baumans, Antoine Moutons, A.K. Williams, and other prominent members of Rose society, were in reality worthless briers, and, what is worse, had been the murderers of the foster children that they had undertaken to support? Ultimately, convinced that such indeed was the case, instead of candidly admitting that the failure had been due to his own negligence, some excuse must be found, and what so easy as to blame the soil. Yes, undoubtedly his soil was unsuited for growing Roses. It is a curious fact that almost every failure in gardening is attributed either to bad soil or climatic influences. Do such men think that all soils should be of the same nature as in that Elysium so happily described by one of England's greatest poets, where it is but necesary to "Tickle the soil with a hoe and it will bring forth a flower? "

Roses, as is well known, will succeed fairly well in the majority of soils where the land is not absolutely too wet, or on the other hand of too light and sandy a nautre. Where the former is the case, it can generally be remedied by providing efficient drainage; this will, of course, mainly depend on the degree of elevation, so as to admit of a free outflow of all surplus water, for there is nothing so prejudicial to the Rose as a stagnant soil. Where the soil is too light and sandy, this may be overcome by the addition of good strong loam or clay; but these must be thoroughly pulverised before being applied, otherwise they cannot be easily incorporated with the natural soil. Of course where this has to be done to a great extent it becomes a rather expensive undertaking, but in Rose growing, as in everything else, unless we are prepared to do our work thoroughly we had better not undertake to do it at all, for a hundred plants well grown will invariably give infinitely more pleasure than a thousand that had no trouble bestowed on them.

Where the soil is also deficient in strength, it becomes necessary to make a careful selection of the varieties that should be grown. It is far better to grow a samll number of vigorous, strong constitutioned kinds, than to extend the list to an indefinite quantity of weak growing sorts, that only succeed properly when grown under the most favoured conditions. The Reverend S. Reynolds Hole, in his admirable work on the Rose, gives the following instructions regarding the preparation and improvement of soils.

"The first thing to do with a cold adhesive clay is to drain it, and to drain it well. When water stagnated around the roots of a plant, they cannot receive the air or the warmth which are alike essential to their health, may life. Cut your drains with a good fall, straight, and 4 feet deep; and do not forget when you have made them, to look from time to time, in seasons of wet, whether or no they are doing their duty. Use tiles, not fagots, which soon, in most cases, become non-conductors.

Having provided channels of escape for the superabundant moisture, make it as easy as may be, in the next place, for the moisture to reach them. Trench your ground, and by exposing it to atmospheric influence, make it as porous and friable as you can. Then consider what additions you may introduce to its improvement. 'Anything', writes Morton, in his work upon *Nature and property of soils,* 'which will produce permanent friability upon clay soils - such as sand, cinders, lime, soot, burnt clay, loose light vegetable matter, or long unfermented manure - will alter its texture and improve its quality.' Of these, having tried them fairly, I have found that which is happily the closest to our hand (like a thousand other privileges and blessings had we but eyes to see them) to be the most advantageous–I mean burnt clay. Some of our modern writers and lecturers speak of it as a recent discovery; but the Romans knew it, and used incinerated soils two thousand years before Sir Humphrey Davy wrote, - 'The process of burning renders the soil less compact, less tenacious and retentive of moisture, and properly employed, may convert matter that was stiff, damp, and in consequence cold, into one powdery, dry, and warm, and much more proper as a bed for vegetable life.' Let those Rosarians, therefore, who have heavy, tenacious soils, having first tapped their dropsical patients, by drain and trench, promote their convalescence by a combination of ancient and modern, external and internal pharmacy. Let them unite the old custom of cautery, as they burn their clay, with the new precepts of homoeopathy, *simlia similibus curantur.* And with this object, let them save every thing, as they were wont to do in our school-days when the festival of Fawkes drew nigh for a bonfire. Keep the prunings of your Rosary, that new Roses, like the Phoenix, may spring from the funeral-pyre; preserve all other prunings, decayed vegetables, haulm, roots, refuse, rubbish, weeds, –

> 'Since nought so vile, that on the earth doth live,
> But to the earth some special good doth give.'

And when you have a goodly *omnium gatherum*, make ready your furnace. Arrange your thorns and more inflammable material as a base, then an admixture of more solid fuel from your stores, lightening and condensing alternately, and in the centre disposing some large *pieces de resistance,* such as old tree stumps, useless pieces of rotting timber, and the like, which, once fairly on fire, will go smouldering on for a fortnight. On this heap, well kindled, and around it, place your clay, renewing it continually as the fire breaks through. The pile must be watched, so that the flames may be thus constantly suppressed, the clay burnt gradually and not charred to brickdust. 'The ashes of burnt soil are said to be best,' writes Morton, 'when they are blackest; black ashes are said to be produced by slow combustion, and red ashes by a strong fire.' Blend these ashes with the parent soil, intermixing lime, rammel, or sand (if you can get them), and then there remains, so far as the soil is concerned, but one addition to be made, and of this we will treat presently.

First crossing, if you please, the little bridge which divides my Rose gardens, and passing over the narrow streamlet, from a cold clay soil, fertilised by cultivation, to a light, porous, feeble loam, best described by a labourer digging it, when he said, 'it had no more natur in it than work'us soup.' Nor was it ever my intention to try Roses in this meagre material, until a friend happened one day to say of it, 'No man in England could grow Roses *there.*' Then, fired by a noble ambition or pigheaded perverseness, whichever you please, I resolved to make the experiment. I took a spade as soon as he was gone, for a happy thought had struck me that this soil might resemble that boy-beloved confection, Trifle, which, thin, frothy, and tasteless in the upper stratum, has below a delicious subsoil of tipsy-cake and jam. So I found out in my garden, not far from the surface, a dark, fat, greasy marl, rich as the nuptial almond-paste, and looking as though the rain had washed into it all the goodness of the upper ground. The lean and the fat, the froth and the preserves, were soon mixed for me by the spade aforesaid; and in this soil, trenched and exposed to the air for a few weeks afterwards, I planted my Briers. Then followed the manure of which I have yet to speak, and in due course the Roses. These in their first summer, 1865, (I do not chronicle my success from egotism but as facts for the encouragement of others), won the two first prizes at Birmingham, and two seconds at the Crystal Palace, with very little assistance from their allies over the water; and in 1868 from "Maiden" Stocks - *i.e.,* from Briers budded in 1867 - I won fourteen prizes out of sixteen collections shown, including that which was then considered the champion prize of all, the first awarded to amateurs at the Grand National Show of the Royal Horticultural Society.

In this case as with the heavy clay, the remedy lay close to the disease, and in very many similar cases it will be found that, by intermixing the stronger and more tenacious sub-soil with the surface, fertility may be secured. If not in actual proximity, the element required for a defective soil - clay, for example, when sand predominates - may be procured generally at no great distance, and may be fetched in a waggon or a wheelbarrow in accordance with ways and means. Let Horticulture in this matter learn a lesson from her younger sister; and let the gardener who is whimpering over his rood of unkindly soil remember what the farmer has done and is doing, the wide world over, amid the forest and the fen. And such pusillanimity is specially comic in the case of a Scotsman or Englishman, who is surrounded by a thousand proofs of triumphant cultural skill; who may walk, from dawn to dusk, among golden corn, where once the antlered monarch spent his life, unscared by hound or arrow; among flocks and herds, knee deep in herbage, where fifty years ago the black cock crowed amid the purple heather, where

> "The coot was swimming in the reedy pond,
> Besides the water-hen so soon affrighted;
> And where, by whishpering sedge, the heron, fond
> Of solitude, alighted."

Chapter VI
Manures

Probably in the whole practice of Rose-growing there is no point on which so much controversy exists, even amongst our most experienced Rosarians, as on that of the most suitable manure for the Rose; every grower of experience has his own nostrum on the subject, and thinks it superior to all others. Some writers (Canon Hole for instance) believe the Rose such a glutton as to be capable of swallowing anything placed within its reach, and would make our Rose beds a veritable dung-hill. Other writers, again, would almost eschew solid manures altogether, being content to feed their favourite on liquid diet only. Many strongly advocate the use of artificial manures, and another school, with equal force, warns us to beware of them all. "Who shall decide when doctors disagree" The truth is, the Rose might exclaim with the apostle, "All things are lawful for me, but all things are not expedient." Or in other words, the Rose can accommodate itself to almost any kind of manure used in moderation, but in the case of many of them, if used at all freely, their evil influence soon shows itself. The effects of different manures on plants is a subject that should be thoroughly mastered by every gardener. There are many manures which, although very powerful, have but a transient effect on plants; others have a tendency to promote a heavy growth of wood. Some again improve the flowering qualities of the plant either in quantity or colour; a few are very slow in assisting the plant, taking months before it has any effect. Therefore, before manuring at all, we ought to know what object we have in view, and giude our actions accordingly. For instance, if our plants are weak and not growing freely, we might use stimulating manure, such as oil-cake, which would make them rush forward at a bound; its effect, however, would be but fleeting, and it must soon be followed by some other more permanent stimulant, otherwise we shall have done more harm than good. If we want more wood we must use seethi (indigo refuse), well decayed horse manure, or guano, all of which are wood producers; the latter must be used very carefully, any overdose of it is liable to have a fatal effect. If we require a manure to have a powerful, and at the same time lasting effect, as, for instance, in making up new Rose beds, we must have recourse to superphosphates, phosphates, or bones in some form or another.

And, lastly, for the production of flowers, we must have a manure, gentle, yet powerful in its action, one that is not fleeting in its effects, but that will act as a lasting store from which the plant can draw its food. And to secure this *sine qua non* of success must be the first thought of every one who desires to grow good Roses. Many of our readers will probably here remark - "Why, everybody knows what manures are best adapted for Roses; there cannot be two opinions on the subject, we have no occasion to search for anything different from what our predecessors have used for years!" But is such really the case - is there any unanimity of opinion even amongst the most experienced growers as to the most suitable food for the Rose? Let us seė what the most successful English Rosarians say on the subject. The Rev. S. Reynolds Hole, the premier amateur Rose champion, says : - "I will tell you where I found the Philosopher's Stone in the words of that fable by A Esop, which is, I believe, the first of the series, and which was first taught to me in the French language, - "*Un coq, grattant sur un fumier, trouvait par hazard une pierre precieuse;* " or, as it is written in our English version, "A brisk young cock in company with two or three pullets, his mistresses, raking upon a dunghill for somthing to entertain them with, happened to scratch up a jewel". The little allegory is complete : I was the brisk young cock, my favourite pullet was the Rose, and in a heap of farmyard manure I found the treasure.

"Yes, here is the mine of gold and silver, gold medals and silver cups for the grower of prize Roses; and not dear all who love them, the best diet for their health and beauty, the most strengthening tonic for their weakness, and the surest medicine for disease. 'Dear me !' exclaims some fastidious reader, 'what a nasty brute the man is ! He seems quite to revel in refuse, and to dance on his dunghill with delight!' The man owns to the soft impeachment. If the man had been a Roman Emperor, he would have erected the most magnificent temple in honour of Sterculus, the son of Faunas, that

Rome ever saw. Because Sterculus, the son of Faunas - so Pliny tells - discovered the art and advantage of spreading dung upon the land; and he should have appeared in the family chariot, the *currus Stercorosus (Anglice,* muck-cart), with the agricultural trident in his hand. As it is, I always think of him with honour when I meet the vehicle in which he loved to drive - have ever a smile of extra sweetness for the wide-mouthed waddling charioteer, and am pained at heart to find the precious commodity fallen, or, as they say in Lancashire, "slattered" on the road. Ah ! but once that fastidious reader will be pleased to hear, the man brought himself to sore shame and confusion by this wild passionate affection. Returning on a summer's afternoon from a parochial walk, I inferred from the wheeltracks on my carriage-drive that callers had been and gone. I expected to find cards in the hall, and I saw that the horses had kindly left theirs on the gravel. At that moment one

Grim spirits in the air,
Who grin to see us mortals grieve,
And dance at our despair,

of those fiendishly suggested to my mind an economical desire to utilise the souvenire before me. I looked around and listened, no sight, no sound of humanity. I fetched the largest fire shovel I could find, and was carrying it bountifully laden through an archway cut in a high hedge of yews, and towards a favourite tree of "Charles Lefebvre,"when I suddenly confronted three ladies, "who had sent round the carriage, hearing that I should soon be at home, and were admiring my beautiful Roses". It may be said with the strictest regard to veracity, that they saw nothing that day which they admired, in the primary meaning of the word, so much as myself and fire-shovel; and I am equally sure that no Rose in my garden had a redder complexion than my own."

And now to be practical, what do I mean by farmyard manure– when and how should it be used?

By farmyard manure I mean all the manures of the straw yard, solid and fluid, horse, cow, pig, poultry, in conjunction. Let a heap be made near the Rosarium, not suppressing the fumes of a natural fermentation by an external covering, but forming underneath a central drain, having lateral feeders, and at the lower end an external tank, after the fashion of those huge dinner dishes whose channels carry to the "wells" the dark gravies of the baron and the haunch (here that fastidious reader collapses, and is removed in a state of syncope) so that the rich extract, full of carbonate of ammonia, and precious as *attar*, may not be wasted, but may be used either as a liquid manure in the Rosary, or pumped back again to *baste the beef.* How long should it remain in the heap before it is fit for application to the soil? The degree of decomposition to which the farmyard dung should arrive before it can be deemed a profitable manure, must depend on the texture of the soil, the nature of the plants, and the time of application. In general, clayey soils; more tenacious of moisture, and more benefited by being rendered incohesive and porous, may receive manure less decomposed than more pulverised soils require.

I will quote in alphabetical sequence the other distinguished public Rosarians who have expressed their opinion, or proved their skill at all events, in the matter. These are Mr. Cant of Colchester; Mr. Cranston of Hereford; Mr. Francis of Hertford; Mr. Keynes of Salisbury; Mr. Lane of Berkhampstead; Mr. Mitchell of Pittsdown; Mr. George Paul, the representative of Messrs. Paul and Son, Chestnut; Mr. William Paul, Waltham Cross; Mr. Prince of Oxford; Mr. Turner of Slough, and Messrs. Wood of Maresfield. There is, of course, a very large number of other nurserymen who grow Roses most extensively and in their fullest perfection - such as Smith of Worcester, the two firms of Dickson at Chester, Harrison of Darlington, House of Peterborough, May of Bedale, Perkins of Coventry, Frettingham of Nottingham, Merryweather of Southwell, Bennett of Salisbury, &c.– one or more near all our cities and towns; but I have selected those who are our principal prize-men, and whose treatises and catalogues are before me.

Mr. Cant says: "In planting Roses, a hole should be made about 18 inches deep, and large enough to contain half a wheel-barrowful of compost; two-thirds of this should be strong turfy loam, and one-third well decomposed animal manure. These should be thoroughly mixed together."

Mr. Cranston writes in his *Cultural directions for the Rose,* which may be followed by amateurs with sure confidence. - "I have found, after repeated trials for some years, that pig-dung is the best of all manures for Roses; next night-soil, cow-dung, and horse-dung. These should stand in a heap from one to three months, but not sufficiently long to become exhausted of their ammonia and salts.

Pig-dung should be put on the ground during winter or early spring, and forked in at once. In using night-soil, mix with burnt earth, sand, charcoal-dust, or other dry substance. Apply a small portion of the mixture to each plant or bed during winter, and let it be forked in at once. Soot is a good manure, especially for the Tea-scented and other Roses on their own roots; so are wood-ashes and charcoal. Bone-dust or half-inch bones forms an excellent and most lasting manure. Guano and superphosphate of lime are both good manures for Roses, but require to be used cautiously."

Mr. Keynes of Salisbury recommended "A good wheelbarrowful of compost - two-thirds good turfy loam, and one-third well decomposed animal manure." He adds - and the words of one whose Roses, in a favourable season, could not be surpassed in size or colour, should be remembered practically - "It is difficult to give the Rose too good a soil."

Mr. Lane of Berkhampstead writes thus : - "The best method of manuring beds is to dig in a good dressing of stable or other similar manure, this being the most safe from injuring vegetation in any soil, and it never does more good to Roses than when it is used as a surface dressing. When placed about two inches deep over the surface in March, the ground seldom suffers from drought; but this is, perhaps, by some considered unsightly."

Mr. George Paul, "the hero of a hundred fights," advises, that "in planting, the ground should be deeply trenched, and well-rotted manure be plentifully added. If the soil be old garden-soil, add good loam, rich and yellow; choose a dry day for the operation, and leave the surface loose. Stake all standards and mulch with litter, to protect the roots from frost."

Mr. William Paul in his interesting work *The Rose Garden*, gives in the introduction the results of his experiments with manure. "In the summer of 1842," he writes, "six beds of Tea-scented Roses were manured with the following substances; 1 bone-dust, 2 burnt earth, 3 nitrate of soda, 4 guano, 5 pigeon-dung, 6 stable-manure, thoroughly decomposed. The soil in which they grew was an alluvial loam. The guano produced the earliest visible effects, causing a vigorous growth, which continued till late in the season; the foliage was large and of the darkest green, but the flowers on this bed were not very abundant. The shoots did not ripen well, and were consequently much injured by the frost during the succeeding winter. The bed manured with burnt earth next forced itself into notice; the plants kept up a steadier rate of growth, producing an abundance of clear well-formed blossoms; the wood ripened well, and sustained little or no injury from the winter's frost. The results attendant on the use of the other manures were not remarkable : they had acted as gentle stimulants, the nitrate of soda and bones least visibly so, although they were applied in the quantities usually recommended by the vendors... I think burnt and charred earth the best manure that can be applied to wet or adhesive soils."

Mr. Prince says : " My plants on the cultivated seedling Brier do not require so much manuring as other forms of stocks. I do not recommend any manure at the time of planting, unless the ground has been greatly impoverished by trees and shrubs or Roses, in which case a portion of the soil should be removed, and a fresh supply given which should consist of the top-spit from a meadow of heavy loam, well decayed; but it should not be forgotten that after the Roses have been planted for two years and are well established they will require a liberal supply of manure. I have found that the worst attacks of mildew first made its appearance on young plants in land which had been manured at the time of planting."

Mr. Turner of Slough does not show his cards, but when he comes to play them on the green cloth or baize of the exhibition table, no man deals more fairly, knows the game more thoroughly, holds more trumps or scores the honours more frequently.

Messrs. Wood of Maresfield, perhaps the largest growers of the Rose in the world, commend a mixture of well-seasoned animal manure with the top-spit of an old pasture, deep trenching, thorough draining, and a free use of the pruning-knife the first year after planting.

Rivers, the patriarch of Rose growers, writes : - "I have found nightsoil, mixed with the drainings of the dunghill, or even with common ditch or pond water, so as to make a thick liquid, the best possible manure for Roses poured on the surface of the soil twice in winter, from one to two gallons to each tree."

We have here the opinions of the ten largest Rose growers in the world - men who grow Roses not by the hundred or thousand, but in tens and hundreds of thousands yearly. Landolicus in his work *The Indian Amateur Rose Gardener,* in referring to the publications of English writers on the Rose, says :- " Many of them are written by nurserymen and those interested in the sale of Roses who do not care to publish to the world what they consider their secrets." This we believe to be an entirely erroneous idea. Were it true, it would brand the nurserymen writers as the most narrow-minded of all individuals, so narrow-minded indeed as to be blind to their own interests. For in what does the prosperity of the nurseryman consist? Certainly not in the failures of his constituents, who may perhaps come to him to replenish their losses, but who more frequently give up Rose growing in despair or disgust. No ! the nurseryman's mainstay are those who encouraged by their successes become enthusisatic on the subject, and year by year launch out on a larger scale, feeling that

"A million scarce would quench desire."

We may rest assured that those who write on the Rose are quite alive to this fact, and give out their secrets unreservedly, knowing that in so doing they are not only promoting the welfare of the Queen of Flowers, but their own also. Undoubtedly there are many who share the opinion of Landolicus regarding professional authors, and for what reason? Why, simply because being imbued with this idea they are either too sceptical to follow the advice given, or, if they do so, do it in a half-hearted fashion, which in itself is generally sufficient to insure failure.

To return, however, to the opinions quoted above; it will be seen that all of them differ more or less from each other, and some of them very materially so. All these growers occupy almost an equally prominent position in the Rose world - men who have year by year fought right royally for the chief honors at the National Rose show and have each in turn been victorious. How then are these differences in opinion to be accounted for ? If each of these growers has secured the maximum of success, and all of them through different channels, it may be supposed that the Rose cannot be fastidious as to its fare, but that like the genus porcine it will fatten on any diet. Such, however, is not the case; the one great secret in Rose-growing–the secret by which all these different methods of treatment are reduced to one level–is simply this, that we must select our manures not so much to suit the Rose as to suit the soil to which it is applied. For instance burnt clay, or incinerated soil, has a wonderful effect on heavy loam or clayey soil, but were these applied to a light porous loam or sandy soil, we should be doing incalculable harm.Dressings of clay or tank earth are very useful in improving very light soil, but were these applied to heavy lands we should probably create a stagnant swamp. We may, however, go further than this; as is well known, the component parts of soils vary immensely, some are rich in nitrogenous elements and almost entirely devoid of mineral matters, in others, the former are almost entirely absent and the mineral elements are superabundant. Now with the former were we to apply a manure rich in nitrogen it would not only be wasted, but would probably cause much injury to our plants; in the same way with the latter, if we applied any stimulant in which mineral properties are superabundant we should do quite as much if not more harm. Our object therefore should be to find out first what properties are deficient in the soil, and supply those wants to the best of our abilities.

There is one point, however, on which the authorities quoted are all more or less of one mind, that is, regarding the value of animal manures as a diet for the Rose. This may be accounted for by the fact that in the majority of them the chemical properties required by the soil are almost equally balanced, or, if present in excess, are in such a mild form as rarely to prove injurious, that is of course provided they have been properly prepared and matured before being applied, for there is no more dangerous enemy of the Rose in the hands of an unskilful practitioner than that of partially fermented manure.

From our own experience we should say that the most suitable manure for the Rose that we have in this country is cow manure and horse manure mixed in equal proportions, the latter should be at least two years old, if older all the better. These, however, differ very much in quality, that from home-fed animals being immeasurably superior to that from bazar cattle. This fact must be borne in mind if we are desirous of using manures to the best advantage. To give some idea of the extent to which the value of animal manures are influenced by the quantity and kind of food consumed, we append the results of experiments made by Sir J.B. Lawes, who is undoubtedly the most reliable authority on agricultural matters.

Table showing the estimated value of the manure obtained from the consumption of one ton of different articles of food, each supposed to be of good quality of its kind.

	Description of food	Estimated money value of the manure from one ton of each food		
1.	Decorticated cotton–seed cake	£6	10	0
2.	Rape cake	4	18	0
3.	Linseed cake	4	12	0
4.	Malt-dust	4	5	0
5.	Lentils	3	17	0
6.	Linseed	3	13	0
7.	Tares	3	13	6
8.	Beans	3	13	6
9.	Peas	3	2	6
10.	Locust beans	1	2	6
11.	Oats	1	14	6
12.	Wheat	1	3	0
13.	Indian Corn	1	11	6
14.	Malt	1	11	6
15.	Barley	1	9	6
16.	Clover hay	2	5	0
17.	Meadow hay	1	10	0
18.	Oat straw	0	13	6
19.	Wheat straw	0	12	6
20.	Barley straw	0	10	6
21.	Potatoes	0	7	0
22.	Mangolds	0	5	0
23.	Swedish turnips	0	4	3
24.	Common turnips	0	4	0
25.	Carrots	0	4	0

"The valuation of the manure resulting from the consumption of different foods is founded upon estimates of their compostion, and upon a knowledge, experimentally acquired, of the probable average amount of those constituents of the food valuable for manure which will be obtained in the solid and liquid excrements of the animlas. In the estimates of the value of the manure from different foods given in the above table, I have based my calculations upon what I consider the average composition of several articles when of good quality."

Liquid Manures

The application of liquid manures to plants is now much more extensively practised than formerly, and there is no class of plants that is so much benefited by it as the Rose, especially when grown in pots. The most useful liquid manures are soluble guano at the rate of two ounces to the gallon of water, and fresh cow manure thoroughly mixed with water and allowed to stand till it becomes perfectly clear : one thing must be borne in mind, that is never to give liquid manures too strong. It is better to err on the side of weakness, as the dosing can always be repeated for plants in the ground; once a fortnight during the growing and flowering season will be ample, but it may be given to pot plants weekly. Soot also makes an excellent manure, especially where worms are troublesome, as it has the effect of driving these troublesome pests to seek other quarters.

CHAPTER VII
PLANTING AND TRANSPLANTING

Where to Plant

In the formation of a new Rosarium the first question that arises is–where shall we find the best situation? Unfortunately, in most instances, it is a case of "Hobson's choice." The amateur gardener, especially in the vicinity of towns, has very rarely any option in the matter; he must take the situation and the soil as he finds them, and resort to artificial means to render the latter a fitting home for the Queen of Flowers, and if he is imbued with that ardent love for his favourite that burns so fiercely in the heart of every true Rosarian, he will think no obstacle too great to overcome so that in the end he may attain success. Many people seem to imagine that the Rose will grow anywhere, and bestow no more care on its cultivation than they would on the most miserable weed in their gardens. They plant Roses indiscriminately among evergreen shrubs, or under the shade of huge trees, and expect them to grow well. It is from this class of growers that we so continually hear– "Oh! it is useless trying to grow Roses in India; neither the soil nor climate is adapted to them." Only a few days since in conversing with an amateur on this subject he informed us that since he saw the grand blooms at the National Rose Show when at home last year, he had determined to give up Rose-growing in despair. We might have asked if he had ever grown Roses at all. He may have put a few plants in the ground, and after that left them to take care of themselves, too careless even to give them the water or food essential to their existence; further than this we believe he never attained, and yet he talks of giving up in despair. Let him first start Rose-growing in earnest; grow them as they ought to be grown, and see how quickly his despair will vanish. The Rev. S. Reynolds Hole says : "he who would have beautiful Roses in his garden must have beautiful Roses in his heart." This is undoubtedly true, and forms an insuperable obstacle to a very large class ever becoming the possessors of beautiful Roses, for the love of pocket so fills the heart as to leave no room for anything else to find a place therein. This is especially the case when the new candidate for admiration draws heavily on the resources of the dearer idol. Good Roses cannot be grown without liberal treatment, and liberal treatment means liberal expenditure.

Has our friend, who was led to despair by seeing such beautiful Roses, any idea of the labour, patience and skill, to say nothing of the expense incurred, in producing these prize blooms? He will probably scarcely credit the fact that in most instances each individual exhibit of 24 or 48 blooms or trusses had been selected from perhaps 5,000 or 10,000 plants, and frequently more. As to these blooms being so far in advance of anything seen in this country, that is simply imagination : there are hundreds of situations in this country in which as fine Roses may be produced as have ever been grown in England. Rest assured the Rose wants no change in our climate, but rather intelligent and liberal cultivation and a careful study of its requirements to enable us to grow it in its full beauty. Above all things the Rose must have a free circulation of air; it must be both exposed and sheltered, and also have sunshine and shade; it must be so arranged that all the plants will have the benefit of the sun during the fore part of the day : this can be effected by extending the garden from north to south, thus making it of an oblong or semi-circular form. The northern fence should be tall and dense, the western should also be tall, but not necessarily so dense as the northern, except in districts where scorching west winds are prevalent. The eastern boundary must be kept at such a height that it will not obstruct one ray of sunshine; at the southern end we may have a dwarf thick hedge to break the force of heavy winds, but this, except in very exposed situations, is not absolutely neccessary. The above remarks apply more particularly to places where sufficient space is available to provide separate quarters for the Rose. In the majority of amateur's gardens, however, no such accommodation is possible, and our favourite must be grown either in exposed beds, on lawns or borders, or mixed with foliage plants. By the former plan, if the beds are properly prepared, Roses may be grown to the highest state of perfection, but they can rarely be induced to thrive satisfactorily when mixed with anything else, especially strong growing shrubs or foliage plants. These not only absorb the food and nourishment essential to the well being of the Rose, but also deprive them of the air, light and sunshine that is indispensable to their existence.

In laying out a Rosarium it is advisable to avoid all intricate figures, for it is difficult to fill them with Roses, and it is rarely expedient to introduce any other kinds of plants among them. Avoid also the too common practice of dividing the grounds up into too many beds. Fifty or a hundred plants in a batch may have a good effect, but if this quantity were divided into a dozen groups, they must necessarily present a paltry appearance. The following design, which is given in Shirley Hibberd's Rose Amateurs' Book, is one of the most suitable we are acquainted with. It is so simple that it can be laid out by any intelligent gardener, and can be modified so as to suit any position. The beds may be of any desired length, but they should not be more than from eight to ten feet in breadth, with a three feet grass or gravel path running between them. This design is a modification of the most celebrated Rosarium in Europe, that of the Jardin du Luxembourg at Paris

Where standard Roses are not available, or cannot be grown successfully, the east and west borders may be planted with dwarfs, with a strong trellis at the back, on which climbing Roses should be trained. The finest Rose garden we have seen in India is laid out on the plan given. In this all the centre beds are planted with hybrid perpetuals, each bed being ten feet wide and sixty-four feet long, and contains 60 plants, there being three rows of plants placed three and a half feet apart. The plants are put at intervals of three feet in the rows, and a grass path three feet wide runs between the beds. A border twelve feet wide surrounds the Rosarium, this is planted entirely with Tea Roses, placed three feet apart each way, about six hundred plants of this family being grown. At the back of the borders, on the north and west, is a stout wire fence ten feet high, on which are trained Marechal Niel, Gloire de Dijon, Climbing Devoniensis, Solfaterre, Cloth of Gold, and a few other vigorous-growing varieties. On the east side there is a similar fence, but only six feet high, and this is entirely devoted to the stronger varieties of Tea Roses or Hybrid Teas, Cheshunt hybrid being a particular favourite, its glowing colour contrasting favourably with the more delicate shades of the other members of the family. On the south side there is a grand hedge of Sweet Brier, about four feet high and

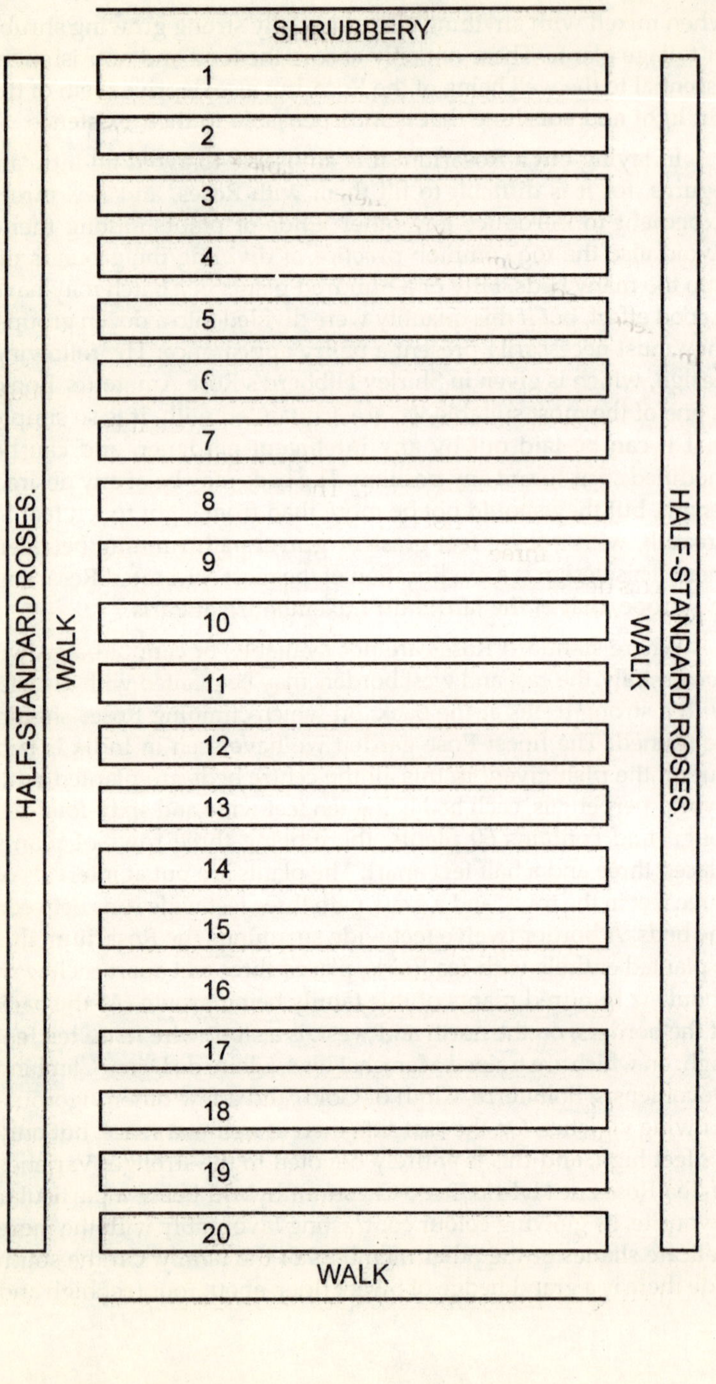
SHRUBBERY
1
2
3
4
5
6
7
8
9
10
11
12
13
14
15
16
17
18
19
20
WALK
HALF-STANDARD ROSES.
WALK
WALK
HALF-STANDARD ROSES.

nearly the same depth; this is kept carefully trimmed, and is almost as regular and perfect in shape as a well kept Box edging. The entire Rosarium contains about two thousand plants, occupying less than three quarters of an acre of ground, its dimensions being 285 X 100 feet. This is undoubtedly on a larger scale than the majority of amateur gardeners would care to embark in. In the formation of a Rosarium the first expense is, of course, the principal consideration, for when once established it is surprising what a small expenditure is necessary to keep it in first rate order - less certainly than many of us bestow on other hobbies or pleasures, frequently of a much more frivolous nature, that give no enjoyment except for the moment, and are entirely devoid of that lasting gratification that is experienced by those who ardently love the Rose, and have the means and the time at command to give their Queen the attention she merits.

When to Plant

The best time for planting Roses in this country is in October or February, the former month for preference, as the plants take more kindly to a new position and experience less check at this period than any other. Plants that have been growing in pots may be put out at almost any season of the year, provided they are kept well supplied with water till thoroughly established. All Roses are the better for being moved every two or three years into fresh soil, for, as with other trees and shrubs, we must induce them to make healthy fibrous roots; and this can only be done by transplanting at intervals. When plants are allowed to remain for a number of years in the same position, they invariably form long bare roots with scarcely any fibres, and, as a natural consequence, the top growth becomes lean and scraggy, and the flowers lose considerably both in size and colour.

How to Plant

How to plant is of as much consequence as when to plant. Every thing must be done with care and forethought,–forethought in supplying them with good healthy stimulants at the roots to keep them for a few years–care not to damage the plants at all in removing. The question of soil and manures has already been fully treated in previous chapters, and it is therefore unecessary for us to say anything on the subject here. In all cases the beds should be thoroughly prepared some time before they are required for planting. The soil should be *at least* two feet deep, this should be filled in first and then the manure added, forking it in well to a depth of twelve or fifteen inches only; if put deeper it has a tendency to draw the roots downward - a danger to be guarded against. We all know that Roses are what are termed "gross feeders," and delight in manure, but even this can be overdone, especially when it is dug in carelessly and allowed to remain in large lumps below the surface. In this state it is positively injurious. It is very important therefore that it should be thoroughly incorporated with the soil; the exact proportion of manure required will depend of course on the nature of the soil–the poorer the soil the more manure will be needed and *vice versa.* To plant a Rose properly the roots should first be carefully examined, every bruised or torn root should be cut off smoothly above the wound lest they should decay and develop fungoid growth, tap roots should be shortened so as to discourage downward growing. Suckers must be carefully removed, and where *Rose Edouard* or *Rosa gigantea* has been employed as a stock, every eye below the planting level should be cut out, so as to prevent the chance of suckers springing up from below the soil amongst the shoots of the genuine Rose, from which it is very hard to distinguish them when young. Have the holes dug sufficiently large to receive the roots when fully spread out. One of the most frequent errors in planting Roses, is that a careful expansion of the roots is not attended to before filling in. Place the plant in the centre of the hole, so that its collar will stand even with the level surface of the ground, unless it is a budded or grafted one, when it should be set two or three inches deeper; them fill in with rich soil, treading down carefully, so that every root and branchlet of root shall be firmly imbeded. Roses require firm planting, that is, the soil ought to be trodden down two or three times while planting is going on, till the task is complete. It will greatly encourage the emission of roots if they are previously plunged into a liquid compost of soil and powdered cow manure of about the consistency of mortar. The method of planting, whether singly, in beds, or in groups, must be governed by the circumstances of the individual planter; but this does not in any way affect the manner of setting in the ground. If planted in groups, the taller growing kinds should be planted in the centre or back ground, grading downwards towards the outside; if placed in rows, they should be at proper distances, so that each shall form a specific object in itself as well as a portion of the row. Plants should never be crowded together; for hybrid perpetuals the rows should be at least four feet apart, and the plants three feet from each other in the rows.Tea Roses of course will not require so much space; if planted three feet apart each way, it will be amply sufficient. Deep planting should also be carefully avoided. The roots should be covered to a depth of about six inches and no more; if planted too deep, plants will neither grow freely nor bloom well. Make the soil fine, round and over the roots, tying each plant firmly to a stake, as it is very important that the roots are not moved after planting. After all is finished give a good watering and lay on a coating of three or four inches of manure over the surface of the beds; this not only retains a proper degree of moisture in the soil, but acts as a kind of reserve store from which the plants will be fed as its nutritive properties are gradually washed into the soil.

The Origin of Red Roses

To sinless Eve's admiring sight
The Rose expanded snowy white,
When in the ecstacy of bliss
She gave the modest flower a kiss;
And instantaneous, lo ! it drew
From her red lips its blushing hue;
While from her breath it sweetness found,
And spread new fragrance all around.

– Hooker

Chapter VIII
Pruning

This is undoubtedly the most important of all operations in Rose-growing. Good soil, rich manures, and, as a consequence, strong healthy plants, all go for nothing provided they are not accompanied by an intelligent system of pruning. Now this is a thing that can only be learnt by experience, and regarding which it is utterly impossible to lay down any hard and fast rules; for we must not only take into consideration the peculiar habits of each plant, that is as to the variety being a weak or strong grower, and the particular group to which it belongs, but we must also bear in mind any peculiarities of soil and climate. Some recommend pruning twice in the year, that is just at the commencement of the rainy season and again in October. From my own experience I should say that, unless under very exceptional circumstances, it is preferable to prune once only, and that not till the end of October or November. Pruning in the hot months is always attended with danger, as at this season any sudden check is frequently attended with fatal results, especially among Tea Roses. Even in October we must not be too eager to commence operations, it is far better to delay a little until we are thoroughly convinced that the rainy season is completely over. Nothing is gained by pruning too early, and frequently much is lost, especially if we have any heavy rains after-wards. Firminger, and several other Indian authorities, state that Roses are best pruned as early as September, or not later than the commencement of October. This I am convinced is a bad practice, and for the following reasons :–at this season, in most parts of India, the rainy season is in full swing, Roses continue to grow vigorously and the wood is full of sap; it is impossible at such a time to open out their roots so as to induce the plants to rest, and promote a proper ripening of the wood, for if we did so we should probably wake up some morning to find most of our plants washed up by the roots. It is equally futile to prune before the wood has been properly ripened, for in such a case the probability is that our Rosarium would resemble a plantation of Briers without a single flower to enliven it, for we all know that the one great secret in the production of prolific crops of either fruit or flowers is to have thoroughly matured wood of the previous season's growth. On the other hand late pruning possesses many advantages. If delayed till November all danger of heavy rains is over; the soil is more easily worked, the superabundant moisture having drained off : this being the case, the roots require to be exposed for a much shorter time than they would at an earlier period. The leaves fall naturally, the wood becomes thoroughly ripened almost to the extremities of the shoots. When such is the case, prune as we may, short or long, we may rely on a bountiful crop of flowers, for they are already there in embryo. I may relate the circumstances that induced me to become such a strong advocate for late pruning. In the season of 1882, through press of work, I was unable to get a fine bed of hybrid perpetuals pruned till about the middle of December, and did so then only to get the plants into reasonable shape, being fully convinced that it was far too late to induce them to flower properly. They were however manured freely and treated in every respect the same as my other plants. Time passed on, they broke most vigorously, almost every bud producing a massive shoot, but all my Rose-growing friends, like myself, was convinced that it was only wood without the chance of a flower, at least any worth naming. We soon, however, had cause to change our ideas on the subject, for as these shoots developed, almsot every one proved to be a flower bearer, and in less than two months from the time of pruning they were in full bloom, and such blooms, for either quantity or quality I have never seen equalled in Calcutta during the fifteen years I have been an enthusiastic Rose grower. And the same opinion was expressed by every one who had the opportunity of seeing them. This, however, in itself could not be taken as a convincing proof of the value of late pruning. My unexpected success might be due to some fortunate chapter of accidents with which I was unacquainted. It was, however, quite sufficient to induce me to repeat the experiment on a larger scale. Accordingly in 1883 I divided my Roses into seven groups, the first was pruned on October 10th and the others at intervals of about 10 days up to December 10th. On this occasion the four last sections were in every way superior to the three groups pruned first. This, however, did not convince several of my Rose-loving friends who had watched the experiment with interest, as in consequence of having had two or three days of very heavy rain early in November it was thought probable that this had a bad effect on those first pruned. In 1884 I proceeded on precisely the same lines, and the experiment was again attended with the same result : the plants pruned in November not only produced finer flowers, and in larger quantities, but were in bloom several days earlier than those pruned in October. Early pruned plants of course grow more vigorously and produce an immense amount of useless wood, the shoots frequently attaining a height of three or four feet before the flower buds are visible. Late pruned plants produce short jointed shoots, in most cases blooming before they are more than a foot in length.

Pruning is an operation that requires much care and intelligence in its performance, and can but rarely be safely entrusted to a native *malee,* few of whom have sufficient knowledge of gardening to be able to distinguish the various families of Roses, or to understand the different requirements of each particular class.

The great point in pruning Roses is to know how much or how far they should be cut back, and what wood should be retained and which removed. Did we know our Roses more perfectly, each variety would have its own special cut that would suit it best. In the absence of such knowledge, we are compelled to proceed on more general lines; first hybrid perpetuals; these may be divided into two classes, namely those of a vigorous habit and those of a weaker growth; the former do not require such severe pruning as the latter, for if these are not cut down closely they invariably break very weakly. Cut out all old flowering wood, also any weak and useless shoots, leaving only those that are well matured.The number of these will of course depend on the size of the plant, but as a rule four or six stems are ample to form a good bush. The vigorous growing kinds may be left twelve to fifteen inches long, and the weaker kinds from six to nine inches only; much, however, must depend on the size and maturity of the wood.

While some do best with only moderate pruning, others require to have one-half or two-thirds of the last season's growth removed; but with all pruning a well shaped top should be kept in view; this can be attained by a combination of cutting and tying to position. The terminal bud at the cut should be left in the position which will most readily promote growth of the desired form : for instance, if a more spreading form be desired, cut so as to leave the bud on the under or outer side; if a compact or upright head be sought, the reverse course should be pursued. Strong, healthy wood is always desirable, therefore in pruning cut out the weaker, reserving the strongest to make the new growth from. Always prune with a definite and fixed form or object in view. Vary the pruning with the requirements of the different varieties, and also for the positions they are to occupy ; as a rule a cup-like form is the best shape at which to aim, each shoot springing away equally outwards and upwards from a common centre. Therefore, prune back to a bud planting outwards, whether it be the second, third, fourth, or fifth bud from the base, in the case of an established plant, and afterwards, when the growth is more advanced, disbud all shoots having a tendency to unduly crowd the centre, or cross or interfere with the others. This is a rule which should guide the inexperienced not only in Rose pruning, but also in that of all other kinds of bushes. In the case of newly planted Roses prune back to three, four, five, or even six buds from the base, bearing in mind what has been said.

The extent to which Roses require pruning not only varies considerably in the case of different kinds, but also as regards the object the cultivator has in view. If you desire quantity, regardless of quality in bloom, cut and disbud sparingly; but if quality is the first object, cut out all weak wood, and then cut away all wood of last year's growth down to one, or at most two eyes, and then you may go still further and cut out one-half of what is left. If with judicious pruning your Roses do not produce magificent blossoms, you may conclude that there is something wrong or wanting in the soil.

For ordinary purposes it is better to prune less severely, as numbers of flowers are generally more acceptable than a few exceptionally large ones. It is difficult to convey in writing the exact method advisable to follow, as even many individual varieties require to be somewhat differently treated to others; but it may be taken as a safe rule that the stronger the natural growth of the variety, and the more vigorous the state of the individual plant, the less pruning is needed, for the obvious reason that a plant in this condition is calculated to support a greater number of shoots with a proportionately larger crop of bloom than one that is weaker either by accident or the less vigorous habit of the sort. In all cases it is advisable to remove completely out from their base the whole of the weak, thin wood, the produce of last or previous seasons, and which has not sufficient substance to push shoots strong enough to flower, for the presence of these uselessly taxes the energies of the plants, drawing support which is better concentrated in the stout, blooming wood. These weak growths also tend to crowd the plants, keeping out both sun and air. With Roses that are naturally weak growers it is necessary to prune to fewer eyes than in the case of the strong ones, otherwise, if left too full, the flow of sap is directed to the formation and support of a much greater number of shoots than are ever strong enough to bear flowers, to the manifest detriment of those which are.

Tea Roses require very careful pruning; many of these have a great antipathy to the knife, and immediately resent any free use of it. Cut away all thin and weakly wood, shorter all the old blooming spurs to one, or at the most two eyes, from the main shoots; this will generally be found suficient for most members of this family. Noisettes again require but very little pruning; thin out all weak and useless wood, slightly shorten the stems or branches left, so as to throw the sap back into the buds and cause them to break freely. That grand old Rose - Marechal Niel - especially dislikes pruning, and should be left as much alone as possible, simply contenting ourselves with cutting out any very weak or spent branches. If, however, plants have become too crowded, it is better to remove some of the main stems at once from the bottom.

Chapter IX
Growing Roses in Pots

How rarely one meets with a good collection of Pot roses in this country. Various reasons may be assigned for this : the first is of course the large amount of extra care and attention required to induce them to thrive satisfactorily as compared with plants in the open ground. The Rose is certainly not an easy plant to cultivate successfully in pots, being liable to suffer from heat, drought, damp, vermin, mildew and mismanagement, these enemies becoming doubly dangerous in unskilful hands. A Rose in the open ground can draw its own moisture, if there is any in the soil within two or three feet of the surface, but plants in pots are entirely dependent on the discretion of the grower for water, food, and all essentials to its existence, failing any of which, or receiving an excess of any, it is in danger of losing both its health and beauty even if it continues to survive under bad treatment. The too frequent practice amongst our ignorant native gardeners is just to pot the plants in any ordinary garden soil, without any preparation whatever; afterwards to give them a regular supply of water daily, whether the plants need it or not, imagining that in so doing he has done everything necessary for the well-being of the plant; as well might we except any animal to thrive and do his work satisfactorily if deprived of his daily allowance of corn; for the Rose is a gross feeder, and if not frequently supplied with a liberal diet in the shape of liquid manure and occasional top dressings of prepared soil, it can never be induced to bloom freely or continue long in good health. Another mistake frequently made is to grow the plants in pots much too large for them. This certainly tends to induce the plants to grow with greater vigour, but unfortunately at the cost of sacrificing all the flowers we look so anxiously for. A leading English Rosarian writes on this subject in the *Garden* as follows: "Accepting the principle of giving more root room when the plants most need it, and only when they need it, it follows that, while some sorts of Roses might need shifting once a year, and not always that; others, such as the evergrowing evergreen Tea Roses, might need to be shifted two or three times a year. This brings us to the extent of the shifts; anything like the one-shift system would prove fatal to Roses in pots (it is this system which is generally adopted in India); on the contrary the shifts should be as small as practicable, from a 4-inch to a 5-inch or 6-inch, from the latter to a 7-inch, 8-inch, or 9-inch, and so on. An inch, or at most two inches at a time, is amply sufficient. This slow progressive enlargement of root room keeps the whole mass of soil filled with rcots; these also speedily reach the sides of the pots and produce that state of things known to cultivators as pot-bound; the effect of this on inflorescence is well known to all practical men, and it is no exaggeration to add that in the case of Roses a pot-bound plant of the same area will produce double the number of flowers as one with its roots in free and loose soil. It is not eay to explain the reason of this, but the fact no one can doubt who is familiar with the cultivation of Roses and other plants in pots."

As to food and water, Roses in pots and out of them are gross feeders and great drinkers. In pots both of these qualities seem intensified by the limited area of their feeding quarters and drinking cisterns. However rich the soil in which they are potted, its feeding properties are soon exhausted by the roots or washed out by the water; hence the necessity of rich solid top dressings and liberal applications of liquid manure. The former can hardly be too rich, the latter may easily be so, for the first are partly decomposed before coming into contact with the feeding roots, the latter goes direct to, and if too strong destroys or cripples them; weak and often, as soon as the Roses are in full growth, should therefore be the rule in regard to all liquid manures. Some of the best for pot Roses are those made of guano at the rate of two ounces to the gallon, or sheep, pigeon or cow manure. The pigeon manure is the strongest, and needs to be used with caution. Either of the others, when thoroughly decomposed, may also be used as solid top dressings, either by themselves or mixed with equal parts of rich loam. Pot Roses should never be allowed to suffer from want of food or lack of water; the amount they use up when in full growth is very great. It must not, however, he supposed that all the water given is absorbed; it very quickly passes through, and the soil becomes dry. The smaller the pots relatively to the area of the plant, and the fuller the pot is of roots, the more frequently must the plant be watered. Over-watering is, however, equally or more injurious than under-watering, and it is needful to steer clear of both extremes. Roses in pots are also much benefited by overhead syringing, especially towards evening, as these prove a capital substitute for heavy dews or rains and also tend to keep the foliage clean.

Proper Compost for Pot Roses

Volumes almost have been written on this subject. Every kind of manure has been recommended, such as blood, bones, night-soil, pigeon manure, malt-combs, etc., etc., until not a few have turned away in disgust from rose-growing because of the unsavoriness of the prescribed aids to growth. Now there is no denying that the Rose in full vigour of growth is what is called a gross feeder, and it is politic not to enquire too nicely at times about the sort of table it has dined or supped at. It is hard to define the best soil for Roses, but it is agreed on all sides that they delight in rich turfy loam from an old pasture, especially if it has been frequently grazed by sleep; if the soil is of a clayey nature all the better. Soil should be collected at least six months before it is required for use. April or May is the best time, as by laying through a rainy season the fibrous matter would be partially decomposed. The surface of the pasture selected should be pared off to a depth of four or six inches and piled in convenient heaps, with the turf downwards, to a height of three or four feet; if very dry, water should be freely added to encourage a slight fermentation; the whole mass should be turned over at least once a month, in fact the oftener the better, and the sooner it will be ready for use. All this can be easily done by residents in the Mofussil or suburban districts, but few living in towns have either the necessary space available, or would care to go to the expense of bringing it from a long distance. In such cases we must make the best possible use of whatever soil is at our command, and endeavour to the best of our ability to add whatever may be lacking to make it fit for our purpose.

But in starting Roses in pots no gross food is needed; they will start and make more roots in less time in a good loam than in any other nostrum whatever. Should it not be sufficiently light, add a fourth part of silver sand. The roots will grip hold of such a soil with avidity, and fill it full of fibre as if by magic; whereas they often sulk and turn away from rich composts consisting of a third or a half of manure, night-soil, bullock's blood, etc. Charred refuse, or earth, may also be used as the plants advance in growth, and even a third or a fourth of well decomposed strong manure. Bone dust, hoof-parings, and horn-shavings have also been used as composts for Roses; these may be sparingly used for the second or subsequent shifts, but at first the great object is to get many roots of moderate strength rather than fewer and stronger ones, and hence fibry, moderately rich porous loam is the best compost for potting up Roses. As soon as the roots show freely through the side of the balls, shift into larger pots, taking care, however, not to overpot Roses on this their first or any subsequent shifts, for, as before remarked, Roses, like most other plants in pots, invariably flower freest when partially pot-bound.

How to Pot Roses

Potting is too frequently looked upon as a very trifling matter that can be done by any *malee* or gardener without supervision. On the contrary, however, it is one of the most imporant operations in the garden, it being what may be termed the starting point either to success or failure. For instance, many plants require to be planted as lightly as possible in the soil, others require a medium degree of firmness, and with many, again, it is impossible to pot too firmly; and, if this is not observed, plants will never thrive satisfactorily.

Having selected the proper size of pots for the plants to be changed, which should not be more than two or three inches larger than those in which they had been growing, fill up with about one-fourth of broken crockery or potsherds; then cover this with about two inches of soil, shake the plant out of the old pot, gently pressing the ball of earth so as to loosen it, place the plant in the centre of the large pot, taking care not to injure the fibrous roots, fill in soil carefully all round, and having armed yourself with a flat-headed stick, ram down the earth all round as hard as asphalte; then put in more and ram down again till the pot is completely filled; then stake firmly and give a copious supply of water, placing the plants in a shady situation for a few days.

Selection of Varieties for Pots

To grow pot Roses successfully, we cannot take varieties indiscriminately as is too frequently done in this country, the consequence of which is the long reed-like stems, with perhaps not a leaf on them for three or four feet of their growth, that we so often see in gardens. The great aim in growing pot Roses should be to produce plants of a dwarf and bushy habit, well clothed with foliage, and, of course, to flower freely. All this may be attained by careful pruning and a judicious selection of varieties, provided, of course, that all the other points in their cultivation are properly attended to. The Tea Roses, hybrid teas, and hybrid China roses are all well adapted for pot culture, these being all dwarf in habit and flowering very freely; but unfortunately amongst these there is not that diversity of colour that is so dear to the heart of every true lover of the Rose; for although these will supply us with every shade of white, blush, yellow, apricot, salmon, and pale pink, it is to the hybrid-perpetuals that we must turn for all the more glowing and brilliant shades of colour. Unfortuantely amongst these there are many of such an extremely vigorous habit of growth as to totally unfit them for growing in pots. The following selection of fifty varieties belonging to this family may, however, be depended upon to produce satisfactory results if properly treated. This list includes many of the finest varieties in cultivation. In a future chapter I hope to give a full description of them.

Alfred Colomb	Duke of Wellington
A.K.Williams	Edouard Morreen
Antoine Ducher	Etienne Levet
Baron de Bonstetten	Elie Morel
Baroness Rothschild	Exposition de Brie
Beauty of Waltham	Ferdinand de Lesseps
Boule de Niege	Francois Michelon
Charles Lefevre	General Jacquiminot
Centifolia rosea	Horace Vernet
Comtesse d'Oxford	Hippolyte Jamain
Duc de Rohan	John Hopper
Duke of Edinburgh	Jules Margottin
Duchess of Edinburgh	John Stuart Mills
Dr. Andry	La France
Dupuy Jamain	Le Havre
Louis Dore	Monsieur Noman
Louise Van Houtte	Mr. Charles Wood

Marie Baumann	Prince Camille de Rohan
Marechal Vaillant	Princess Mary of Cambridge
Marie Rady	Reynolds Hole
Mdme Clemence Joigneaux	Sir Garnet Wolseley
Mdme Hippolyte Jamain	Sultan of Zanzibar
Mdme Victor Verdier	Victor Verdier
Mdme Therese Levet	Pierre Notting
Monsieur E. Y. Teas	Xavier Olibo

Resting Period

One of the greatest difficulties to contend with in the cultivation of the Rose in pots is to give the plants a certain period of rest, so as to ensure a thorough ripening of the wood, without which it is hopeless to expect a satisfactory production of flowers. In a cold climate, where the plant remains in a dormant state throughout the winter, this object is thereby attained, but here, where the plants are always more or less in an excited state, we must necessarily resort to artificial means. At the end of the rainy season remove all the soil from the pots to a depth of from three to six inches (according to the size of the pots) so that the roots are fully exposed to the sun, and withhold water entirely for at least ten days or a fortnight, after which re-pot those that may require a shift, giving the others a top dressing of manure mixed with an equal quantity of rich loam, water must then be supplied freely, and as soon as the plants show signs of starting into growth prune them as may be required.

Pruning

Probably more Pot Roses are entirely spoiled by injudicious pruning than from any other cause. The usual course is to prune and simply to allow them afterwards to grow in whatever form they may choose to take. On their own roots, in genial soil, they yearly acquire strength such as necessitates, at the time of annual pruning, the specimens being allowed to get to a larger size, especially in height, the result of which is that the strong shoots, from which the greater portion of the flowers are produced, grow to a considerable height, at which point most of the blooms are borne, leaving the plants comparatively thin and bare at the base. Although it is anything but desirable to train Roses in a way that gives any approach to formality, still such an arrangement of the shoots may with advantage be employed as will keep them well furnished with a fair proportion of vigorous growth and full-sized flowers down to the pot, at which point the plant should have the greatest breadth, gradually tapering up to the top. At the time of pruning, or soon after growth has commenced, a portion of the strongest shoots should be bent down and tied out horizontally over the edge of the pot; this is easily effected by fastening a stout wire just beneath the rim, to which the branches may be tied. The remaining growths should be shortened back to different lengths, to assume the position such as will lay the groundwork for the specimen which later on will be clothed with foliage and flowers. The central branches, according to the more or less strong-growing erect habit of the variety, may require a few sticks to hold them in their places, but the whole of such supports will be effectually hid by the foliage, and no trim outline should be attempted.

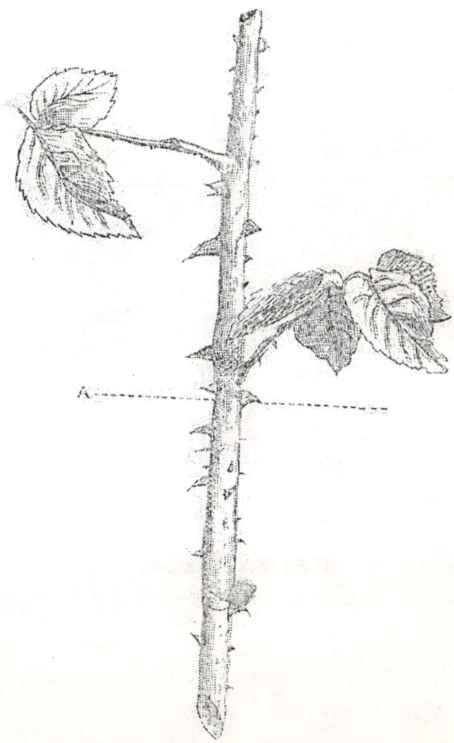

Plate 2 : Cutting Prepared for Planting

(H.P.) Mrs. Laxton

Tea, Devoniensis

Chapter X
Rose Enemies and their Consequences

The grower of Roses who is not troubled with insects injuring either foliage or blossom is indeed a highly favoured and fortunate individual : I fear there are not many such in this country, nor indeed in any other. The Rose, throughout the whole civilised world, has been recognised as the Queen of flowers, and this admiration seems to have extended to the insect kingdom also, for there is certainly no other plant in cultivation that has attracted the attention of so many distinct species and forms of insects as the Rose. It would be almost impossible to recount all the ills that Rose flesh is heir to. Its enemies are legion, but probably the most dangerous is the unskilful or careless cultivator, for it is generally owing to his negligence or ignorance that the Rose suffers from the majority of other evils to which it is liable. We trust, however, we have already said sufficient in previous aricles regarding our "Queen" and the treatment she appreciates, to enable him to see the error of his ways and form a determination to show her becoming homage in the future.

Mr. G. Baker, one of the most successful English Rosarians, gives a very complete list of the enemies of the Rose in that valuable little work "The Rosarian's Year Book" for 1882. With one or two exceptions the whole of these pests are found in this country; I think, therefore, I cannot do better than give his remarks in extenso.

The Cockchafer- We know that the caterpillars of many small beetles and moths are most destructive to the buds and young shoots of our Rose trees, one of which we are too familiar with to need a description of its appearance - the cockchafer (Melolontha vulgaris). In its perfect state it is a terribly destructive insect, working sad havoc among the leaves and flowers, as those whose Rose plants are surrounded with trees know to their bitter experience and vexation; as its work of spoilation is carried on during the night, it is consequently the more difficult to cope with. We fear all that can be done with this wolf of insect pests is to endeavour to kill all we can, both of the grubs and perfect insects; the grubs are unsightly looking objects, having the end of the body curved, so that the creature cannot crawl in the ordinary way, but is obliged to lie on its side.

Bracken-clock (Phyllopeztha horticola) - This is a very troublesome insect, both in its larval and perfect state; the eggs are deposited in the ground about July, after which they are speedily hatched; the grub grows most rapidly, and in appearance is very like that of the cockchafer. It feeds most greedily on the roots, but when it attains its perfect state, it leaves the ground and does much violence to our Roses, among the petals of which it may be often found; nor does it confine its ravages to the flowers, for it gnaws round holes in the leaves as if made by shot. Now as to treatment– We have tried several modes, but with very little success; the surest way to get rid of them is to destroy the grub, which may be done by hoeing over the ground pretty often, and carefully looking up the grubs and picking them out, then dressing the ground with equal parts of gas lime and soot, or ammonial liquid from the gas-works, mixed one part to ten of water, will effectually destroy them.

Earwigs (Forficula) - These baneful insects are constant in their habit, frequently dodging in and out, disturbing the petals of the flowers; they are nocturnal in their vissitations, and hide themselves deep among the petals, soiling the beauty of the bloom in a most vexatious manner by nibbling round and destroying the uniformity of shape in the petals. They are very destructive, but can easily be destroyed by placing pieces of reed or bean stalks where they visit (these are chiefly the standard Rose trees). Being intolerant of light, they avoid the sunshine by every means in their power; you can blow them out of the reeds or bean stalks into a can of hot water, or what may be more convenient, a glass bottle with a little oil in it; you will also find the entomological forceps very handy in enabling you to draw out these most troublesome intruders.

Sawfly (Hylotoma rosae) - This is most appropriately named from the peculiar formation on its under surface. On close examination by a powerful lens, there will be seen a sort of double notched ridge extending the whole length of the body, which the creature can bring into action like a saw, and thereby effect a groove in the part on which she rests, and therin deposit her egg, after which she moves on and acts in the like manner. If you examine your plants in the autumn, you will find the stems and nervures on the under surface marked with little notches - these are the grooves made by the sawfly - from which young grubs have been hatched. Now, as to getting rid of them - We have here again often failed, and at the best have met with mere partial success. We recommend assiduous search and hand-picking, though unfortunately the mischief is done before we can catch the destroyer; these grubs, however, are often discovered in the ground, and I therefore strongly advise the free use of the hoe, afterwards a good dressing of equal parts of gas lime and sulphur.

The leaf-cutter Bee (Megachile centuncularis) - These insects are solitary in their visits, and when one has selected a plant to its liking, she settles on a leaf, and with the greatest agility cuts a semi-circular piece out, pursuing her work with the utmost mathematical precision, at the same time supporting the severed piece, which she carries off as soon it is detached, to form a lining for her nest. The bee invariably visits the same plant or one near it, and often takes two or more scollops off one leaflet. Yet we feel inclined to forgive these little depredators the injury they do; but if anyone can find heart to destroy them, the best way is to watch the plant or plants they visit, and with a piece of board in each hand, when the bee is busy at work, put one piece under and the other over, then quickly clap them together so as to secure the insect.

Winter Moth (Cheimatobia brumata) -This is a curious little insect, and appears in winter, and though small is capable of doing much mischief; the female has no wings, consequently cannot fly, but she may be seen creeping along and seeking the unopened buds, and lays her eggs upon them and the young shoots also, and when the spring comes and the leaves expand, the eggs are hatched, and give forth a number of caterpillars, which speedily bury themselves in the bud. The little birds lend us their aid to seek out these troublesome intruders, but unfortunately, we have found they have dragged forth the bud as well as the insect with it.

Swallow-tail Moth (Ourapteryx sambucaria)–The caterpillars of these moths are called Loopers. When one of these desires to advance, it grasps the object firmly with its fore feet and draws the hinder feet close to them, forming the body in an arched shape. The hind feet then take a firm hold, and the body is projected forward until the fore feet can repeat the process. These caterpillars resemble very closely dead twigs, so that they can hardly be distinguished from the branches on which they cling. They feed on the leaves and flower buds. The list of moths classed under the family name of Tortricide, or

Leaf rollers, supply many destructive agents to the Rose, including the following : Tortrix heparana, Tortix ribeana, Lozotoenia rosana, Pardix tripunctata, and Spilonota roborana. The grubs of the above make their appearance with the first opening of the leaves, of whose structure they take advantage to construct their summer abode, banqueting, in the meantime, on the leaves that shelter them, and, if unmolested, after working havoc among the foliage, make for juicy buds, which they soon disfigure and render entirely useless. The larvae have the peculiarity, when disturbed, of lowering themselves with a web-like thread. The only remedy for their destruction, and also those of the winter moth and swallow - tail moth, is assiduous hand-picking.

Nepticula anomalella and angulıfas-ciella – The larvae of these moths feed on the pulp of Rose leaves, making long galleries and blotches under the epidermis, and generally making their appearance in July, August, and September. The best way to destroy them, is merely to squeeze the leaves together, or have them picked off and burnt.

Red Spider (Tetranychus tellarius) - These little creatures, are unquestionably very injurious to Roses, either when trained to walls or grown under glass. They increase most rapidly, and though so minute in size, they have extraordinary powers of extracting the juices from the leaves; and to further aggravate the deadly mischief thus caused, they spin tiny webs over the leaves and points of the young shoots, so as to completely clog up the pores of the leaves, thereby stopping their powers of transpiration and absorption, and giving them a parched or burnt appearance. As these little nuisances abhor damp, the best remedy is the constant use of the syringe. We have found a wash, composed of a large wine-glassful of petroleum in two gallons of soft water, most effectual. Before playing on the plants, draw up a syringe full and force it back again into the vessel two or three times, so as to mix the petroleum as much as possible with the water. The wash may be used every day, or as long as is found necessary.

Ants (Formica sanguinea) are occasionally very troublesome pests, being very determined and incessant in their attacks, generally eating into the flower buds, and thereby rendering them perfectly useless. A little arsenic mixed with moist sugar, and placed in their runs, will soon destroy them.

Aphides (Aphis rosae), or, as they are more commonly called, green fly or plant lice, I am sure need no description. They are, unfortunately, but too well-known, especially to the Rose grower. They are wonderfully prolific, completely smothering, in a few days, the leaves, branches, and buds of the plants they infest. The injury they do very soon arrests the growth and progress of the plants, and their leaves and branches become twisted and distorted by the twisting of the tissues, for the extraction of the juice, and the plants if not attended to, become at length almost paralysed by the injury thus occsioned. The autumnal broods of these insects are egg-layers- and those produced from the eggs in the spring are viviparous. Tobacco water, Tobacco powder, or, where possible, fumigating them with Tobacco paper, are the most certain remedies. Violent syringing with clear water will also clean the plants for a short time, but those not disabled will quickly return to their feast. They are killed with the slightest pressure, so that you have only to draw your fingers over the infested parts, and destroy thousands at once. On the leaves and stems of trees much infested with aphides, may be observed a glutinous substance that adheres to the fingers and is sweet to the taste. This substance is propely called honey-dew, and is secreted from the aphides. Bees and ants are very fond of this honey-dew, and the ants may be seen feeding on the sacharine secretion as it exudes from the insect. Thousands of ants may be seen traversing the trees on which aphides are plentiful. Some are of opinion that ants do not feed on the Rose, but follow after the aphides; however this may be, we have no doubt many rosarians, like ourselves, have found swarms of the black ants on the top of Rose buds, busily at work; and certainly where this is the case, however you may fairly dislodge them for the time, the little creatures you will find return again boldly to their work, and assuredly where they have visited the bud, it never is seen to open its blossom in its known natural form and beauty. Yet we have been anxious to forgive these little busy workers the mischief they have created when watching the marvellous power possessed by ants, and how they make known to their comrades any store of food they have discovered.

Mildew - We should be careful, by every possible means, to guard against producing any check to the plants, either by watering the roots or overhead with cold water during very hot weather, and thereby rendering them susceptible to fungoid attacks. In preference to watering at such a time, we would advise a good mulching, or a constant moving of the surface soil, to prevent radiation. We can strongly recommend the following wash: Boil 1 lb. of soft soap in two gallons of water–syringe the plants daily with half-a-pint of this mixture, put in two gallons of rain water, and dust the affected parts with sublimated sulphur when wet from syringing. We have also used, with much good effect, an insecticide called Fir Tree Oil, prepared by a Mr. Hughes, chemist, at Manchester, and sold by most nurserymen - half-a-pint to four quarts of water. It is rather an expensive preparation, but we have used it through a very neat little instrument that has, within the last few months, been brought out by Mr. Wells, of Earlswood Nurseries, at Reigate, called Wells' Improved Spray Diffuser. It is worked with great facility, and can be directed to any part of the affected plant. It is a great saving, as a small bottle will do as much good as two gallons of insecticide with the oridnary syringe; or a wash consisting of soft soap dissolved in boiling water, and then add sulphur and tobacco, stirring the mixture well together when using.

Orange fungus - There is, however, no disease to which the Rose is liable that is so destructive in its effect as a virulent attack of Orange fungus. It is most subtle in its action; attacking the foliage sometimes in an early state of its growth, and spreading rapidly over a collection of plants, it makes its appearance on the under side of the leaves, in the form of the heads of very small pins. These, however, rapidly increase in number, until the leaves look as though they had been dusted with cayenne pepper and their vitality is quickly consumed through its effects. By its ravages the plants are denuded of foliage long before the wood has time to ripen, consequently they are in too delicate a state to stand against very severe weather, and those that have that ordeal to undergo, invariably start weakly the following spring. The remedies we can speak of are, unfortuantely, not very successul; and though we have but faint hopes of being able to effectually cure this pernicious disease, the next best thing is to endeavour to check its vegetative powder of spreading growth and prevent its reppearance. This can be attempted by raking off all loose materials and as much of the soil as possible, and burning them. At the same time give the ground a good dressing of quicklime. The burnt soil and other matters can be returned to the Roses greatly improved by the change they have undergone. At pruning time, carefully collect everything cut from the plants and destroy it. Then give the plants–stems and branches, stakes and ties (if any)–a good coating of the following mixture, applied with a suitable brush: Quicklime and soot, mixed to the consistency of paint in a pailful of which add half-a-pound of sublimated sulphur and a small handful of coarse salt; stir and mix well together before applying, the object being to destroy the resting spores of this troublesome fungus. We have tried washes of all kinds, carefully syringing and brushing over the leaves with various compounds, but with little success, and in some instances finding the remedies even more fatal than the disease. We have most faith in an infusion of Hellebore root, four ounces to half-a-gallon of boiling water, then add half-a-drachm of bichloride of mercury (first dissolve the mercury in a little spirit), and lastly, add half-a-gallon of lime-water. We have certainly sen good results from this application, though we must also admit it has sometimes failed. We have observed that we get this Orange fungus, or mildew, in long continued dry weather, and chiefly on the lower leaves of the smooth-wooded class of Rose plants, such as Victor Verdier, Comtesse d'Oxford, Hippolyte Jamain, and the like; but it is worthy of remark that neither Madame Clemence Joigneaux, William Warden, or Edouard Morren, and those of the same character of foliage, &c., are subject to these forms of fungoid disease.

Black fungus - This appears on the leaves in blotches. The edges are irregular or star-shaped. It most commonly makes its appearance in poor and exhausted soils, or after a long continued drought, causing an insufficient supply of nourishment to the plant. Though these are the causes, it is most undoubtedly contagious after it has obtained a footing. As a remedy, syringe with a solution of soft soap, 6 oz. dissolved in a gallon of water, adding 2 oz. of sulphur, mix well together; or, nicotine soap, 4 oz. to a gallon of water; or, sponge the leaves with the following wash : 2 oz. of sulphate of copper dissolved in hot water, and then add two gallons of cold, soft water.

Root fungus - This frequently attacks the Rose; it is brought about by the soil in which they are planted containing matter favourable to fungoid growth, such as dead woo, leaf-mould, &c., hence the necessity of removing all such substances; stumps also of rotten stakes should be carefully taken from the ground. We know some regard with suspicion the Manetti stock; their opinion is that Roses on this stock being planted somewhat below the union, so as to induce this stock to swell, and with the view of the Roses becoming established on their own roots, the stock then dies and becomes a suitable breeding repository for this fungus, the mycelium of which permeate the dead tissues, and instead of being the medium of giving existence or maintaining vigour of life in the Rose, it becomes the means of imparting its death-blow. We mention the matter, though we do not share the opinion. The best chance of remedy is to lift the plant and remove all decayed portions of the root, then thoroughly wet the roots, and dust with quicklime, and plant in fresh soil.

Curl - This generally occurs when the Roses have been occupying the ground for a very long period of time consequently the constituents of the soil necessary to their well doing become exhausted, and they are thereby rendered very susceptible to climatic changes. Under these circumstances I advise that the plants be lifted and re-planted in improved soil.

Canker - This disease is, as a rule, confined to that most glorious Rose, Marechal Niel, and arises from the plant's weakness and inability to take up and make use of sufficient nourishment to sustain its growth and prolific blooming. As a remedy, I suggest the removal, if possible, of the affected parts, and the enrichment of the soil both by solid and liquid manures.

Lichen and Moss - Sometimes form on the stems of standards and dwarf standards, and if allowed to accumulate, are decidedly injurious to the well being of the Rose, stopping the pores of the epidermis of the stem and young branches, besides forming suitable niches for all kinds of insect eggs and spores of fungi. The winter dressing we have mentioned above for Orange fungus, will also remove and prevent this cause of disease.

The Queen of Flowers

Would Jove appoint some flower to reign,
In matchless beauty on the plain,
The Rose (mankind will all agree),
The Rose the Queen of flowers should be :
The pride of plants, the grace of bowers,
The blush of meads, the eye of flowers;
Its beauties charm the gods above;
Its fragrance is the breath of love;
Its foliage wantons in the air,
Luxuriant, like the flowing hair;
It shines in blooming splendour gay,
While Zephyrs on its bosom play.

– ***Sappho***

CHAPTER XI
FORMS OF GROWTH

The Revd. S. Reynolds Hole in *A Book about Roses,* says : – "In a Rose garden no formalism, no flatness, no monotonous repetition should prevail. There should the Rose be seen in all her multitudinous phases of beauty. There should be beds of Roses, banks of Roses, bowers of Roses, hedges of Roses, edgings of Roses, pillars of Roses, arches of Roses, fountains of Roses, baskets of Roses, vistas and alleys of the Rose. Now overhead and now at our feet, there they should creep and climb; new tints, new forms, new perfumes should meet us at every turn. Here we come upon a bed of seedlings so full of interest and of hope. Here is the sunny spot where we gather, like Virgil's shepherd, the first Rose of spring or the last of autumn. Art is here as the meek admiring handmaid

"Rosa quo locorum Sera moretur,"

of nature, gently smoothing her beautiful hair, checking only such growth as would weaken her flowing riglets, but never daring to disfigure with shams and chignons - with pagodas, I mean, and such like tea-garden trumpery. Art is here to obey, but not to dictate- to work as one who counts such service its own reward and honour. If before the Fall, before the earth brought forth brier and thorn, man was put into a garden to dress it and to keep it, with his will and with his might must he labour now in that plot of ground where he would fain realize his fond idea of Eden. He must work hard, but only as one who copies some great masterpiece - not as one who designs but restores. He must keep order, but only as replacing an arrangement which he had himself distrubed. Thus, and thus only he may hope to make himself a garden

"Where order in variety we see,

And where, though all things differ, all agree."

We have here undoubtedly a very glowing picture of what a Rose garden should be, and amongst our more fortunate brethren at home, probably with patient industry and a liberal expenditure, such a glorious dream might be realized; but in this country I fear that we must be content with a much lower standard of perfection, for it would certainly be futile for us to attempt to grow Roses in many of the forms mentioned. Mr. W Paul, in the *Rose Garden,* states that much confusion has arisen from there being no acknowledged standard of reference for the names of particular forms of Rose Trees. Thus the terms *low standard, half standard* and *dwarf standard* are used synonymously by some. The following explanation is given of the terms employed in the above work : -

Weeping Roses are kinds of vigorous and pendulous growth worked on stems of 4 feet and upwards.

Standard Roses are any kinds on stems above 3 feet.

Tall Standards Roses are any kinds on stems above 4 to 5 feet.

Half Standards are any kinds on stems above 1½ to 2½ feet.

Dwarf Standards are any kinds on varying from 6 to 18 inches.

Dwarfs are budded or grafted close to the ground and termed *worked dwarfs,* or are grown from cuttings or layers and spoken of as *on their own roots.*

Climbing Roses are the most vigorous kinds selected from various groups.

Pillar Roses are analogous to the last; but the best forms of these are kinds of more erect, habit and less flexible in growth than those usually chosen for climbing Roses.

Dwarf Roses

Dwarf Roses, as mentioned in the above table, are divided into two sections. First, those that are grown from cuttings or layers, which are termed "Own Root Roses," and second, those that have been propagated by budding, grafting, or inarching; these are known as "worked Dwarfs." Until comparatively a very recent date a strong prejudice has existed against Roses on their own roots, under the belief that plants grown in this way did not thrive so vigorously, flower so freely, or produce such fine blooms as those that had the support of foster parents. Gradually, but surely, however, this prejudice is disappearing, and the majority of the

Rose-growing public are beginning to believe that it was based on entirely fallacious ideas. For my part, I am persuaded that the best mode of growing Roses is on their own roots, and I believe this opinion will become confirmed and we shall find it ere long generally adopted, though of course, there must be positions in every garden where Standards, Half Standards or Pillar Roses may be planted with good effect; but to my mind, Roses, like all other flowers, look best when planted in masses, and therefore as plants they will be seen to most advantage when on their own roots and producing the finest bloom. A writer on this subject, in a recent edition of the *Rose Annual*, says : –

"At the present moment, perhaps, more than at any other time, the opinion of the Rose-growing public seems setting in strongly in favour of plants which have never been budded or grafted. Dazzled for a long time by the extraordinary vigour and celerity of growth of plants worked on the Manetti, and also by the enormous size of the flowers produced under careful and generous cultivation, to the mass of Rose growers own-root Roses were a long-forgotten thing of the past, which the mind associated only with the idea of the old Gallicas, Hybrid Chinese, and other favourites of a byegone generation Valubale, indeed, as the Manetti stock is, on account of its easy adaptability to soils and climates generally considered unfavourable to the cultivtion of Roses, and granted also the excellence of the seedling Briar as a dwarf stock, especially when Rose flowers in autumn are a desideratum, it is, nevertheless, we think, a matter of congratulation that more attention is being paid to plants on their own roots. It is true that they take longer to establish themselves, and do not, therefore, make large plants so rapidly or yield such a quick return of quantities of flowers as budded plants, but without taking into consideration the fact that certain kinds, such as Marechal Niel, are best suited to this mode of growth, this is more than compensated for by the longer duration of the plant's existence, and by the exemption from the plague of suckers and offshoots which require constant watching for on worked plants, but which we so often see developed through neglect in private gardens to such an extent as to imperil the existence of the Roses themselves. We are also of opinion that there is generally a refinement and finish about the blooms on own-root plants which contrast favourably with the coarseness and roughness apparent in so many of the flowers cut from worked plants, especially when produced on maiden or one-year-old plants. It is often taken for granted that if worked plants be planted sufficiently deep as to ensure the burying of the junction between the scion and stock, the former will throw out roots, and by taking the plant up at the proper season, and cutting away the stock, a plant on its own roots will be the result. By this means the end aimed at would of course be attained, but we are rather sceptical as to the adaptability of the mass of varieties to this treatment, and are of opinion that it is better to start at once with plants that have been struck from cuttings or layers.

As a rule, plants on their own roots, especially when pot-grown, are not so large as worked plants of the same age, owing to their slower growth; for this reason, also, they are rather apt to try the patience when first planted out, but when once established, they grow so well, and give so little trouble, that the extra time they take in their early stages is easily forgiven and forgotten."

Another competent authority in discussing the same subject, but from what may be termed the commercial point of view, remarks that –

"The slaughter of the last winter has done more to alter the form and fashion of Roses, than all that has been written against them; nevertheless, it will be a long while before standards disappear. It is just as well that it should be so. Violent changes of fashion are hardly consistent within the domain of high art, and no one can deny that Standard Roses belong to the latter. The trade may also be said to have a vested interest in standards : of course, we mean a legitimate vested interest. Their stocks at the present moment are doubtless many millions strong. In some of the Rose farms there can be hardly less than half a million Briers budded, or about to be budded, this year. The whole of the vigour and all the root-force of this dense forest of Briers will speedily be diverted to the service of our best Roses with as much certainty and almost as much ease as each private water cistern is filled from the main.

"It is all very well for us or others to advocate Roses on their own roots, but to the trade, with all the stem and root force of Briers ready to force the Rose buds into bushes with leaps and bounds, it must seem very like telling the householder who has his connections with water mains complete to dig a well for his own use, as to urge the trade to strike their Roses from cuttings. In the latter case they have to create, or at least, develop force; in the former they have simply to divert it. It must also be confessed that the Briers, standards or dwarfs, are like horses in the stable ready harnessed to be put-to at the shortest notice, whereas Rose cuttings are more like unbroken colts at large in the meadows. We do not say these are our views, but they are those that must needs strike the trade, and no one can fail to admit their force. And it must also be admitted that the greatness and success of horticulture in most of its branches is largely based on the imprisonment of the strength and energy of wild plants for the service of cultivated varieties. Logically and physiologically there seems no more cogent reasons why Roses should grow on their own roots than fruit trees or other shrubs or plants. The fact is, an enormous number of cultivated plants borrow roots, not flowers, from other plants; and the arrangement cheapens production, and hastens, beyond all calculation, the multiplication of species and varieties.

"The trade in Roses may be said to be built up on borrowed roots. They are time and money-saving expedients, of enormous power and importance, and for these reasons alone they will be certain to be used for many years. The tastes, the interests, the power of the trade, in this matter suits the means and the wishes of their customers. Rapid, moderately cheap, and large supplies are what is chiefly desiderated by the public. The trade has purchased, prepared, furnished these Rose farms to meet and satisfy these demands; it would seem well nigh impossible to satisfy them without the use of borrowed roots, and for the present that consideration may settle the matter.

"In the Rose trade it is almost the same as if the ordinary maxims of political economy were being reversed - that the supply was creating and sustaining the demand; but having given the masses a taste for the best and sweetest Roses, the cry is still for more. Thus the trade in Roses is sure to prove a growing one, and to keep pace with the growth of wealth, intelligence, and culture. In regard to the latter the Rose is likely to exert a powerful influence, for if it be true – and it is – that men become assimilated to the objects of their pursuits and affections, surely close companionship with the Rose will form a centre of sweetness, a source of light, to many, and a refined and ennobling pleasure for all."

Although the above writer makes out a very strong case in favour of the employment of artificial stocks for the propagation of

Roses, it is very evident that he is writing entirely in opposition to his own convictions on the subject. Were it a question of propagation only, every Rose grower who has had any experience in the matter would certainly be in favour of budding, grafting or inarching, for he knows that by any of these means he can not only raise a much greater number of plants in a given time, but can also produce strong blooming specimens quite a year in advance of those grown from cuttings or layers. This is of course the view that the trade grower takes of the matter, and he is quite justified in doing so; but the amateur rosarian is fettered by no such considerations, and must view the matter from another standpoint. To him propagation is a matter of secondary importance when compared with the formation of a permanent Rosarium, the healthy development of his plants, and the production of an adequate supply of bloom, and we are convinced that in no way (except under very exceptional circumstances) can these results be secured so well as by growing plants on their own roots.

All of us are of course aware that one of the main objects in adopting artificial methods of propagation, such as budding or grafting, is to secure for the scion certain good qualities, such as a strong constitution, vigorous or compact growth, a floriferous habit or other good points that it does not naturally possess; Every one who has had much experience in these operations must have observed that the influence of the stock on the scion, as a rule, varies in proportion to the degree of affinity that exists between the two species that are brought together; in many cases the result of a union may be all that could be desired, in others its effects are scarcely perceptible, and in some instances this influence is productive of evil results, occasionally being so powerful as to entirely alter the character of the plant either in foliage, habit, or flower.

In this country the two species that are generally employed as stocks are *Rosa gigantea* and *Rose Edouard.* The former is a plant of very vigorous growth, but of a loose, straggling semi-scandent habit, and although not actually flowerless, as described by Firminger, has but very rarely been known to bloom under cultivation. Now what good quality does this species possess that could be utilised to improve our garden Roses? A union with such a stock no doubt tends to promote a vigorous growth, but as a rule, Hybrid Perpetuals in our climate make too much wood naturally, and Tea Roses rarely do well on it.

Rose Edouard, a grand old Rose in itself, as regards habit, is better adapted as a stock for general propagation than the preceding; it has, however, one unfortunate defect, which it too frequently transmits to the plants worked on it, that is, that during the cold season it almost invariably refuses to expand its blooms.

Although we so strongly advocate the growing of Dwarf Roses on their own roots, we certainly do not advise that budding or grafting should be entirely dispensed with, there are certain situations and particular soils in which it is almost imperatively necessary to provide a strong, free-rooting foster-parent for most of our Roses. Then, again, there are some varieties with such a delicate constitution that unless supported on a more vigorous variety would inevitably succumb to the enervating effects of our climate. The various methods of propagation referred to have already been fully described in previous chapters, so that it is unnecessary for me to say anything further on the subject here.

Pegged-Down Roses

This is a comparatively new system of growing Roses that is coming much into practice in England, and one that could be introduced into this country with much advantage; as for the greater part of the year our rose-beds at best present a vey unsightly appearance with their long leafless stems towering in mid-air, especially during the hot and rainy seasons, when it is impossible to prune them into a reasonable compass, as by so doing we should run the risk of losing many of them. The following description of the *modus operandi* is given in a recent number of the *Garden* : -

"Only those who know the glorious displays that Roses are capable of making when grown in this way can rightly estimate their value. Hybrid perpetuals are the most effective for this purpose. I find the best growers to be Alfred Colomb, Charles Lefevre, Marechal Vaillant, Madame C. Wood, Annie Wood, General Jacqueminot and Docteur Andry. The best light varieties in our beds are *Centifolia rosea*, John Hopper, Anna Alexieff, Souvenir de la Reine d'Angleterre, Madame Vidot, Jules Margotin and Madame Rivers. They should all be on their own roots, as plants budded on any other stock are not to be depended on, for the suckers they usually send up will be a constant source of trouble and unless they are cut away as fast as they show themselves, they seriously check the growth of the Rose itself . It requires an experienced eye to detect the difference between the Rose and the stock, consequently own root Roses are in every way the best."

Preparation of the Beds

As the beds are to be permanent, any extra care in the way of time or materials that may be expended on them will be amply repaid in after years, indeed without thorough preparation Roses cannot be expected to last many years in a satisfactory condition. The amount of labour required will, in a great measure, depend on the nature of the soil to deal with: if of a poor light character, all the old soil should be taken out to a depth of eighteen inches and a mixture of three parts of good strong loam and one part rotten manur substituted. If possible all this work should be done when the weather is fine and dry, as the materials incorporate in a very much better way in dry weather than in wet, and as a result the roots will take more kindly to the new soil. There are many places in which good Roses may be grown without the aid of new soil, and in such cases a good dressing of thoroughly rotten manure incorporated with the soil to a depth of eighteen inches will be all that is necessary. In other cases the removal of a portion of the old soil, and the substitution of an equal quantity of loam and manure will suffice. In every case, however, the soil must be trenched from eighteen inches to two feet deep, and if this is done three weeks or a month before the Roses are planted, the soil will have time to settle down, and be in a better condition for the reception of the plants than it would otherwise be.

Planting

If the plants are in pots they may be put out at any time, but the best months for planting Roses from the open ground is in October on November.

Pruning

Of this little will be necessary for the first two years, as all the growth must be pegged down to cover the beds. The plants should be planted one foot from the sides of the beds all round and two feet apart, and the centre should be filled in with plants at the same distance from each other. This will give ample space for the shoots to be laid down to meet each other, which they will readily do in three years from the time of planting if all goes well. As soon as there is young growth enough to take the place of that which has flowered, the old flowering wood must be cut away every year, and the young shoots pegged down to supply its place. If the points of these shoots overlap each other they must be cut back.

A well furnished bed of pegged Roses should have the surface covered all over with shoots about nine inches apart. Until there is growth enough to cover the sufrace the old wood must be allowed to remain for another year, by pruning in the lateral growth to a spur with two or three buds they will flower again. When the pruning takes place all the old pegs should be removed and fresh ones supplied; the plants must be kept liberally supplied with water, and if manure water can be had so much the better. In any case it is important to remember that in order to produce satisfatory growth they must have plenty of moisture. It is best not to be in a hurry to peg down the young growth, as it gains greater consistency by being allowed to grow erect.

Chapter XII
Standard Roses

We but very rarely see this method of growing Roses attempted in this country, owing, probably, to the difficulty in obtaining a suitable stock for them. With patience, however, it is quite possible to form very good plants either on *Rosa gigantea* or *Rose Edouard*. For this purpose we must select the strongest plants possible, leaving the stoutest stem and cutting all the rest of the wood away below the level of the ground line; then shorten the stem back to the required height, and carefully remove all buds along the stem except three or four at the top. These must be left to form lateral branches on which to bud. Some proceed to bud at once on the main stem, this is not, however, advisable, as the union is much more liable to injury from high winds than when placed on a lateral branch. As soon as these are sufficiently firm to operate on, proceed in accodance with directions given for budding in Chapter III. Standards may also be formed by layering any very vigorous shoots from old plants; as soon as these are well rooted and growing freely, they should be planted in the place where they are intended to remain; then cut back to the height needed, carefuly disbudding the entire stem except the three or four topmost eyes which must be left to form the head. As soon as these have pushed about four or five leaves they should have their tips pinched out to induce them to branch freely. Standard Roses however, no matter how formed, rarely if ever, thrive satisfactorily in the plains. I have even imported plants from England on two or three occasions, and never met with any great success with them. I am inclined to believe that the cause of failure is owing to the large amount of bare stem, exposed to the full force of the sun becoming so heated and dried up as to be no longer capable of acting as a channel through which the necessary nourishment for the support of the plant must flow. I have tried to remedy this by binding the stocks with moss, hay or straw, and even khus-khus grass, keeping them moistened in dry weather, but none of these seemed to do any permanent good.

Now the question arises, why should we attempt to grow Roses in this unnatural style? And the reply can only be that it is the fashion to do so. We of the noble sex would have the weaker ones believe that it is only they who are influenced by fashion and its many changes; and yet can we point to any greater absurdity than that of attempting to grow plants on the top of broomsticks, for literally speaking, it is little more or less. Happily even in England the days of Standard Roses seem to be numbered, and in a few years will probably be reckoned as a thing of the past. A recent writer in the "*Garden*" makes the following remarks on this subject : "One reason why Standard Roses die so soon, or grow so slowly, arises, I believe, from the barenness of the ground. The tops at first are too meagre to afford either shelter or shadow, and before the struggling tops have made sufficient progress to provide either the one or the other, the roots have succumbed either to sunstroke or frost-bite. There is nothing in nature analogous to our Standard Roses mounted on stilted stems borrowed of the wild brier and set on a smooth even surface exposed to all sorts of meteorological and other severe changes of temperature and physical conditions. No, it won't do : even the growth of weeds that cover the surface is not in vain. The safety and longevity of our Roses demand either that we grow them in bush form, or that we sub-crop the soil under our struggling Standards to conserve their moisture, preserve their strength, and protect the roots from extremes of temperature and of aridity. The Roses of olden times had at least one thing that their modern competitors lack – shade and shelter for their roots; and hence partly, at least, their greater longevity and better health."

Pillar Roses

These when properly trained are undoubtedly very attractive objects. But, probably on account of the great care and attention required to produce anything like a satisfactory result, this mode of training is but very rarely attempted in this country. The following description of the *modus operandi*, by one of the most eminent of English Rosarians, will probably prove both interesting and instructive to those who may desire to attempt their culture.

"The culture of Pillar Roses certainly demands some skill; but it is a skill that is easily acquired by the observant and enquiring cultivator. Let us consider the several points in regular order, so as to dismiss all simple matters with a word and deal with difficulties as they come before us at such length as their relative importance may demand.

Planting Pillar Roses

In any case the soil must be well drained, liberally manured, deeply stirred and in a sound condition. It should be of such quality as to produce good wheat on cauliflowers, or it will never produce Pillar Roses. A Pillar Rose will require at least one square yard of soil, which must not be occupied with shrubs or grass, and every autumn this soil must be enriched with a dressing of half-rotten stable manure. Whatever tends to increase the vigour of a Rose – such as top dressings in summer, abundant supplies of water, &c. – must be given to Pillar Roses; for it is not only desirable to clothe the Pillars, but to do so with *stout wood* which can only be accomplished by feeding liberally. Let us suppose the Roses planted, they are then to be cut down to within one or two buds of the base and allowed to grow the first season as they please, and the more vigorously the better.

Pruning Pillar Roses

The second season they will require pruning. Now to prune them properly the Rosarian must bear in mind that it is much easier to induce a tree to grow to its full height than to induce it to form regular tiers of flowering wood all the way from its root to its summit. This is true of Apples, Plums, Pears, Vines, and hundreds of other trees. Keep the leading shoot upright, and do not prune it at all, and it will grow with great vigour, so as continually to increase its length until it reaches its maximum height; but in the meantime the leading bud having monopolised the sap, there will be but few side branches formed, and consequently there will be little or no flowering wood produced. It is true that trees do produce side branches without the aid of the pruner, and that these take a horizontal or oblique direction; nevertheless the general tendency of the sap is upwards, and one of the first consequences of allowing a tree to grow in its own way is to cause the formation of a bare stem for some distance from the ground line; and that tendency is of itself a sufficient argument for pruning Pillar Roses. In a word, if the pruning is neglected they soon acquire their full height but have naked stems; whereas, if properly pruned, these stems will be clothed from head to foot with flowering branches. The pruning in the second year will consist in removing by a clean cut, to within one or two buds of their base, all long weak shoots, reserving two or three of the strongest shoots and shortening these about one-third or one-half of their length. If any doubt as to the application of these instructions let the Rose itself furnish a hint. If it has attained to a great height, and is so regularly furnished with side shoots as to be already nearly sufficient to cover a pillar prune all the side shoots back to three or four buds and the leaders only a fourth or fifth of their whole length. If it has not grown much cut it back very hard, removing quite half of the entire growth so as to conform pretty nearly to this rule – the more growth, the less pruning; the less growth, the more pruning. Having accomplished the pruning, lay the shoots down full length along the ground and fix them with a few strong pegs so that the wind may not blow them about. This will cause the buds to break – that is to say will cause the formation of side shoots the whole length of the rods : as soon as these burst freely they must be tied up to their poles or pillars.

The third season's pruning must be on the same principle as in the preceding year; the cultivator must be more anxious about obtaining plenty of furniture – that is, of hiding the pillar with a plentiful side growth from the ground upwards. He need not think much about getting the Rose to the top of the pillar; it will go there in time and perhaps sooner than will be good for its ultimate beauty; and if it does not, it is only necessary to leave one or two long rods unshortened and they will soon mount to the summit of their ambition. To begin, then, with the pruning, let us first determine about the furniture of the base of the pillar. Here we find already plenty of weak spray, some well placed strong shoots, and perhaps a certain proportion of wiry twigs that produced flowers last season. All the weak spray should be cut clean out, leaving only the buds at the base to break again; the same with the wood that flowered the previous year, but the strong side shoots may be cut to six or eight buds from the base. Where the pillar is bare, cut a few shoots very close so as to get some vigorous growth to fill up the gaps; where crowded, thin away the weakest of the shoots, and leave those that are best placed for flowering. Proceed thus till you arrive at the top, then shorten back the leading shoots according to their length and strength, but not severely, to a plump bud to carry the growth upward the next season.

After this pruning there ought to be an abundant bloom; and from this time forth there must be very little pruning; the cultivator's principal care will be to keep the tree liberally nourished and provide for the occasional *renewal of the main shoots*, for those originally formed will in time be debilitated through excessive production of flowers.

The renewing or repairing of the pillar is accomplished by means of the strong shoots that rise from the base. As these appear tie them in loosely, so as to induce a free growth, prune them as recommended for the first formation of the pillar, and as soon as they reach half way up the pillar and are tolerably well furnished with side shoots remove one of the old leaders, and let the young one take its place. When an abundance of young shoots are produced some must be cut away entirely to within one bud of their base; from the bud left a flowering shoot will generally be developed next season, or it may be another strong shoot, which may be useful though not wanted the previous year, in which case keep it, if not pinch it back and cause it to form a mass of laterals, or leave it to grow to its full length and then cut it back as before. Two more remarks seem needful to complete these directions. By training the leading shoots straight up the pillars they will grow with more vigour; by training them regularly round and round the pole the growth will be more moderate and regular, and there will be an earlier disposition to form flowering wood. It is well in all cases to allow new shoots to go straight up and to twist them the next season after the pruning. This secures strong wood in the first year and plenty of laterals in the second. The last remark is, that poles and pillars should not exceed twelve feet, and when it is determined to have them of that height the most robust growing Roses should be selected. The better kinds of hybrid-perpetuals and Bourbons do best on pillars of six to eight feet; if taken higher it is difficult to keep them furnished at the bottom.

We may now offer a few remarks as to the poles and pillars themselves. It is best not to insert them till after the Roses have grown two years, and when inserted, it must be in a way to stand firm in a gale. In all cases it is best if the lower parts of the posts can be charred, as this prevents the growth of mycelium, by which so many Roses are destroyed by the proximity of decaying wood to the roots. The superiority of iron must not be overlooked, for not only is wood perishable, but the soundest wooden pole may be snapped short off by a gale. If iron poles are adopted they should be one inch in diameter with triple prongs proportionately stout, and the prongs should be from one to two feet in length, according to the height of the poles above ground.

Chapter XIII
Climbing Roses

Climbing Roses certainly receive less attention from writers and cultivators than almost any other class of these popular flowers; but why this should be the case I do not pretend to know, unless it is perhaps that they require more attention to ensure their being in first rate condition. However that may be, it is very certain that there are many good Roses which require support in some shape or form to bring out their good qualities. For poles, pillars, arches, arbours, &c., only those Roses are suitable which have more or less of what is called a climbing habit of growth - I say what is called a climbing habit of growth, because, strictly speaking, there is no such thing as a climbing Rose. Roses do not climb or cling to anything in the same way that such strictly climbing plants as the Vine, the Honeysuckle and the Ivy do. Roses which make long rambling growths, whose shoots are unable to stand up without support of some kind, these are the kinds which do duty as climbers. Before determining on the kind of climber to plant, however, the height the plants are required to attain must be considered. Fortunately in this country we have a very wide field from which to make our selection. What are known, however, amongst English Rose growers as climbing Roses, such as the Ayrshire, Banksian, and Boursault groups, are entirely unsuitable for cultivation in the plains, although they thrive vigorously enough in the Himalayas at an elevation of 4,000′ to 8,000′. Their absence, however, is more than counterbalanced by the large number of other species which are here well adapted for this purpose. Most of the vigorous Hybrid Perpetuals and Teas may be relied on from 8ft. to 15ft. if the soil be good. The extra strong growers of the same classes with the Noisettes and Hybrid Noisettes will cover well up to 15 ft. or even 20ft. or more in height. I purpose now to mention a few of the best of scandent habit; I had better, however, say at once that it is not my intention to enumerate all that are good, because to do so would take up too much space and also perplex my readers.

For positions not exceeding 8 to 10 feet in height many of the hybrid perpetuals are eminently suitable, not that they can be said to be climbing Roses, but there are many of them sufficiently vigorous in growth to reach the height mentioned within two years from the time of planting. Especially is this the case when they are on their own roots and planted in a good soil. Barrone Prevost is an excellent climber; Marechal Vaillant, Charles Wood, Dr. Andry, Annie Alexieff and La Ville de Saint Denis are also good; nor must I omit to mention climbing Countess of Oxford, climbing Jules Margottin, climbing Charles Lefebvre, and climbing Victor Verdier. These possess all the good qualities of the verieties in their original form, combined with a wonderfully vigorous habit of growth. As a general rule all varieties of this group that are described as of very vigorous growth may be employed as dwarf climbers.

Those who require varieties of a more scadent habit than the preceding must search amongst the Teas, Hybrid Teas and Noisettes, and may select from the following with perfect safety:– Marechal Niel, Solfaterre, Safrano, Cloth of Gold, climbing Devoniensis, Lamarque, Reve d'Or, Gloire de Dijon, Celine Forestier, Cheshunt Hybrid and Duchess of Edinburgh. The last two are red Roses of great merit : Cheshunt Hybrid I consider one of the most useful Roses yet introduced, and certainly deserves more attention than it has yet received from Rosarians in this country, I have heard complaints of its being a shy bloomer. I think, however, in these cases, this must have arisen from over-pruning, for with me it has proved extremely free flowering, and has more than sustained the high character given it by Rosarians in England. The first nine varieties named bear yellow flowers of different shades, most of which are too well known to need any description here. In this small group we have certainly the two finest Roses in the world, namely, Gloire de Dijon and Marechal Niel; regarding the former variety the Reverend S. Reynolds Hole says : - "Its flowers are the earliest and latest; it has symmetry, size, endurance, colour and perfume. It is what cricketers call an "all-rounder," good in every point for wall, arcade, pillar, standard, dwarf, *en masse,* or as a single tree. It is easy to cultivate; it forces admirably, and you may have it almost in its summer beauty when Christmas snows are on the ground. With half a dozen pots of it carefully treated, and half a dozen trees in your garden, you may enjoy it all the year round; and if ever, for some heinous crime, I were miserably sentenced, for the rest of my life, to possess but a single Rose tree, I should desire to be supplied on leaving the dock with a strong plant of Gloire de Dijon." And the same writer is scarcely less enthusiastic regarding the Marechal; he says:- "Since the time when a baby in floriculture I first began to 'take notice' of Roses, more than thirty years ago, three new stars of special brightness have glittered in our firmament - Gloire de Dijon, Charles Lefebvre and Marechal Niel. The latter is, I think, the greatest acquisition, because we had, previous to its introduction, no hardy yellow Rose, realising as this does - in the wonderful beauty of its flowers, their size, shape, colour, fragrance, longevity, abundance, in the amplitude of its glossy leaves and the general habit of the plant - our every desire and hope. We possessed some approximation to Gloire de Dijon in our Tea and Bourbon Roses. Charles Lefebvre was a development of General Jacqueminot, but of a hardy Golden Rose, more precious and more welcome a thousand times than those Golden Rose which Popes have sent to favoured Kings, we saw no harbinger. Even the Marechal's own mother, Isabella Gray, had displayed such feeble charms that no one mourned her sterility. Suddenly, unexpectedly she produced a paragon."

It may be observed that climbing Roses, as a rule, suffer more from indifferent preparation of the soil than from neglect of any other part of their management, and I shall direct special attention to this point. To grow them in a successful manner they require the same care as is devoted to the other classes of Roses. Indeed in some cases it is necessary to take more than ordinary care in the preparation of the soil, as they have frequently to be planted in hot dry positions, and when such is the case it is necessary to make the border somewhat deeper than would serve for a bed of Roses on the lawn. These positions also require the soil to be of the very best description to ensure a free and continuous growth; for unless a Rose tree, no matter what the form it may be grown in, does not continue to make growth, it cannot flower in a satisfactory manner. In all cases where there is a doubt about the soil, or the spot being of a suitable character, it should be taken away to a depth of two feet and a width of two feet six inches, and be replaced with good soil. A rich fibrous loam, if it is to be had, with one-third part rotten manure, is decidedly the best, but any good mellow loam with the addition of manure will do.

Vigorous-growing varieties of Roses, especially such as Marechal Niel, Gloire de Dijon, or Lamarque, that do not flower freely if pruned to any great extent after the principal flowering is over, require attention. Whilst the plants are young, and before they have filled the space which their heads are destined to occupy, they need not be much reduced, but when they have filled anything near all the room available, if cutting back is not carried out some time in the year, they get crowded with useless, weak wood, little able to produce handsome, full-sized flowers. To avoid this a portion of the large, strong, old branches may be cut out near to point on the main stem from which they spring, leaving a stump, the latent eyes of which may be expected to immediately break into growth. These will form strong, vigorous branches, which will produce the best flowers next season. This removal of a portion of the old wood annually, to be replaced by new, may be carried to the extent of one-third or one-fourth the entire plant, which, so treated, will always contain a sufficient quantity of young, vigorous flowering growth, and will not attain a dimension beyond that which there is space for, and that profusion of weak, useless shoots that results from insufficient pruning will not exist. The plants at the same time sould be thoroughly well washed, so as to free them from insects. If there is any mildew upon them, a liberal application of water impregnated with sulphur will be found useful. Where planted in a position where the root space is confined, manure water, given so as to soak the whole mass of soil as far as the roots can extend, will be of the greatest possible use. This may with advantage be repeated from time to time.

Chapter XIV
Hybrid Perpetuals

This class or group of Roses has been aptly likened to Moses' serpent, swallowing up all the rest, for it is a combination of almost every species. Here we have varieties containing a mixture of Bourbon, Damask, China, or Noisette blood, and embracing almost every shade of colour except pure white or yellow; the latter has been frequently announced by many of the French raisers, but up to the present time it has never not become an accomplished fact.

The Rose has, perhaps, undergone greater improvement within the last twenty years than it ever previously attained, and this improvement may be attributed in a great measure to the introduction of this class having opened out such a large field for hybridising and raising seedlings. Until within the last few years this was almost entirely in the hands of the French-raisers, and consequently the market has been surfeited with an immense number of new varieties, a very large percentage of which, after trial, having been found entirely worthless. Probably during the last twenty years, there has been an average of upwards of fifty new varieties sent out yearly, and yet at the present time there is certainly not more than one-third of these in cultivation, the others having gradually dropped out of sight. It seems strange that none of our great English rosarians have ever made any attempts to arrange this grand heterogeneous mass into proper groups or families; neither the English term of "Hybrid Perpetual" nor the French "Hybrid Remontante" convey anything more than a description of their flowering qualities, ignoring altogether all family distinction. It would undoubtedly be a very difficult task to classify such an extensive group, especially when we consider that, until within the last few years, every new variety sent out was but the result of accidental or self-fertilisation – the first Rose that could claim any pedigree at all, and that of one generation, only having been introduced in 1865 or 1866.

The celebrated American rosarian, Ellwanger, has, however, taken a step in the right direction by dividing them into certain typical sections, each having for its head a well-known old Rose. This will prove of great assistance to the amateur, for when we know the particular strain of blood flowing in the veins of any variety, we shall the better know what treatment it requires. Too many would-be gardeners commence rose-growing under the impression that all the many different members of this family are amenable to one form of treatment; experience will, however, soon convince us that what will suit one particular group is almost certain to kill another. As an instance, I remember early last November visiting a certain garden in Calcutta where a large collection of Roses is grown; the pruning season was just over, and what was my astonishment to find that every variety, whether Tea, Bourbon, Noisette or Hybrid Perpetual, had all been treated precisely alike – every plant cut back to within twelve or eighteen inches of the ground. I asked the unfortunate owner the reason of this barbarous treatment, and he innocently replied that such and such an authority says "that the harder plants are cut back the more vigorously they will grow again." This is all very well for some of the Hybrid Perpetuals, and no doubt it was for these that the remark was intended, but what about the delicate slender stemmed Teas, or the climbing Noisettes? The result can easily be imagined. Those unfortunate Teas lost so much blood in the struggle that they had not sufficient strength left to start into growth again, and the majority of them succumbed. The Noisettes, such as Cloth of Gold, Solfaterre, Truimphe de Rennes, and Marechal Niel stand today as living monuments of Folly, with stems stout enough and long enough for fishing rods, but lacking all those "golden drops of beauty" they produce so freely when treated rationally.

It is, of course, more easy to understand a unit than a hundred, and in the same manner if most of our Roses could be classified or arranged round a certain small number of distinct, well known popular varieties as types, we would undoubtedly be able to understand their character and treatment better. Mr. Ellwanger's paper on this subject is a very comprehensive one, and I think I cannot do better than give it *in extenso,* feeling assured that it will

(H.P.) Mrs. Jowitt

prove of service to any of my readers who take a really practical interest in the "Queen of Flowers."

Typical Roses

To know the peculiarities which pertain to certain families of Hybrid Remontant and other Roses would be advantageous to different people in many ways. There are some types, such as La Reine, Jules Margottin, Victor Verdier, and the Giant of Battles families which are quite marked in their characteristics. If all new Roses were classified or described as being of such and such origin, or as belonging to a certain class, it would be of great value. The nurseryman is unwilling, with some exceptions, to undertake the propagation of a kind that will not root and grow freely; he also desires such as are of healthy habit, and good constitution in addition to excellence in colour and form of flower. The amateur, perhaps, would not knowingly purchase a variety devoid of fragrance, or that was not a free bloomer. The florist would perhaps require that a variety should be of steadfast colour and one that does not quickly fade, or that it should be useful to force, yielding flowers in abundance, &c. If, therefore, new Roses were described as belonging to the La Reine or Victor Vedier type, we shall have some very important knowledge of their qualities, since those Roses have imparted to their progeny certain distinct attributes by which they may readily be distinguished from others. A consideration of the different prominent types found amongh Hybrid Remontant Roses may be studied with interest and profit.

Baronne Prevost Type

The year 1842 ushered in to rosarians what is now the oldest type of Roses in the class, namely Baronne Prevost. This is not a numerous family, and is also of less importance to us than many others, but we can well imagine what pleasure it gave in years gone by to the rosarians of the day. This type makes long stout shoots, fortified with red thorns of unequal length, but generally short, foliage rather oval, somewhat crimpled; flowers large, or very large, of flat shape, very full, fragrant, and of some shade of rose : it is the most hardy type we have. Varieties : Boildieu (1877), Colonel de Rougemont (1853), Madame Boll, and Oderic Vital; they are all free bloomers.

Geant Des Batelles Type

The founder of this family was raised by Nerard in 1846, and doubtless has Bourbon blood in its veins. The colours are various shadings of crimson, very rich and effective when in perfection, but very fleeting; the sun soon gives them a muddy hue, the flowers are well shaped but small, and have slight fragrance; they are very freely produced in the spring and summer months, but, as a rule, not in autumn. The shoots are of moderate or short growth, short-jointed, erect, very stiff, and covered with very numerous reddish thorns. The foliage is of lustrous dark green, very subject to mildew. They are difficult to propagate from cuttings, and are liable to injury from frost. The leading sorts are : Arthur de Sansal, Cardinal Patrizzi, Crimson Bedder (1874), Empereur de Maroc, Eugene Appert, Evique des Nesimes, Lord Raglan, Louis Chaix, Mrs. Standish, Vainquer de Solferino, (very few of this type thrive at all satisfactorily in the plains).

Jules Margottin Type

In 1853 Jules Margottin of Bourg-la-Reine near Paris, sent out a fine Rose, which he called after himself; though he has been raising seedling Roses ever since, none of them have quite come up to this in worth. Wood light green, sharp red thorns, somewhat numerous, shoots rather stout and generally of vigorous growth, crimpled foliage. Flowers of large size, very full, somewhat flat shape, mostly shades of rose and carmine, almost without perfume, generally flowers freely in the autumn. They are very hardy; as a rule difficult of propagation by cuttings, but making very vigorous plants when budded. Abel Grand, Achille Gounod, Berthe Baron, Besie Johnson (quite fragrant), Charles Margottin (reddish crimson), Claude Bernard, Comtesse de Serenye, Duchesse de Vallambrosa, Edouard Morren, Egeria, Emily Laxton, John Hopper, Magna Charta, Madame Gabrielle Luizet, Madame La-charme, Madame Louis Levique, Mademoiselle Therese Levet, Marchioness of Exeter, Marguerite de St. Amand, Marquise de Castellane, Miss Hassard (scented), Monsieur Noman, Peach Blossom, Princess Mary of Cambrige, Rev. J.B.Camm (very sweet), are the leading sorts.

Victor Verdier Type

The head of this family originated with Lacharme of Lyons, and was sent out by him in 1852. It is doubtless of the La Reine type crossed with some monthly Rose, probably a Bourbon. The descendants are very numerous, and, in spite of their rather tender habits, form a valuable group, being the most free flowering of them all; had they but fragrance they would be unrivalled; but, alas ! they are devoid of scent, and cannot therefore rank as high as the others Fine feathers alone do not constitute fine birds, and surely fragrance is to the Rose what song is to the bird. The shoots are of moderate growth, stout, upright, nearly smooth, of a reddish green with an occasional reddish thorn; the foliage is very large and of a deep lustrous green, very attractive. The flowers are large, well built up; generally shades of rose and pink prevail. It is the best adapted for forcing in winter of all the families. The leading varieties grown are - Andre Durand, Capitaine Christy, Rosy Morn, Charles Verdier, Countess of Oxford, Etienne Levet, Hippolyte Jamain, Julius Finger, Madame George Schwartz, Madame Deverts, Madame Eugene Chambeyran, Madame Louise Donadme, Madame Maxime de la Rocheterie, Mademoiselle Eugenie Verdier, Marie Cointet, Marie Finger, Mrs. Baker, Oxonian, President Thiers, Pride of Waltham and Souvenir de President Porcher.

La Reine Type

In 1844 Laffay introduced what he loyally named "Rose of the Queen" (Rose de la Reine). This variety bore royal sway for many years; it not only still sells well, and is to be considered a very useful Rose, but it should also have our esteem as being the parent of a most useful family.

The wood is light green, furnished with occasional thorns, of strong growth; foliage pale green and crimpled. Flowers various shades of rose, generally of semi-globular form, large, somewhat fragrant, free in the autumn, quite hardy, enduring more cold than any of the other families, except Baronne Prevost. The leading sorts are Anna de Deisbach, Antoine Monton, Auguste Mie, Belle Normande, Francois Michelon, Gloire de Vitry, Louis de Peyronny, Loelia, Madame Alice Dureau, Madame Nacharry, Paul Neron, Reine du Midi, La Ville de St. Denis, Elizabeth Vigneron.

General Jacqueminot Type

In 1852 the head of what is now considered the most valuable type made his bow to an admiring world; clad in rich apparel and marshalled under his generalship is the army of dark crimson livery, Roses which so excite and please our senses by their charms and loveliness. This family probably originated from the old Hybrid China Gloire de Rosomanes; they are moderately hardy, but less so than those of the Baronne Prevost, La Reine and Jules Margottin types. The flowers are invariably shades of red and crimson, generally highly perfumed, freely produced in the spring but varying greatly as to thier autumnal bloom. As a family they are much more shy in the autumn than any of the others. The shoots are of vigorous growth, not very thick, generally upright, with quite numerous light green spines; the foliage handsome, rather pointed. It is now the most numerous of the families, popular taste leaning more towards crimson than to light colored Roses. The leading varieties are Alfred Colomb, Andre Leroy, Anna Alexieff, Beauty of Waltham, Camille Bernardin, Oriflamme de St. Louis, Charles Lefevre, Duke of Edinburgh, Empress of India, Francois Fontaine, Gloire de Santhenay, Marie Baumann, Marie Rady, Marechal Vaillant, Maurice Bernardin, Pierre Notting, Prince Camille de Rohan, Prince de Porcia, Prince Arthur, Senateur Vaisse, Triomphe de Amiens, Triomphe des Beaux Arts, Triomphe de Rosomanes, Xavier Olibo. Sub-divisions of this type occur which may be classed as follows; Charles Lefevre family with light reddish-green wood and foliage, and occasional pale red thorns; the flowers are more wavy in outline than in the other families; the growth is somewhat less vigorous, the wood more smooth. Dr. Andry, Glory of Cheshunt, Harrison Weir, Horace Levet, Lord Macaulay, Madame Anna de Bresabrassoff, Mrguerite Brassac, Mrs. Harry Turner, Paul Jamain and W. Wilson Saunders are the leading kinds. A second division of this type would be the Duke of Edinburgh family with long growing light green wood, and a few small light green spines. Flowers are thinner in petal than the others, rather smaller, burn much more quickly in the sun, and are not constant in autumn. It is a very beautiful family when grown in a moist, cool climate, but there are few of the members that will do well under our hot sun. The varieties best known, mostly or recent origin, are: Brightness of Cheshunt, Dr. Hooker, Duke of Connaught, Duke of Teck, Robert Marnock, Reynolds Hole, Sultan of Zanzibar, The Shah. A third division takes in the Alfred Colomb family, having a similar habit of growth to the General Jacqueminot type, but the thorns are less numerous, and of a more yellowish hue. The flowers are more globular, stand the sun better, and are much more freely produced, constituting a most valuable family. The varieties are : A. K. Williams, Fisher Holmes, William Roelle. A fourth division includes the Senateur Vaisse family. This is of moderate growth with smoother wood than most of the others, and rather more perfectly formed flowers. The foliage is more round, and perhaps of a deeper green. Madame Victor Verdier, Mousieur E.Y.Teas and Mrs. Laxton form the leading members.

Monsieur Boncenne Type

This type was introduced in 1864 by Liabaud, and gives us the darkest roses we have. From appearances we should think it originated in a natural cross between varieites of the Giant of Batelles and General Jacqueminot types. They are of dark green wood, with few thorns, rather long shoots of somewhat spreading habit. The two varieties first named are of very vigorous growth, and resemble each other so much as to be considered synonymous. None of these bloom freely in the autumn, but they are magnificent in their dark velvety shades as seen in the spring. Baron Chauraud, Baron de Bonstetten, Abel Carriere. Henry Bennett Jean Cherpin, Jean Liabaud, Jean Soupert, and President Leon de St. Jean comprise the family. This about exhausts the divisions that can be considered distinct types. Though there are other roses that stand aloof, they have no followers. Such are Baroness Rothschild, Mabel Morrison, Caroline de Sansal, and a few others.

On examination it will be found that none of these types combine all excellencies, but that the Alfred Colomb, Charles Lefevre and Senateur Vaisse families have more good points concentrated in them than any of the rest. It is from these types that we have the most to hope for, as the seed parents of the better varieties that shall be raised in the immediate future; but hybridisers should seek to blend the excellencies which pertain to other families with the good features of these. Having this aim in view, we may hope in confidence for a deep crimson Marie Baumann of vigorous growth, a fragrant Eugenie Verdier, and a white Alfred Colomb.

Taken as a family the hybrid-perpetual has found in India a home in every way congenial to it. There are, however, exceptions to every rule, and amongst such a large and varied family, whose many primogenitors were originally scattered over almost the four quarters of the globe, we must expect to find some who cannot stand the vicissitudes of an Indian life, and consequently, either succumb entirely or bloom most indifferently, and in a few instances obstinately refuse to bloom at all. For our own guidance it is advisable to divide this large family into two groups. First, those in which the Provence, French or Damask blood is predominant; second, those that are nearer allied to the China, Bengal or Bourbon families. Now all the Roses of the latter class invariably thrive to perfection in this country; many of them better even than in Europe. The former group are much more uncertain, some of them are all that could be desired, but, as a rule, the nearer affinity any particular variety has to any of the three species mentioned, the less probability is there of its succeeding satisfactorily. The reason for this is not far to seek, as they are all descended from species indigenous either to Europe or Western Asia. The second group being all inhabitants of Eastern Asia, accounts for their thriving so satisfactorily in our climate. I should explain here that *Rosa Bourbonica,* the parent of all the Bourbon Roses, is believed to have been a nutural hybrid from *Rosa Indica,* probably crossed with some species of Damask Rose, and is consequently always classed with Roses of Eastern origin.

Selection of Varieties

Having divided the family into distinct groups as above mentioned, we must next proceed to the selection of varieties, a task of no ordinary difficulty when we consider the immense number of varieties that are now in cultivation, some of the English rose-growers' catalogues descirbing four to five hundred kinds; this is even eclipsed by some Continental raisers, one Belgian firm in particular giving the names of over 1,000 varieites of hybrid perpetuals. It is hardly necessary to remark that lists of this description must contain an immense number of worthless kinds, and also innumerable synonyms, or varieties so closely resembling each other as to completely baffle the most experienced rosarian to distinguish them. We must first determine what space we have at command for Roses, and what proportion of it we can set aside for this class only, for it should be the aim of every Rosarian to grow each group or class separately, as it is only by this means that we can attain any degree of neatness or uniformity in our Rose garden. If we indiscriminately mix Bourbons, Hybrid Perpetuals, Teas, and Noisettes together, our beds must present a straggling uneven appearance, baffling every attempt to reduce it to any degree of neatness. Having decided on the space to be planted, and the number of plants required, we next come to the selection of varieites, and we should here aim rather at quality than quantity. For instance, suppose we have space for a hundred plants only, it would be much more judicious to plant fifty good kinds in duplicate than to plant a hundred varieties. In making a selection we should also arrange to balance the various shades of colour as much as possible.

I will now endeavour to give a list of this numerous family divided into groups of each colour, and for this purpose adopt the classification of that veteran rosarian "Rivers," as given by him in his "Rose Amateur's Guide," adding only the names of the many new varieties introduced since the publication of the last edition of that invaluable little work.

Dark Crimson

There are but few varieties of this class of colour - I mean with those dark velvety petals so common among the French Roses and hybrid Chinas, and with flowers full and perfect in shape. It has always been a curious fact in rose culture that dark, almost black roses have either been semi-double or ill-shapen, so that it is only within very recent times we have received varieties with flowers large, full and tolerably shaped, still we ought not to give up the culture of Emperor de Maroc : its flowers are very double, not large, and slightly reflexed. It forms a pillar rose of much beauty, its flowers are so rich and deep in their colouring. Alexandre Dupont, Prince Camille de Rohan, Reynolds Hole, Roseriste Jacobs, Souvenir de Charles Montault, Souvenir de Victor Verdier, Sultan of Zanzibar, Vicomte de Vigier, Xavier Olibo, Abel Carriere, Auguste Neumann, Clovis, Comte de Flandres, Crown Prince, Dingee Conard, Dr. Hogg, Due de Rohan, Duke of Wellington, Empereur de Bresil, Fontenelle, Jean Cherpin, Jean Soupert, Lord Beaconsfield, Monsieur Boucenne, and Monsieur Eugene Delair are all dark roses, generally shaded with purple.

Crimson and Scarlet

There are many shades of this colour in the Roses of this family, depending for their brilliancy much on climate, season and situation. Among the most brilliant is the well known Geant des Batelles, now old, and almost forgotten, the most bright and brilliant of all Roses, and at the same time one of the most hardy and free-growing. No Rose of late years has been so popular. As an instance of this I may mention that in the autumn of 1849, eight thousand standards and dwarfs of this variety were dispersed over the whole face of the country from this place (Mr. Rivers' Nursery).

This beautiful and favourite Rose is now the parent of a numerous family, every member of which, when first ushered into the rose-world, has been pronounced more beautiful than its far-famed parent. After a time, however, most of these promising children have settled down into esteemed members of the Geant family, but have not totally eclipsed their parent.

In enumerating the fine Roses of this range of colour one is almost bewildered, so numerous are they. It would seem when one sees a fine flower of Senateur Vaisse just on the point of expanding, that no Rose, or indeed no flower, can be more brilliant, more beautiful; yet I have sometimes bent over Gloire de Santenay, and thought it still more so; the flowers of both are so perfect in shape, so brilliant, and so exceedingly beautiful. Charles Lefevre, Francois Lacharme, Alphonse Damaizin, Maurice Bernardin, Professor Koch, Madame Julie Doran, Oliver Delhomme, Alfred Colomb, Le Rhone, Lord Macaulay, Antonie Ducher, Baronne Adolphe de Rothschild, Comtesse de Oxford, Dr. Audry, Duke of Edinburgh, Fisher Holmes, Louis Van Houtte, Marie Baumann,Vaniquer de Goliath and Lord Clyde form a perfect galaxy of Rose beauty. I cannot see the possibility of surpassing the above by new varieties, and yet they come, or pretend to come, every season from France. Every spring some fine new varieties are ushered into the rose-world of England, and some thousands of francs have been sent over to our neighbours in exchange for a host of new names, to be added to the rose catalogues of the day so as to perplex both buyers and sellers. This incessant introduction of novelties without novelty, is, I fear, bringing rose cultivation to Charlatanism, which can only be stemmed by the English growers being well assured of the qualities of a new Rose before they recommend it. We must not pass over some old friends in this class of colour. General Jacqueminot, with its luxuriant growth and magnificent clusters of flowers, has always been a favourite, and will continue to be so although its large crimson flowers are not so full and perfect in shape as those of the varieties I have enumerated. The following are the principal varieties belonging to the class besides those above mentioned: – A. G. St. Hilaire, Alfred de Rougemont, Auguste Rigotard, Camille Bernardin, Charles Darwin, Crimson Bedder, Dean of Windsor, Docteur Baillon, Dr. Hooker, Dr. Sewell, Due de Montpensier, Duchess de Caylus, Duchess of Bedford, Duke of Tech, Edouard Pynaert, Empress of India, Eugene Appert, Exposition de Brie, Ferdinand Chafrolette, Francois Louvat, Glory of Cheshunt, Henry Bennett, Horace Vernet, Jean Liabaud, Jules Chretien, Lady Sheffield, La Rosiere, Lord Raglan, Madame Charles Crapelet, Madame C. Wood, Madame Ferdinand Jamain, Marechal Vaillant, Marguerite Brassac, Masterpiece, May Quennell, Monsieur Etienne Levet, Monsieur E.Y. Teas, Pierre Seletsky, Mrs. Baker, Mrs. Harry Turner, Mrs. Laxton, Pierre Notting, Prince Arthur, Red Dragon, Robert Marnock and Star of Waltham.

Carmine

The Roses of this range of colour are perhaps the most chaste and pleasing of all, as their flowers are for the most part so elegantly shaped. Prince Leon is a gem, and is remarkable for its vigorous habit and fine foliage. To this now old variety we may add Jules Margottin, which, taking all in all - its fine colour, shape, fragrance, robust habit, and freedom of flowering - may be pronounced the finest Rose known. How grand are its early flowers, the personification of our old cabbage-rose, with a perfume quite equal, and a bright rosy pink colour far more interesting.

The following kinds will be found perfect and beautiful : – A.K. Williams, Amicet Bourgeois, Baron Haussmann, Beauty of Waltham, Boildieu, Constantin Fretiakoff, Devienne Lamy, Dupuy Jamain, Ernest Prince, Francois Courtin, George Baker, John Hopper, J.S. Mill, King's Aere, La Ville de St. Denis, Le Havre, Louise Dore, Madame Clemence, Joigneaux, Madame Ducher, Madame Therese Levet, Mdlle. Marie Rady, Marie Louise Pernet, Marquis de Castellane, Paul Verdier, Richard Laxton, Sir G. Wolseley, Thomas Mills and Ulrich Brunner Fils, these form the *creme de la creme* of this group, and no Roses can be more charming; these all, or nearly all, have an intensity of rose colour, if the expression may be used, which is of all colours the most pleasing, for do we not say "the rosy morn," "the rosy hues of life," and employ many other expressions all denoting the invariable charm of this most delightful of all tints?

Roses Coloured and Pink

Almost numberless are the Roses of this tint, so that it is really difficult to select a few that are most worthy of the attention of every amateur. Our old friend La Reine is still in dry seasons most beautiful and fragrant; but her daughter Louise Peyronny is still more so, for, owing to this charming Rose not being quite so double, it opens well in all seasons. The following kinds are distinct and very beautiful :– Abel Grand, Alice Dureau, Ana Alexieff, Annie Laxton, Baronne Prevost, Calliope, Catherine Bell, Centifolia rosea, Duchess of Edinburgh, Elie Morel, Hippolyte Jamain, Julia Touvais, Lady Sheffield, Madame Caillat, Madme Eugene Verdier, Madame Fillion, Madame Montet, Mdle. Eugenie Verdier, Magna Charta, Marchioness of Exeter, Marguerite de St. Amand, Monsieur Paul Neron, Nardy Freres, Oxonian, Pierre Durand, Queen of Waltham, Royal Standard, Victor Verdier, William Warden, William Griffiths; but let us not forget a Rose of a charming silvery rosy lilac colour, Madame Vigneron, which the raiser declared, when describing it, "glistened as if powdered with silver."

Are there yet more gems ? Yes, new names and new and fine Roses; for such are most perfect in all that constitute fine Roses. Another and another still, for who can pass by and not admire Comtesse de Chabrillant? No Rose can be more perfect or beautiful; and yet we may add Duchess de Cambacres, a most vigorous growing rose, blooming in immense clusters, giving flowers with a powerful fragrance. Of all the Roses in this group, the Comtesse de Chabrillant is the most perfect in shape and colour, like Senateur Vaisse or Charles Lefevre among crimson roses : it is quite impossible to imagine a rose more beautiful.

Blush and Flesh Coloured

Among the most desirable varieties in this class of colour is Madame Rivers, with flowers nearly white; it is a vigorous grower and appears to bloom well in all climates. With this very fine Rose we may class Madame Vidot, of the same exquisite shape, but tinted with delicate pink so as to be wax-like and most beautiful. Besides these we have Bessie Johnson, Captain Christy, Charles Rouillard, Comtesse de Serrenyi, Duchess de Vallambrosa, La France, Baroness Rothschild, Madame Marie Finger, Marquise de Montmart, Miss Hassard, Peach Blossom, Pride of Waltham,

Princess Louise Victoria, Rosy Morn, Sophie Coquerelle, and Marguerite D'Ombrain.

White

We have as yet not a long list of Roses of this desirable colour, though several very choice varieties have been introduced during the past few years, among which are, Baron de Maynard, Boule de Niege, Helene Paul, Julius Finger, Mabel Morrison, Mervielle de Lyon, Madame Francois Pettit, Madame Hippolyte Jamain. Madame Lacharme, Madame Noman, Mdlle Bonnaire, Reine Blanche, Violette Bouyer and White Baroness.

Chapter XV
Hybrid Perpetual Roses

In the foregoing groups I have briefly noticed the best known and most popular kinds in each section, and will now endeavour to give a descriptive list of the leading members of this large family. In compiling this, the aim has been to include only those of proved sterling merit, both new and old. There is no questioning the fact that, taken as a body, there is a vast improvement year by year in the new varieties introduced, not only in colour and form of flower, but also in the habit of growth, (a point too often lost sight of in the selection of varieties). On the other had it must also be admitted that amongst the older kinds there are gems of the purest water, take for instance Paul Neron, Marie Baumann, Senateur Vaisse or Xavier, Olibo. If we except A.K. Williams, and perhaps Mervielle de Lyon, there has not been a single new variety introduced during the past ten years to equal them in their respective classes.

In the column describing the habit of growth the following abbreviations are used :-

Vig. – for vigorous, being varieties which form large heads, and produce long vigorous shoots, nearly all of which are adapted for Pillar Roses.

Rob. – robust varieties which produce long shoots and large wood; these form good Standards, and some of them good Pillar Roses.

Free – varieties which are very good growers, forming fine full-sized plants.

Mod. – moderate, these are compact, yet good growers, although they never make large heads.

Dwf. – dwarf, are mostly dwarf delicate-growing sorts, which should only be grown as dwarfs.

The letter S is affixed to all the fines Show Roses; these may be depended on as being the best and most constant for the purpose of exhibition.

The letter P indicates those varieties which are best adapted for Pillar Roses.

Name	Description	Habit of Growth
Abel Carriere........S	dark velvety crimson, colour of *Prince Camille de Rohan,* large and well formed, good shape, and one of the best dark Roses ...	vig.
Abel Grand...........S	clear silvery pink, flowers large, full, and well-formed; a good Rose, and very sweet	vig.
Admiral Seymour....S	deep velvety purplish red, flowers large and full	vig.
A. Egeria............S	beautiful bright rosy pink, very large, full, and well formed	vig.
A.G. St. Hillaire....S	bright crimson, flowers Camellia-formed, dwarf habit; a good Rose	vig.
Alfred Colomb....S	brilliant carmine-crimson, flowers very large, full and globular; superb	rob.
Alfred de Rougemont..	very rich deep velvety crimson, flowers medium size, smooth, beautifully formed, double	mod.
Alfred K. Williams....S	fine carmine-red, large, full, and imbricated; one of the most beautiful and perfect	vig.
Alexandre Dupont....	Purple velvety red, shaded with crimson, very large	vig.
Andre Gill...............	Bright carmine-red, large, full, well formed, globular	vig.
Antoine Chantin......	Dark cherry-red, edge of petals whitish, flowers large, full and well formed	vig.
Alphonse Soupert.....	Pure vivid rose, the flower in the way of *La Reine*	vig.
Alice Dureau..........S	rosy lilac, centre deep red rose, flowers very full, globular, very fine and sweet-scented	vig.
A. M. Ampere........	purple-red, with bluish reflex, medium size, full, cupped	vig.
Amicet Bourgeois....	bright cherry-red, large, full, cupped, blooming in clusters	vig.
Anna Alexieff.........P	fresh rosy pink, a good and abundant blooming Rose	free.

Name	Description	Habit of Growth
Annie Laxton..........S	deep rose, beautifully shaded with cherry-crimson; very early	free.
Annie Wood...........S	brilliant crimson-scarlet, flowers double and perfectly imbricated; a first-rate Rose	vig.
Antoine Ducher.......S	very rich crimson-rose, large smooth thick petals, flowers large, full, deep, and well formed	mod.
Archiauchesse Eiizabeth D Autriche.....	fine pink-rose, very large, full, free flowering	vig.
Auguste Neumann...S	rich velvety crimson and violet-purple, very dark, and colour stands well, full and of good size; a good Rose	mod.
Auguste Rigotard....S	clear brilliant crimson, petals large, even, and smooth, flowers cupped; a fine Rose	vig.
Avocat Duvivier.......S	deep purplish red, very large, full, and perfect	vig.
Baron de Bonstettin..S	rich velvety purple, in the way of and similar to *Monsieur Boncenne;* a fine Rose	vig.
Baron de Maynard...P	pure paper-white, flower of moderate size, full and well formed	mod.
Baron Haussmann...S	clear carmine-crimson, flowers of good size, beautifully inbricated and full; a fine Rose	vig.
Baronne Prevost....P	brilliant rose, very large and full; forms a fine Pillar	vig.
Baroness Rothschild..	*Madame la Baronne de Rothschild.*	
Barthelemy Joubert.S	bright cherry-red, large and full; fine	vig.
Baron Nathaniel de ...	right crimson-red, large, full, fine form *Rothschild*........	vig.
Beauty of Beeston....	fine brilliant velvety crimson, a dwarf-growing *Charles Lefebvre,* but not so full, foliage fine; very free flowering, and sweetly scented	
Beauty of Waltham...S	cherry-crimson, petals large and well disposed, flowers cupped, large, and finely formed, very sweet	free.
Bessie Johnson......S	blush-white, flowers very large and full, and highly fragrant; good light Rose	vig.
Boildieu..................	bright cherry, very large, full globular flowers	rob.
Boule de Neige.......P	pure white, centre delicately shaded with cream, flowers of beautifully imbricated form; a good white Rose,	vig.

Name	Description	Habit of Growth
Brightness of Cheshunt.......S	peculiarly vivid brick-red, a medium sized flower of open imbricated form, very free	
Calliope............S	centre beautiful bright pink, outer petals paler; long handsome buds, very large and full; fine and distinct	
Camille Bernardin....S	bright red, beautifully formed, large, full, and deliciously sweet	
Captain Christy....S	blush, centre delicate flesh colour, flowers large, full, and beautifully formed; a superb Rose	mod
Capucine Liabaud....	capucine-red, medium size, double	vig.
Catherine Bell........	flowers very large, deep rose, back petals delicate silvery pink, and very fragrant, vigorous climbing habit	vig.
Centifolia rosea....S	rich rose-pink, flowers large and cupped, a very distinct and beautiful Rose with abundant foliage	vig.
Charles Darwin....S	deep crimson, with a brownish tint, and slightly shaded with violet; a good boomer and thoroughly distinct	
Charles Lefebvre..SP	rich velvety shaded crimson, smooth thick petals, flowers extra large, quite full, and most beautifully formed; a superb Rose	vig.
Charles Rouillard	pale rosy peach, changing to pale lavender-rose, flowers cupped, large, full and exquisitely formed	vig.
Charles Fanquet	scarlet-red, large, full, well formed	vig.
Climbing Chas. Lefebvre	a wonderfully vigorous sport from that superb old Rose *Charles Lefebvre;* producing shots 8 to 9 feet in a season; as a crimson perpetual climbing Rose, this is a great acquisition	vig.
Climbing Jules Margottin	a sport from *Jules Margottin;* flowers exactly similar to its parent; a free and vigorous climbing habit; not in a robust form, but branching as freely as an evergreen climbing Rose	vig.
Climbing Victor Verdier	bright cherry-red, strong climbing habit; a good pillar or climbing Rose	vig.
Clothilde Rolland	pinkish rose, colour clear and good, flowers of moderate size, well filled and nicely imbricated, fine globular form	vig.
Clovis	violet-red, shaded, distinct and good	vig.

Name	Description	Habit of Growth
Colonel Felix Breton	velvety grenata-red, large and full, regularly imbricated form, a new colour	vig.
Comte de Mortemart.........SP	fine clear rose, of very large size, full, in the way of *Centifolia,* beautiful circular shelled form; a very distinct variety in every way	vig.
Comte Frederick de Thun Hohenstein......	deep crimson, shaded with carmine, large, full, and fine form	vig.
Comte Horace de Choiseuil..........	ver milion, lighted with velvety scarlet, shaded, large, full imbricate form	vig.
Comte de Flandres...	purple-red, large, full, well-formed; a seedling from *Madame Victor Verdier*	vig.
Comte Adrien de Germiny.........	bright rose, large, full, well formed, imbricated; a seedling from *Jules Margottin*	vig.
Comtesse Henriette Combbs........	bright rose, with silvery reflex, large, full, in the way of *Marie Baumann*	vig.
Comtesse de Paris.........S	very bright clear red, and of fine form; a good Rose	free.
Comtesse Cecile de Chabrillant.........S	beautiful satin-rose, flowers very compact and perfect, very sweet	free.
Comtesse de Camondo.........S	fine bright rose, shaded with violet, very large, full, imbricated form; extra	vig.
Comtesse de Serenyi.........S	blush centre, beautifully shaded rose, cupped and perfectly formed; one of the best light Roses	vig.
Comtesse Nathalie de Kleist	coppered red, reverse of petals carmine, a new colour; large, full, cupped	
Comtesse de Casteja.................	rich deep scarlet, large, full, perfect imbricated form; opens freely, first class variety. A seedling from *Alfred Colomb;* is quite as good, but a different colour	vig.
Comtesse de Mailly-Hesle...........	flesh colour, shaded, large, full, well formed	vig
Comtesse de Paris...	bright rose, large, full, globulous, well-formed	vig.
Constantin Fretiakoff.........S	flowers very large, very full, well formed, beautiful brilliant cerise-red, much deeper in the centre; a superb Rose and sweet scented	vig.
Countess of Oxford.........S	carmine, with soft violet shade, velvety, flowers large, full, and cupped, petals smooth; a fine Rose	vig.
Countess of Roseberry.......S	flowers brilliant carmine-rose, large, full, and finely cupped; a vigorous-growing variety, blooming freely all through the year	vig.

Name	Description	Habit of Growth
Crimson Bedder, introduced, 1874......	as a crimson bedding Rose this variety surpasses every other for brilliancy of colour and continuous blooming; its habit of growth is moderate, and short-jointed, producing a mass of flowers the whole season; colour scarlet and crimson, very effective and lasting, clean glossy foliage and free from mildew	mod.
*Crown Prince.........*S	flowers bright purple, the centre shaded with lurid-crimson, very large and double	
*Dean of Windsor....*S	clear rich vermilion, sometimes slightly shaded with crimson, large, full, and good symmetrical form; free and constant	mod.
*Devienne Lamy.......*S	deep carmine a large full flower of imbricated form; a very fine Rose....................	mod.
*Dingee Conard.......*S	rich velvety crimson, a well-formed compact flower, fine even petals and good high centre; a fine dark Rose	mod.
Directeur Alphand......	deep blackish purple, large, full, well formed	vig.
*Docteur Andry.........*S	rich rosy crimson, flowers large, fine smooth petals; a superb Rose	free.
Docteur Baillon......	bright crimson-red, shaded with purple, large, full and well-formed	vig.
*Dr. Hogg.........*P	deep violet, nearest to the blue colour sometimes desired in Roses, pretty shell-shaped petal, and very hardy	vig.
*Dr. Hooker.........*S	deep crimson and velvety purple good petals, large, even, and well formed	vig.
*Dr. Sewell.........*S	brilliant crimson-scarlet, shaded with purple, back of petals bright red, large, full, and finely cupped	vig.
*Duc de Montpensier.........*S	rich velvety crimson, flowers large, full, and well formed; a superb Rose......................	mod.
*Duc de Rohan.........*S	fine brilliant carmine, superb colour; a good old Rose	vig.
*Duc de Wellington..*S	rich velvety crimson, flowers good size, cupped and well formed; a first-rate Rose	mod.
*Duchesse de Caylus.........*S	glowing rosy crimson, flowers large, full and beautifully cupped, with high centre and fine outline	free.
*Duchesse de Vallombrosa.........*S	blush, centre delicate flesh, flowers large, full, and cupped; an exquisitely formed and beautiful Rose	vig.

Name	Description	Habit of Growth
Duchess of Bedford.S	flowers dazzling light scarlet-crimson, large, full, and of perfect globular shape	
Duchess of Connaught.......	dazzling crimson, shaded with dark velvety purple, highly perfumed, free bloomer	mod.
Duchess of Edinburgh.........S	pale rose, flowers large and globular; a well formed flower, but not constant	vig.
Duke of Albany.......	flowers vivid crimson when first opening, changing to a darker shade of colour as they expand, very large and full	rob.
Duke of Connaught..S	velvety crimson and purple, rich deep colour; compact, well formed, and a very good Rose.	mod.
Duke of Edinburgh..S	rich velvety crimson, shaded, flowers large and very attractive; a superb Rose	vig.
Duke of Teck.........S	bright crimson-scarlet, clear and distinct, in the way of *Duke of Edinburgh*	free.
Dupuy Jamin.........S	brilliant carmine-crimson, colour very fine, petals large, broad, and smooth, flowers well formed, luxuriant foliage; a good Rose	vig.
Earl of Pembroke.....	colour very soft velvety crimson, enlivened on margin of petals with bright red	
Eclair........................	bright fire-red in the way of *Charles Lefebvre* .	vig.
Edgard Jolibois..........	velvety-scarlet, shaded violet, flowers large and very double;	vig.
Edouard Morren.......	brilliant glossy pink, very large; a magnificent Rose	rob.
Edouard Pynaert...SP	deep crimson, shaded violet, compact, well-formed even flowers; very fragrant	vig.
Elie Morel.........S	lilac-rose, flowers very large, full, and of very fine form; a beautiful Rose	free.
Emilie Hausberg....S	light rose, changing to pale satin-rose, large and full, exquisitely formed	vig.
Emily Laxton.........S	a large full flower with globular pointed buds, flowers large and well formed; a good Rose	vig.
Empereur de Bresil..S	red, shaded with blackish violet, very large and very full	vig.
Empress of India....S	dark crimson and purple, well formed, moderate size	vig.
Ernest Prince.........S	clear red, deeper in the centre, very large, well formed and globulous	vig.

Name	Description	Habit of Growth
Eugene Appert.......P	bright scarlet and crimson, colour superb; a fine pillar Rose	rob.
Exposition de Brie...S	rich glowing crimson, flowers large and of good form; very fine	free.
Ferdinand Chaffolte.......S	deep velvety crimson, colour very bright and beautiful, flowers large and full, outer petals smooth and shell-shaped	
Fisher Holmes.......S	rich purplish crimson, flowers large, cupped, double, and of fine imbricated form; a superb Rose	free.
Fontenelle.......P	dark velvety crimson and purple, very large and full, blooms in clusters	vig.
Francois Courtin.......	purplish cerise, outside rose with white stripes, flowers large, full, and of a fine cup shape	vig.
Francois Levet.....SP	Chinese rose, medium size	vig.
Francois Louvat......S	deep crimson, shaded with lilac, very large and fine cupped form; a superb Rose	vig.
Francois Olin...........	cherry-red, mixed with white, large, full, well formed, blooming in clusters	vig.
Geant des Batailles....	brilliant crimson, large, full, and very sweet; a well-known old Rose	mod.
General Jacqueminot.......S	brilliant scarlet-crimson, most superb glowing colour, and a most abundant bloomer; a fine bedding Rose	vig.
George Baker.......S	a pure lake, shaded with cerise, good form	free.
Georges Moreau......S	very bright, shaded red, very large, opening well; globulous	vig.
Glorie de Bourg La Reine...............	fine brilliant scarlet red, and crimson, flower large and full; a superb Rose	vig.
Gloire de Rosomene	brilliant crimson, semi-double; most effective and beautiful as a Pillar Rose	free.
Glory of Cheshunt....S	this is a seedling from *Charles Lefebvre*, with flowers of a rich shaded crimson, very bright and vivid	free.
Guillaume Guillemot.......S	carmined rose, with pale reflex, very large, full, and globulous; a seedling from *Madame Charles Wood*	vig.
Harrison Weir.......S	beautiful rich velvety crimson enlivened with scarlet, flowers large, full, very smooth	rob.

Name	Description	Habit of Growth
Helene Paul.......S	very fine white, sometimes shaded with rose, very large, of globular form	vig.
Henrich Schultheis....	delicate pinkish rose; sweet scented; very vigorous; flowers exceedingly large, of first-rate form, and very full	vig.
Henry Pages............	bright rose, large and full, fine form, good habit	vig.
Henriette Petit.......P	fine deep amaranth red, large, full, well formed; in the way of *Beauty of Waltham*, but more vigorous	vig.
Henry Bennett.......P	intense violet-crimson, colour very rich, flowers cupped, good even petals, but not sufficiently full	vig.
Hippolyte Flandrin...S	rosy pink, colour glossy and good, petals large, smooth, and firm, flowers very large, imbricated	mod.
Hippolyte Jamain....S	fine bright rose, shaded with carmine, very large and full, flowers very even and well formed; a fine rose	vig.
Horace Vernet.......S	rich brilliant velvety crimson, petals large and smooth, flowers large, full, and of a most perfectly imbricated form; a truly superb Rose	free.
Hortense Mignard.....	soft rose, a well-formed smooth flower, petals shell-shaped; a good flower	free.
Jean Cherpin.......S	rich violet-plum, a superb colour, petals smooth and well formed, and the flowers cupped	mod.
Jean Liabaud.......S	fiery crimson, centre rich velvety crimson, flowers large, double, and well-formed; one of the finest dark Roses	vig.
Jean Soupert.......S	plum-purple, almost black, flowers good size and evenly firmed	vig.
Jeanne Sury.......S	bright claret and crimson, a large handsome Rose	free.
John Hopper.......S	centre brilliant rosy crimson, the outer petals lilac-rose, flowers cupped, full, and well formed; a first-class Rose	rob.
John Stuart Mill......S	bright clear red, large, full, and beautiful form, fine shell-like petals of good substance; a good Rose	vig.

Name	Description	Habit of Growth
Joseph Metral.........	deep grenata-red, large, full; a new colour	vig.
Jules Chretien.......S	bright crimson-red, shaded with purple, very large, full, and well formed; a superb Rose	vig.
Jules Margottin.......S	brilliant glossy pink, a glowing flesh colour, flowers large; a beautiful old variety	vig.
Julius Finger.......S	pure white, lightly tinted with rose at the end of the season, large, full, and perfect form	vig.
Julia Touvais.......S	soft pink, with silvery rose tint, large, full, and distinct	rob.
King's Acre.......S	bright vermilion rose, flowers of extra large size, globular; a fine Rose for forcing	vig.
La Duchesse de Morny.................S	bright pleasing rose, flowers large, full, and beautifully formed, having petals of good susbtance	vig.
Lady Sheffield.......S	brilliant rosy cerise	
La France...........S	satin pink, outer petals pale flesh, flowers large and globular, partakes somewhat of the China Rose, very fragrant, distinct, and beautiful	free.
La Reine............SP	brilliant glossy rose, large and full	free.
La Rosiere..........S	amaranth, large and full, somewhat resembling *Prince Camille de Rohan;* a superb Rose	vig.
La Ville de St. Denis.......S	rosy carmine, flowers as large as those of *La Reine,* and exquisitely formed	free.
Loelia.......S	satin-rose; a noble Rose, with fine large smooth petals, and of exquisite form	mod.
La Souveraine.......SP	beautiful lively rose-carmine, reverse of petals whitish, very large, habit very robust, and very sweet; similar to *Madame Clemence Joigneaux*	vig.
L'Esperance..........S	rosy cerise, colour clear and satiny, flowers large, well formed and double, highly scented	mod.
Le Havre..............S	brilliant vermilion, flowers smooth and well formed; a fine Rose	mod.
Leopold I., Roi des Belges...............S	crimson, with a soft tint of violet, flowers large, full, and imbricated; a beautiful Rose	vig.
Lecocq-Dumesnil.......	dazzling red, strongly marbled and tinted with brown, crimson and violet flowers extra large, full, and perfectly imbricated	vig.

Name	Description	Habit of Growth
Leon Say............	bright red shaded with brown, lilac-rose, large, full; a good variety for bedding	vig.
Lord Bacon...........	flowers deep crimson, illumined with scarlet and shaded with velvety black, large and full	rob.
Lord Beaconsfield	blackish crimson, very fine large globular flower of good habit	vig.
Lord Frederic Caxendish............	bright dazzling scarlet, being much brighter than *Duke of Edinburgh* or *Duke of Teck;* form unique, globular, and finely finished	vig.
Lord Macaulay.......S	rich dark velvety crimson, colour dense and glowing, flowers large, double, and well formed; a superb Rose	free.
Lord Raglan.......SP	deep crimson, changing to mottled crimson, large and superb	vig.
Louis Dore..........S	fine cherry-red, shaded with purple, fine form, large, full, a free bloomer, and a fine Rose	vig.
Louis Van Houtte....S	deep red-amranth, shaded with dark claret, good and distinct, flowers cupped and well formed; a fine distinct Rose, and very fragrant; superb	mod.
Lydia Martey...........	pale pink, flowers large, and of good substance	vig.
Mabel Morrison.......	a sport of *Baroness Rothschild,* pure white; not sufficiently double	mod.
Ma Surprise.......	bright scarlet, sometimes violet, not always perpetual; a seedling from *Eugene Appert*	vig.
Madame Alexandre Julien.......	fine delicate fresh rose, large and full, beautiful elongated bud	vig.
Madame Appoline Foulon.......	fine light salmon, shaded with lilac, flowers large and full	vig.
Madame Alfred Leveau.......S	bright carmine rose, large, full, fine form	vig.
Madame Auguste Perrin.......	fine rose, reverse of the petals whitish, of medium size, large, well formed	vig.
Madame Bertha Mackart.......	deep rose, reverse of the petals silvery, flowers extra large, cup-shaped, and somewhat globular; described as thoroughly perpetual	vig.
Madame Boutin.......S	cerise, a beautiful clear colour, flowers very large and full, petals broad and even	rob.

Name	Description	Habit of Growth
Madame Caillat.......S	clear brilliant rose, flowers large and full, petals broad and even; a first-rate Rose, and quite distinct	rob.
Madame Charles Crapelct..............S	rosy scarlet, large smooth petals, flowers beautifully formed; a superb Rose	free.
Madame Charles Wood..................S	beautiful clear rosy crimson, petals large and of good substance, flowers very large, expanded, full, and well formed	mod.
Madame Chevrot....S	satin-rose, cheerful colour, smooth, well-formed flowers; seedling from *Victor Verdier*	vig.
Madame Clemence Joigneaux.......S	brilliant rosy carmine, flowers very large, deep, and very full, fine stout petals; a superb Rose	rob.
Madame Crosy.........	China rose, very large petals; sedling from *Souvenir de la Reine d' Angleterre*	
Madame Dorlia.......	bright cherry-red, shaded with purple, very large, full, and expanded	vig.
Madame Ducher........	bright carmine, very large, flowers evenly and well formed; a superb Rose	
Madame Eugene Chambeyras.......S	light rose, shaded with copper, large, full, globulous, very fine form; a seedling from *Victor Verdier*	vig.
Madame Eugene Verdier.......S	light silvery rose, clear and good, of large fine-petalled glomular shape	vig.
Madame F. Bruel.......	carmine-rose, large, full; seedling from *Comtesse d'Oxford*	
Madame Ferdinand Jamain.......S	rosy claret, deep petals, large and bold flowers, distinct and good; very fragrant	vig.
Madame Fillion.......S	fresh rosy pink, flowers large, full, and of good form; very fragrant	vig.
Madame Francois Pettit......P	beautiful white, form globular............................	vig.
Madame Furtado.....S	brilliant carmine-rose, colour fresh and beautiful, flowers globular, of great depth and fine outline; highly scented, delicate habit	mod.
Madame Gabriel Luizet.......S	fine satin-rose, a very delicate and beautiful tint, large, full, and well-formed; a distinct and very beautiful rose, very sweet	vig.
Madame Georges Schwartz...............S	glossy rose, with soft lavender shade, flowers large, full, and cupped; a fine deep flower and a superb Rose	vig.

Name	Description	Habit of Growth
Madame Hippolyte Jamain.................S	white, slightly tinged with rose, extra large, and a very fine show flower	vig.
Madame Jacquier...S	lavender-rose, veined, and shaded bright rose, flowers globular, petals deep and shell-shaped; a handsome Rose	vig.
Madame John Twombly................	deep currant-red, large, full, well-formed, in the way of *Alfred Colomb*	vig.
Madame Jules Grevy.......	interior salmon-white, outside salmon-red, medium size; a sport between *Triomphe de l'Exposition* and *Madame Falcot*	vig.
Madame Julie Daran................S	violet crimson, flowers cupped, beautiful form, large smooth petals, of good quality	vig.
Mdlle. Julie Gaulain...	fine rose, shaded with salmoned-orange, large, almost full	vig.
Madame Knorr...........	deep brilliant rose, outer petals whitish, distinct; very beatiful in bud	free.
Madame La Baronne de Rothschild.......S	palest flesh, petals large and smooth, flowers large, double, and of fine globular form, very distinct and beautiful; one of the best	mod.
Madame La Marquise d'Herve...............YS	violet-red, shaded with bluish slate, large and full; this is the nearest approach to a blue Rose	vig.
Madame Lacharme..S	white, centre the palest blush, cupped, exquisitely formed and highly scented; a beautiful white Rose	free.
Madame Laurent.....S	bright rose, fine large globular flower, handsome and distinct	vig.
Madame le Lievre de la place................	bright shaded currant red, and whitish edge, flowers very large, full, and well formed	vig.
Madame Louise Vigneron..................	beautiful bright rose, with darker centre, flowers large, full, and well formed	vig.
Mdlle. Louise Aunier..	bright rose, large, full, imbricated form	vig.
Mdlle. Louise Chretien.................	deep rose, salmon in the centre, globulous, very large and full	vig.
Madame Louise Donadine................	flesh colour in the centre, lighter on reverse of petals; a sport from *Countess of Oxford*	free.
Madame Marie Bianchy..................	lilac colour, brighter in the centre, large, full, imbricated form	vig.
Madame Marie Finger.................S	flesh, centre deep salmon-pink, well formed; a fine distinct Rose, very free blooming	vig.

Name	Description	Habit of Growth
Madame Marie Raederer............S	bright cherry-rose, shaded carmine, large, full; a seedling from *Jules Margottin*	vig.
Madame Martha d'Halloy.............	cherry-carmined red, large, full, well formed; a seedling from *Madane Boutin*	vig.
Madame Marie Lagrange...........	brilliant carmine, large, or very large, almost full	vig.
Madame Melanie Vigneron.............	beautiful lilac-rose, edge of petals silvery, flowers large, very full	vig.
Madame Montet......S	very soft rose, large, almot fully; very fine	vig.
Madame Nachury...SP	fine satin-like rose, with a soft lavender shade, a new colour; flowers large, full, and cupped, distinct and well formed	free.
Madame Noman......S	pure white, with peach centre, exquisite form; one of the best light Roses	mod.
Madame Olympe Torestchenko	rosy white, or carmined rose, large, full, well formed	vig.
Madame Oswald de Kerchove	white, rosy with coppered yellow at the base of the petals, of medium size, full, with imbricated form	vig.
Madame Pierre Margery.......S	very fresh rose, lighter in the centre, large, full	vig.
Madame Prosper Laugier..................	rich clear rose, flowers extra large size, somewhat expanded, petals even and well formed	vig.
Madame Rochet	fresh satin-rose, large, full and globular	vig.
Madame Sophie Fropot.................	pale satin-rose, broad, smooth, even petals, flowers cupped; a beautiful and distinct Rose	free.
Madame Therese Levet.......S	bright-cerise, large and full, and beautifully formed; a distinct and very beautiful Rose	vig.
Madame Thevenot....	bright lively red, flowers very large, full, and globular; very sweet	vig.
Madame Veuve....... Alexandre Pommery...	pink rose shaded with bright rose, very large, full	vig.
Madame Victor Verdier.......S	brilliant rosy crimson, colour very beautiful, flowers large and well formed; a distinct and beautiful Rose	vig.
Madame Vidot.........S	palest flesh, mot beautifully formed; a most perfect Rose	mod.
Mdlle. Bonnaire.......S	pure white, centre beautifully shaded with clear flesh, flowers of medium size and well formed; a very beautiful free-blooming Rose ..	mod.

Name	Description	Habit of Growth
Mdlle. Catherine Soupert....................S	white bordered and shaded with rose, large, full, of perfect form; a fine Rose	vig.
Mdlle. Emilie Fontaine........................	bright crimson-red, shaded with fire, large, very full, and well formed	vig.
Mdlle. Eugenie Verdier.....................S	centre clear satin-pink, outer petal pale satin, colour clear and beautiful, flowers large, full, and cupped; a superb Rose	vig.
Mdlle. Ilona d' Adorjan......................	pale salmon-rose, reverse of petals silvery, very large, full, and excellenty formed; a full distinct Rose	vig.
Mdlle. Julia Dymonier.................S	pink, changing to blush, flowers compact, beautifully and evenly formed, large and full; an improved *Marie Cointet*	
Mdlle. Louise Margerand.................	light rosy pink, with lilac reflex; somewhat resembling *Mrs. Rivers*	vig.
Mdlle. Maric Cointet...	bright satin-pink, outer petals paler, glossy thick petal; a very beautiful and distinct Rose .	dwf.
Mdlle. Marie Closon....	delicate rose, whitish edge, very full and well formed, very fragrant and free blooming ...	vig.
Mdlle. Marie Digat......	fine crimson red, large and globulous, free bloomer	vig.
Mdlle. Marie Rady.......	brilliant red, flowers large, very full, and beautifully imbricated; one of the most perfect..	vig.
Mdlle. Marie Verdier...	bright rose, good cupped form; a beautiful Rose	vig.
Mdlle. Marguerite D'Ombrain..............S	satin-rose, flowers large, full, and globular; a distinct and fine Rose, very fragrant	vig.
Mdlle. Marguerite Manoin........................	deep carmine-rose, beautiful fresh colour, very large and full; a fine Rose	
Magna Charta...........S	flowers bright pink, suffused with carmine, very large and full, and of good form	vig.
Marchioness of Exeter.....................S	bright rose, flushed with carmine, a large, cup shaped, and well-built flower; good habit and distinct	vig.
Marechal Vaillant....S	rosy crimson, colour bright, flowers large, double, and well formed; a fine Rose	vig.
Marguerite Brassac.S	dark velvety crimson, similar to *Charles Lefebvre,* very smooth and even in form	vig.
Marguerite de St. Amand...............S	glossy satin-rose, a beautiful flesh colour, flowers extra large, globular, and well formed; a good distinct Rose	free.

(H.P.) Mary Pochin

Name	Description	Habit of Growth
Marie Baumann.......S	rich carmine-crimson, flowers large and of exquisite colour, perfectly formed; one of the best Roses	free.
Marie Louise Pernet.S	deep rosy red, a fine large globular flower and well formed; a very good and distinct Rose	mod.
Mary Pochin..............	Lake, shaded with rich velvety crimson, colour very bright, flowers moderate size.	
Marquise Adele de Murinais..................S	flesh, large, compact full flower; a very beautiful Rose, and very sweet scented	mod.
Marquise de Castellane...............S	deep cerise, colour clear and good, flowers large, circular, and perfect; one of the finest	rob.
Marquise de Gibot...S	pale rose, flowers large, full, and globular; a fine and distinct Rose	vig.
Marquise de Mortemart................S	blush-white, centre pale flesh; beautiful, rather delicate	dwf.
Masterpiece.............S	bright rosy crimson; the flowers are very large, full, and of perfect globular shape; habit good, and foliage fine	vig.
Maurice Bernardin...S	rich crimson, shaded with violet, colour superb, flowers very large and double; a splendid Rose	free.
May Quennell..........S	brilliant magenta carmine, shaded with crimson, very large and full, and of perfect globular form	vig.
Mervielle de Lyon.......	fine pure exquisite white, slightly rosy, finely cupped and opening freely, flowers large, four to five inches in diameter, one of the best new Roses	
Miss Hassard.........S	beautiful delicate flesh colour, large, full, and fine form, very sweet; a free bloomer	vig.
Monsieur Alfred Dumesnil................S	deep rose, bright centre, flowers globular, large, and well formed; distinct and very sweet	
Monsieur Boncenne..............SP	intensely rich plum, superb, flowers well formed; one of the best dark Roses	vig.
Monsieur Benoit Comte.......................	brilliant scarlet-red, shaded with vermilion inside, large, full, globulous and cupped	vig.
Monsieur Etienne Levet.......................S	vermilion, with a soft velvety lavender shade, flowers very large and full, petals exquisitely smooth and shell-shape; superb	vig.

Name	Description	Habit of Growth
Monsieur Eugene Delaire.....................	velvety, lighted with fire-red, large, full; extra	vig.
Monsieur E.Y. Teas..S	deep red, large, full, and of the most perfect form; one of the best Roses grown, and very fragrant	mod.
Monsieur Fillion.......S	fine rose, striking colour, a large, full, and well-formed flower	vig.
Monsieur Francois Michelon.................S	fine deep rose, reverse of petals silvery white; large and full; very beautiful........	vig.
Monsr. Francisque Rive...........................	bright cherry-red, very large and full, well formed..	vig.
Monsieur Gabriel Tournier.................S	rosy crimson, flowers extra large fine large petals, globular flower; a distinct and good Rose	vig.
Monsieur Jules Monges	beautiful carmined rose, very large, full, cup shaped..	vig.
Monsieur Norman....S	delicate rosy pink, flowers large, deep, and of fine globular form; a superb Rose	mod.
Monsieur Paul Neron.....................S	pale soft rose, violet shade, flowers immensely large and full	rob.
Monsieur Pierre Seletski......................	rich violet and crimson, petals even, smooth and good; a fine cup-shaped flower, distinct, and very good; handsome foliage	free.
Monsieur Thouvenel..............S	velvety red, large and full	vig.
Mrs. Baker.............S	beautiful shaded crimson, large, full, and well formed; very beautiful	free.
Mrs. George Dickson..................	bright satiny-pink, flowers large, not too full, opening freely. First Class Certificate, Royal Horticultural Society	vig.
Mrs. Harry Turner....S	colour intense crimson-scarlet, with rich maroon shading, flowers large and beautifully imbricated, the foliage dark and handsome; somewhat resembling *Charles Lefebvre*	
Mrs. Jowitt...............	brilliant glowing crimson, shaded with lake, flowers very large, globular, fragrant	
Mrs. Laxton...........S	bright rosy crimson, large and perfect, as perfect as a Ranunculus; a first-class Rose	vig.
Mrs. Rivers..............	pale flesh, nearly white, petals beautifully formed, cupped, large and full; good habit	free.

Name	Description	Habit of Growth
Nardy Freres..........S	rose, shaded soft lavender; flowers very large, full, and well formed; a very distinct and first-rate Rose	vig.
Oxonion..................S	shaded rose, large and full, fine globular form; a good exhibition Rose	free.
Paul Verdier..........SP	rich rosy crimson, flowers large, double, and of the fine imbricated form; a fine pillar or wall Rose	vig.
Peach Blossom.......S	delicate peach, a new and beautiful colour, large, full, and fine shape	vig.
Penelope Mayo........S	brilliant carmine-red; fine, distinct, similar to *Duchesse de Caylus*; perfect form	vig.
Pierre Carot ....S	deep red changing to clear red, of medium size, large, perfect form	vig.
Pierre Durand...........	fine bright rose, large, almost full	vig.
Pierre Notting.........S	deep velvety shaded crimson, globular, beautifully formed flower; fine and distinct	vig.
President Senelar......	deep cherry-red, changing to purple, very large and full	vig.
President Willermoz...S	rich brilliant carmine, with a very soft and pleasing violet tint; flowers of moderate size, double, and well formed	free.
Pride of Waltham....S	delicate flesh colour	
Prince Arthur..........S	very rich crimson shaded deeper colour; a dark form of *General Jacqueminot;* distinct and good	vig.
Prince Camille de Rohan.................S	rich dark maroon crimson, flowers moderate size, double; one of the finest dark Roses	free.
Princess Beatrice....S	foliage large, bright and handsome; flowers deep pink, with clear blush margin, large, full, and globular form	vig.
Princess Louise Victoria..................P	flesh changing to blush, moderate size, compact, very pretty and clustering; a good pillar Rose.	vig.
Princess Mary of Cambridge.............S	pale silvery pink, flowers large, full, and high in the centre; a beautiful and desirable Rose	free.
Princess Antoinette Strozzio.................S	fine deep rose, flowers large, very effective and finely formed; a flower similar to *Marie Rady*	vig.

Name	Description	Habit of Growth
Princess Charlotte de la Tremouille.......S	fine satin-rose, very large and full, globular form free bloomer; in the way of *La France*........	mod.
Princess Radziwill....	bright carmine, large, full and imbricated	vig.
Profesieur Edouard Regel........	red-cerise shaded silvery, flowers large, well formed, and in the way of *Annie Wood*.....	vig.
Prosper Laugier........	brilliant reddish-scarlet, flowers large, double, and of splendid form........	vig.
Queen of Queens......	flowers pink, with blush edges, large and full, of perfect form, and a continuous bloomer	
Queen of Waltham....	beautiful rose-cherry, a very distinct and lovely colour; large, full, and double	free.
Queen Victoria.........S	flesh, shaded with pink, very large, full, and beautiful	mod.
R.C. Sutton........	deep rose, the reverse of petals white; a fine form; very free blooming; foliage exquisite; one of the most sweetly-scented Roses.	
Red Dragon...........P	a hybrid climbing Rose, colour brilliant crimson, very bright and striking........	vig.
Red Gauntlet........	bright scarlety crimson	
Reine Blanche.........S	pearly white, centre palish flesh, flowers large, full, and cupped	vig.
Reine du Midi.........S	fine satin-pink, flowers large, and of a fine globular form; a fine Rose	vig.
Reynolds Hole.........S	maroon, shaded with crimson, flowers of good size, perfectly formed; a fine Rose of a new and distinct colour	free.
Richard Laxton........S	colour reddish crimson, large, full, and cupped; beautiful shell-like petal and a fine Rose	vig.
Robert Marnock......P	rich brownish crimson flowers, large, imbricated, and well formed	mod.
Rosieriste Jacobs...S	fine velvety red, shaded with black, large full, well formed, globulous; extra fine	vig.
Rosy Morn........	delicate peach colour, richly shaded with salmon-rose, large and full........	mod.
Royal Standard........S	beautiful soft satiny rose, large, very full, and exquisitely formed	vig.

Name	Description	Habit of Growth
Senateur Vaisse......S	intense glowing scarlet, fine thick petals, flowers perfectly full, large, exquisitely formed, and highly fragrant; a superb Rose	free.
Sir Garnet Wolseley...S	rich vermilion, shaded with bright carmine, and the colour well maintained throughout, flowers very large, full, and perfectly formed. This Rose is distinct from *Exposition de Brie, Ferdinand de Lesseps* and *Maurice Bernardin*	vig.
Sophie Coquerelle...S	blush, centre flesh, colour clear and good, flowers very large; a fine Rose	free.
Souvenir d' Arthur Sansal......S	beautiful clear rose, colour of *Jules Margottin,* but brighter; flowers large and well formed	vig.
Souvenir de Charles Montault	velvety purple and crimson, double, very fragrant; a free-flowering and fine bedding Rose	free.
Souvenir de Madame Robert	salmon-pink, deeper in the centre, large, full, cupped, opening well, growth very vigorous, extra; a seedling from *Jules Margottin*	vig.
Souvenir de Madame Berthier......S	fine bright red, very large and full; a seedling from *Victor Verdier*	vig.
Souvenir de Victor...S *Emmanuel*......S	vermilion red, velveted with purple and crimson, very large and full; extra	vig.
Souvenir de Victor Verdier......S	bright dark red, shaded purple	
Star of Waltham.......S	crimson, very large, double and of fine form, smooth petals and of good substance; a superb Rose	mod.
Tatiana Oneguine.....S	clear lilac-red, shaded with carmine, large, full, and well formed	vig.
Sultan of Zanzibar...S	blackish maroon, shaded with crimson, flowers globular	vig.
Thomas Mills..........S	flowers extra large, full and of fine cup shape; colour dazzling bright rosy carmine with whitish stripes; a very free bloomer	vig.
Ulrich Brunner Fils....	carmined rose, very large; seedling from *Paul Neron*	vig.
Vicomte de Vigier......	intensely rich, velvety crimson and lilac, colour superb, large petals; a well-formed globular flower, distinct	vig.

Name	Description	Habit of Growth
Victor Verdier..........S	deep rose, centre brilliant rose, a charming colour, flowers very large and full; an excellent Rose	free.
Violette Bouyer........S	white, shaded with pink, large, full, fine form....	vig.
White Baroness........	pure white; much fuller than *Mabel Morrison* ...	vig.
William Warden.......S	a sport from *Madame Clemence Joigneaux*, but of a very lovely shade of pink	
Xavier Olibo...........S	rich velvety crimson, colour superb; distinct and very beautiful	mod.

CHAPTER XVI
TEA ROSES

Next to the Hybrid Perpetuals the most important group are the Tea Roses. The former have maintained their pre-eminence on account of their greater diversity of colour and form, and also to the fact that they are more hardy, more easily grown, and withstand rough treatment much better than the more delicate Teas and many other clasess of Roses.

The Teas, however, are, so to speak, much more refined, more distinct as a class, and certainly more chaste and beautiful; and though embracing comparatively but a limited range of colour, the blending of tints in these colours almost bids defiance to any proper description being given of them; their peculiar delicate fragrance is also distinct from any other group.

Mr. Shirley Hibberd, in his "Amateurs' Rose Book," thus eulogises this beautiful family : "These are universally regarded as ranking higher than all other Roses in the scale of floral excellencies. They are of less value, certainly, than the Hybrid Perpetuals, because less hardy and less variable in style and colouring, but their delicious fragrance, refined colours, and highly finished outlines fill the true rosarian with highest rapture, and engage him to bestow upon Tea Roses the best of his attention and the largest share of his love. To grow Tea Roses is indeed an object worthy of the ambition of the most ardent horticulturist – the more to be esteemed perhaps because it is attended with difficulties. The shallow pretender who thinks to accomplish wonders without first preparing his mind and hands for the task, will surely be disappointed, for it is to skilful management alone that these coy and capricious flowers make the response that is desired. They appear to have been designed by Nature to furnish the highest test of skill and patience in Rose culture, and to afford constant evidence

(T) Gloire De Dijon

of the fact that the cultivation of Roses does not consist in merely buying the plants and sticking them in the ground, and then pruning them with a knife and fork, according to the plan of the jobbing gardener, who thinks that trees of all kinds should be cut down and done away with.

The prevailing characteristics of the group are the production of long rods armed with hooked spines of a brownish or purplish colour; the leaves large, glossy, rather distant; the flowers large, semi-double, borne on long footstalks, and hence often presented drooping - an attitude favourable to their protection from wind and rain, though not desirable as regards their appearance. The colours vary from white to citron and rose pink, and the odour they emit may be likened to that of the finest sample of Tea newly opened; say for the sake of being precise, it is a sublime edition of first-rate orange-scented pekoe."

As will be seen from the foregoing remarks, in England this family is looked upon as exceedingly delicate and requiring the greatest care and attention to ensure any degree of success. In this country, however, they seem to have found a home in every way congenial to them, and under intelligent cultivation never fail to reward our labours with their beautiful flowers in profusion. In the whole family of Tea Roses there is not a single variety that can be called a shy bloomer, much more any that fail to bloom entirely, as is so frequently the case among Hybrid Perpetuals.

The first important point in cultivating this group is the choice of a suitable position. The most favourable site is one that is entirely open to the east and south, and partially shaded on the north and west; and the latter more especially so. One hour's sunshine in the early morning is more valuable to most plants than the whole of the rest of the day; on the contrary, western sunshine is frequently very prejudicial to plants, and for the following reasons : After a plant has been fully exposed to the morning and mid-day sun, its sap must of course attain to a high degree of heat; if this is continued till sunset, the plant has not regained its normal temperature before the chilly night air, which at some seasons sets in very quickly in the plains, falls with withering effect on the plants when quite unprepared to withstand its influence, being almost identical with checked perspiration inthe human being, for we all know that plants live, breathe, and even perspire through their foliage. On the other hand, where plants are shaded after mid-day, their temperature gradually sinks to the ordinary level, and they are then prepared to withstand the change, which of course falls on them in a much smaller degree. One thing must be carefully noted, that the position selected should be well raised above the ordinary ground level, so that any excess of moisture may be carried off at once, as they are very impatient of anything like stagnation at the roots, "Landolicus," in his "Indian Amateur Gardener," gives the following advice regarding the formation of rose beds : "A soil for Roses cannot well be made too rich. I would suggest that at a depth of about three to four feet, according to the sort of Rose to be grown, a double layer of slates should be placed, drainage put down and the whole soil filled in, after being prepared with good stiff loam, cow-dung and stable manure. By this means the whole earth will be good, and the roots would not go down deeper than the good soil, and this soil might be renewed."

Few of us would probably care to incur the extra expense needed to make up beds according to the above plan for Hybrid Perpetuals, or any other of the vigorous growing families of roses. We cannot, however, too strongly recommend it for Tea Roses, knowing from our own experience how soon they repay the additional outlay. We know a bed of Tea Roses that was made and planted long before the "Indian Amateur Gardener" was published, and differ somewhat from the plan given above in a few minor points, though having practically the same effect and has the additional advantage of cheapness.. This consists of a piece of ground fifty feet square; all the old soil was removed to a depth of three and-a-half feet on the north and four feet on the south side, thus giving it a gradual slope; the bottom was then beaten down firmly, and on this three inches of old building rubbish was laid mixed with a small quantity of fresh lime to bind it together. This was again well beaten, and another inch of new kunker and lime added (at the rate of one part in three), was again beaten down, the whole, when finished, having the appearance of a pucea floor. This was allowed to dry for a fortnight, and a layer of coarse brick rubble or khoa, similar to what is used in the lower strata for road-making, was then added to the depth of ten inches. The soil, which had been previously prepared, was then filled in and pressed down firmly, and when finished off was about four inches on the sides and eight inches in the centre higher than the ordinary level. The soil was prepared as follows:– Two parts of the original soil (which was a good light loam that had grown first-rate vegetables for years), one part turfy loam, and one part old cow manure and half a ton of bone phosphates added to the whole, the bed was allowed to remain a month to permit of its settling down and the plants were then put in three feet apart each way and treated liberally from the first with liquid manure and top dressings at intervals. This was completed in 1878, now more than seven years ago. The first season they were not pruned at all; in 1879, 1880 and 1881 they were pruned and manured in the ordinary way; in 1882, however, the plants had become too large and woody; all the old wood was then cut back to within three or four eyes of the main stem, leaving on each plant two, or at the most three, strong shoots of the previous season's growth; they were then heavily manured and a surface dressing of about three inches of old manure forked in over the entire bed, and this was supplemented by frequent dressings of liquid manure. By the end of the flowering season the plants were larger than ever, though of course the quantity of bloom had been materially reduced as compared with former years, as the vigorous succulent shoots they had thrown up so freely from the base produced but very few flowers, a matter of regret for the moment, though there was the consolation of knowing that the foundation for a grand crop the following season had been laid.

In October 1883, the plants were again pruned; this time all the old wood that had been left the previous year was cut back to within three or four eyes of the main stem; the new wood was simply shortened back to the first well ripened joints. Instead of opening the roots in the usual way to manure the plants, these were left intact, and trenches were cut between each row of plants about one foot wide, going quite down to the layer of brick rubble. These were allowed to remain open for a fortnight, and were then filled in with a compost of equal parts of old cow manure and fresh turfy loam, with about five hundred weight of bone phosphates added to the whole.

The result exceeded even the most sanguine expectations; the flowers were not only borne in endless profusion, but were of grand size and quality – certainly the best we have ever seen anywhere in the neighbourhood of Calcutta, where, as most of us know to our cost, it is a very difficult thing to grow really good Roses. It will be observed that by the plan of pruning and manuring adopted, there was obtained, so to speak, new plants on old established roots and in new soil. The wonderful profusion of bloom may be attributed to two causes : first, in cutting the trenches the plants were subject to a partial pruning of the roots, as the soil when cut through was found completely filled with fibrous roots, (root pruning, as we all know, increases the floriferous qualities of nearly every description of plants); second, after these trenches had been filled with the new soil, the roots, which had been cut in removing the old soil, would naturally break freely into it, thereby securing fresh food and nourishment for the plant, for it is on the fine fibrous roots, often wandering a long distance from the main stem, that the plant has to depend for its sustenance. This is a fact very difficult to instil into the minds of our native gardeners – aye, and many amateurs also, who when removing plants think it is quite sufficient if they secure the main roots intact, ruthlessly sacrificing what they foolishly imagine to be unnecessary appendages, but which in reality are the life and soul of the plant. This acounts for so many plants succumbing to the operation of transplanting, and others, if they do survive, sometimes remain at a standstill for months, that is till new fibrous roots, or what we may term food-seekers, are formed. The Chinese gardeners have shown us to what extent root-pruning may be carried in stunting or dwarfing plants. The whole of the miniature plants raised by them being treated in this way, they have reduced this to such a science that even with shrubs that in their natural growth attain a height of twenty or twenty-five feet, they will produce perfect flowering speciemens not more than six inches high, and it is even stated that one species of conifer or pine has been dwarfed to such an extent that a complete plant, several years old, can be used instead of a button-hole flower.

To return, however, to our subject, we ought to have mentioned that from the south side of the bed in question there are four subsoil drains placed at intervals of ten feet and on a level with the pucca bottom of the bed; these carry off all surplus moisture to a tank close by.

I can safely say that plants grown in this way will produce double, or even treble, the quantity of flowers, and of much better quality than they will when grown in the ordinary way. Another advantage, in the rainy season, generally a very critical period not only for Tea but also many other families of Roses, they will stand any quantity of water without flinching. I ought also to mention, on the other hand, that during dry or hot weather they require to be supplied with two or three times the amount of moisture that plants do when grown in ordinary soil. During the seven years this bed has been in existence, not more than twenty of the original plants have had to be replaced from any cause whatever – awonderfully low death-rate averaging but a little more than one per cent per annum.

And now as to the question of cost. Herein lies the only stumbling block to the whole system, and before which all the increased health and vigour, all the enhanced quantity and quality of the flowers, will wither in the mind's eye of many a would be enthusiast. The bed in question contains sixteen rows, each comprising sixteen plants, that is 256 plants in all, and it was estimated at the time that it cost a rupee for each Rose planted in addition to their original value – undoubtedly a very large sum, but it has been repaid tenfold, if not in actual specie, at least by the grand measure of success it ensured.

It is a curious fact that, until within the past two or three years, with the exception of Devoniensis, which still maintains its position as one of the very finest Roses, not a single seedling variety of this group had ever been raised in England, and this was an accidental seedling found growing wild in a Devonshire garden. Another English raised variety is Letty Coles; this is, however, only a sport from Madame Willermoz, supposed to have resulted from inter or cross-budding. Some of the best Roses in cultivation have been produced in this way. I will content myself by giving two ro three well known popular varieties as examples. First, let us take Marechal Neil, which, it is said, originated in this way (although at the time it was first sent out it was described as a seedling variety): Buds of Cloth of Gold were inserted on the American Rose, Isabella Gray, the result of the union being "The Rose of Roses." Then we have that grand Rose, Mabel Morrison, the result of bud variation, caused by the inoculation of Baroness Rothschild and Niphetos; and, lastly, we have Belle Lyonnaise, the result of Gloire de Dijon being budded with Celine Forestier.

A curious instance of the influence that buds have on the stock occurred to me a few years since. A fine shoot of Xavier Olibo had been accidentally broken off, containing several eyes in prime condition for budding. I looked round in vain for suitable stocks, for every one had been worked previously. At last I espied an old favourite, Marechal Neil, that had thrown up a monster shoot that season. Without a second thought I headed it down to about four feet and inserted the whole of the eyes, seven or eight in number, at intervals of five or six inches along its entire length. Two of these broke almost at once, and made shoots about three feet in length the first season. It is not of these, however, that I have to speak, but of the Marechal himself. To my astonishment, on the flowering season coming round, every bloom on the plant had each petal striped with deep crimson; this became intensified as the flowers matured, till, before withering, they were almost entirely of this colour. I felt I had gained a prize, indeed, and in all probability had done so, but it was the old tale of the cat and the mouse over again, for played with it till we lost it. Instead of propagating it at once, as I certainly ought to have done, I foolishly determined to leave it alone till the following season, so that this curious freak might be confirmed or otherwise. Dame Nature, however, decreed that I should be disappointed for before the next season came round my poor Marechal had been laid low by that fell disease, *canker,* by which so many of his noble ancestors had been made to bite the dust, this disease in fact being almost exclusively confined to this noble Rose.

I may mention that Marechal Neil is classed with Tea Roses by many authorities. Others again make a separate group termed "Tea Noisettes" in which they also include Cloth of Gold, Triomphe de Rennes, Celine Forestier, &c. The more general practice, however, is to class all these, including the Marechal, as *Noisettes,* and it is under this head that I hope in a future article to describe them. I will now endeavour to give a short description of the best varieties of Tea Roses, selecting the most distinct kinds, but of course in a group like this, where the range of colour is but limited, there will be found a certain amount of sameness in many varieties.

Descriptive List of the Best Tea Roses.

(*For explanation of the abbreviations used* *see page 145*)

Name	Description	Habit of Growth
Abricote....................	pale fawn, wih deeper centre; an excellent hardy free Rose	mod.
Adam......................S	flesh, centre salmon and fawn, moderately hardy and beautiful	mod.
Adele Fragrans..........	pale yellow, beautiful in the bud	
Adrienne Christophle..............S	yellow, centre copper and apricot, shaded with rosy peach; sometimes deep yellow; highly fragrant	mod.
Alba rosea...............S	white, tinted with rose, distinct and beautiful	free.
Aline Sisley.............S	varying from deep purple-rose to shaded violet-red; medium size or large; scent most delicious	vig.
Anna Olivier...........S	flesh and buff, shaded with rose, flowers tolerably large, smooth, and beautiful	vig.
Baron Alexandre de Vrints........................	pink, striped with red and white, a new colour; of medium size, full	vig.
Beaute de L' Europe...	deep yellow with reverse of petals coppered, very large and full, extra fine form (*Glorie de Dijon* type)	vig.
Belle Lyonnaise.....SP	deep canary-yellow, flowers globular, large and full; a fine pillar Rose	vig.
Belle Fleur d' Anjou.S	light flesh colour, shaded, large, globular and double, somewhat like *Souvenir d'un Ami*	
Bougere....................	very large, full, and hardy	free.
Caroline	blush-pink, centre delicate rose, large and full	vig.
Catherine Mermet....S	bright flesh-coloured rose, large, full, and finely formed; a superb Rose	vig.
Climbing Devoniensis..........SP	like the *Devoniensis,* but more vigorous in the habit; forming a fine climbing Rose	vig.
Clotilde....................	creamy white, centre bright salmon-pink, flowers of moderate size and full	vig.
Comte de Paris........S	pale flesh, very large and full; a moderately hardy and superb Rose	dwf.
Comtesse de Nadaillac..................S	orange and copper, centre salmon colour, fine deep petals and hadsome bud, highly fragrant; a superb Rose	mod.
Comtesse de Sembui....................S	salmon-rose, reverse of petals silvery, large, full, and well formed; growth very vigorous, very distinct and good	vig.

Name	Description	Habit of Growth
Comtesse Ouvaroff..S	delicate cream, suffused with pink, petals of good substance	mod.
Comtesse Riza du Parc..S	metallic rose, changing to pink, flowers large and well formed; distinct	mod.
David Pradel..S	pale rose and lavender, mottled; a peculiar flower, distinct and pretty	mod.
Devoniensis..S	creamy white, centre sometimes blush; a most superb and deliciouslly-scented Rose	mod.
Duc de Magenta..	pale flesh, delicately tinted with fawn, petals large and of fine waxy substance, flower large	mod.
Duchess of Edinburgh..S	deep glowing crimson, very free flowering; distinct and very beautiful	free.
Etoile de Lyon..S	fine striking sulphur-yellow, deeper in the centre, very large, full, and very fine form; one of the best yellow Roses ever raised	vig.
Flancialloc de la Princess Stephanie....	salmon-orange-yellow, medium size; a seedling from *Gloire de Dijon*	vig.
Gloire de Dijon..SP	buff, with orange centre, very large and double, handome foliage, and vigorous free-blooming habit; the most useful of all the Tea-scented Roses	vig.
Goubault..S	salmon-pink, highly fragrant, most beautiful in the bud	mod.
Homere..	blush, with deeper centre, very free and hardy; beautiful in the bud	free.
Innocente Pirola..S	very light fawn, changing to white; a charmingly formed flower of medium size; beautiful in bud	vig.
Isabella Sprunt..S	orange-yellow, fine buds for bouquets	
Jaune d'Or..	fine golden-yellow, flowers full and globular; medium size, beautiful	dwf.
Jean Ducher..S	salmon-yellow, shaded with rose-peach in the centre, large, full and globular, growth very vigorous; distinct and superb	vig.
Jean Pernet..S	light orange-yellow, outer petals paler, flowers of moderate size and double	free.
Jules Finger..S	bright red, passing to clear red, shaded outside of flower, large, full, and fine form	vig.
La Boule d'Or..S	outer petals pale-yellow, centre rich nankeen-yellow, flowers globular and very large, with fine broad smooth petals	free.

Name	Description	Habit of Growth
La Sylphide............S	outer petals cream, tinted with pale carmine, centre fawn, large, full, and well formed: highly fragrant	free.
L'Enfant Trouve..........	see *Vicomtesse de Cazes*	
Letty Coles...............	shaded pink, a sport from *Madame Willermoz.*	
Louise de Savoie......S	clear pale yellow, very large and full, good shape, and vigorous habit; very fragrant	free.
Louis Richard...........	copper-rose, changing to deep red in the centre, large, full, and well formed	
Ma Capucine.............	orange-yellow, nasturtium colour, small and semi-double	
Madame Angele Jacquier.................S	flamed cerise with coppered yellow at the base, charming bright colour, flowers large, full, and well formed; a distinct and beautiful Rose	vig.
Madame Barillet Deschamps.............	white, centre cream, large and well formed; very free bloomer, and excellent	mod.
Madane Berard......SP	bright buff or fawn colour, with enlight salmon tint, flowers very large, full, and well formed; a superb robust-growing Rose for pillar or wall	rob.
Madame Bonnet Eymard....................S	pure white, sometimes yellow in the centre, full, and of medium size, blooms freely	vig.
Madame Bravy..........S	see *Alba Rosea*	
Madame Camille........	delicate rose, violet shaded, veined flowers, very large and full; a fine Rose, free habit	free.
Madame Caro............	salmon-yellow, of medium size, fine form, very full	vig.
Madame Celina Noirey......................S	salmon rose, flowers large and full	mod.
Madame Chenadane Guinoisseau.............	sulphured canary-yellow, beautiful bud in the shape of *Madame Falcot;* distinct	vig.
Madame Cusin.........S	purple-rose with white centre, tinted with yellow, large, full, and well formed	vig.
Madame Damaizin.....	buff, with salmon tint, outer petals cream, flowers large and full; distinct and beautiful	free.
Madame Denis........S	waxy white, centre fawn and flesh, flowers large, full, and cupped; a distinct and very fine Rose, a peculiar must scent	vig.

Name	Description	Habit of Growth
Madame de St. Joseph..................	fawn, shaded with salmon-pink, large and beautiful	mod.
Madame de Vitry......S	centre bright pink, slightly tinted, outer petals paler, good size, full.................................	free.
Madame Emilie Dupuy...................SP	pale fawn, flowers large, full, and well formed; a good Rose for wall or pillar	vig.
Madame Falcot.........	deep rich orange-yellow, petals large, flowers double, rich dark foliage; a beautiful Rose	free.
Madame Hippolyte Jamain....................S	white, centre copper colour; peculiar	
Madame Joseph Halphen....................	white, beautifully tinted with carmine; full and free blooming	mod.
Madame Joseph Schwartz.................S	white, tinged with flesh-rose, full, medium size; a seedling from *Comtesse Labarthe;* extra fine	vig.
Madame Jules Margottin................S	copper and rosy cerise, variable, distinct and very pretty...	mod.
Madame Lambard....S	fine, bright red, large, full, and well-formed buds; beautiful and distinct	
Madame Levet..........P	buff, centre shaded salmon, very much resembling *Gloire de dijon,* large, cupped,................ and full	vig.
Madame Margottin...S	rich yellow, with salmon-pink centre, full, and of good form	free.
Madame Maurin.......S	cream and fawn, flowers large, full, and finely formed; a beautiful and distinct kind	mod.
Madame Serlot........S	white, see *Alba rosea*	mod.
Madame Trifle..........P	pale fawn, changing to cream, shape and habit like *Gloire de Dijon,* flowers somewhat paler; a good Rose	vig.
Madame Welche......S	flowers very large and double, of the finest form, the outside petals pale yellow, the centre deep orange, often shaded reddish copper	
Madame Willermoz..S	creamy white, centre tinted with fawn, petals very thick and finely formed....................	mod.
Mdlle. Cecile Berthod....................S	golden yellow, colour clear and beautiful flowers cupped, tolerably large and full; distinct.	mod.

Name	Description	Habit of Growth
Mdlle. Francois Janin..........S	orange yellow, sometimes coppery in the centre, flowers small	vig.
Mdlle. Lazarine Poizeau..........S	deep canary-yellow small conical-shaped buds; quite a gem for button-hole flowers	mod.
Mdlle. Marie Arnaud...	fine canary-yellow, centre deep golden yellow	
Mdlle. Marie Berton..P	pale yellow, changing to white, very large and fine; a good Rose	vig.
Mdlle. Mathilde Lenaerts..........P	fine bright rose, bordered with white, of medium size or large, full, and very well formed; climbing variety	vig.
Mdlle. Therese Genevay..........S	fine peach-rose, large, full, and of fine form, blooms freely, very effective	vig.
Marcelin Roda.........S	pale lemon, centre canary-yellow, flowers good size, globular and full; a beautiful Rose	
Marechal Bugeaud.....	bright rose, very large and full; a moderately hardy and excellent Rose	mod.
Marie de Medicis.....S	centre fawn, outer petals mottled with crimson, highly fragrant	mod.
Marie Ducher..........P	cream and fawn, flowers large, full, and well formed, the shape of the flower and habit of the plant resembling *Gloire de Dijon;* a good Rose	free.
Marie Guillot...........S	beautiful white, large, globular, full, of very fine form; a superb Rose	vig.
Marie Sisley............S	cream, deeply margined and shaded with rosy salmon, size moderate, full, and very fragrant	free.
Marie Van Houtte.....S	white, slightly tinted with yellow, border of the petals tipped with rose, flowers quite full and well formed; a superb Rose	mod.
Marquise de Sanima..	copper rose, centre sometimes light rose, in the way of *Reine du Portugal,* large, full, and fine form	
Miss May Paul.......SP	white, lilac in the interior, outside petals red, large, well formed, and of a climbing habit	vig.
Moire	pale yellow, shaded with buff and rose, large and full; distinct	
Monsieur Furtado......	very bright sulphur-yellow, medium size, full, and finely formed	mod.
Narcisse................S	fine pale yellow, beautiful, an abundant blooming and good kind	mod.

Name	Description	Habit of Growth
Nina	blush, very free blooming and beautiful, but the flowers a little loose	mod.
Niphetos	white, centre pale straw, long buds, very large, thick petals in dry weather; a superb Rose	free.
Pactolus	lemon, centre pale yellow; a good and moderately hardy Rose	free.
Pauline Labonte......S	outer petals flesh tinted cream, centre deep salmon-buff, very large, full, and fragrant; a distinct Rose	mod.
Perfection de Montplaisir	clear lemon, handsome buds, good and distinct	
Perle de Lyon..........S	deep fawn and apricot, colour of *Madame Falcot,* petals large, flowers globular; a beautiful yellow Rose	vig.
Perle des Jardins....S	fine straw-yellow, sometimes deep canary-yellow, very large, full, fine form, and one of the best yellow Roses	vig.
Princess Prosper d' Aremberg	salmon-red, carmine in centre, reverse of petals clear carmine, of medium size; full	vig.
Red Safrano	this is a sport from *Safrano,* and in every way equal to that well-known variety, but is of a bright red colour	vig.
Reine du Portugal	golden yellow, flowers large, full, and globular; a distinct and good yellow Rose	mod.
Reine Maria Pia	deep rose, crimson in the centre, large, full; a seedling from *Gloire de Dijfon*	vig.
Rubens..................S	white, delicately tinted with rose, flowers large and beautifully formed; a superb Rose	mod.
Safrano	bright apricot, fine dark foliage, moderately hardy; a most beautiful Rose in the bud	free.
Shirley Hibberd	nankin-yellow, medium size, cupped, full, a new colour, blooms freely	vig.
Socrates	deep rose, fawn centre, large and full	free.
Sombreuil...............S	pale straw, large, double, and very beautiful; hardy	free.
Souvenir d' Elise.....S	petals large, flowers full and generally perfect, though occasionally it produces a hard centre; superb Rose	mod.
Souvenir de Paul Neron.......................S	white with rose and buff tint, flowers large and full; distinct and good	

Name	Description	Habit of Growth
Souvenir d'un Ami....S	salmon and rose, very large and full, large and handsome foliage; a superb Rose	free.
Souvenir de Madame Pernet......................	salmon-pink, petals broad, smooth, and even; a good Rose	
Triomphe de Milan...S	pale yellow, deeper in the centre, form and colour of *Triomphe de Rennes;* a good and distinct Rose	mod.
Unique........................	white ground, flamed with rose and purple; a distinct Rose, but delicate	dwf.
Vicomtesse de Cazes......................S	yellow, centre copperish yellow, tender	dwf.
Yellow........................	pale yellow, very large and fine petals, beautiful in the bud, but very tender	mod.

Chapter XVII
Hybrid Tea Roses

This is an entirely new family of Roses that has sprung into existence during the past few years, and owes its origin almost exclusively to artificial hybridisation, most of the varieties being crosses between some species of tea and hybrid perpetuals. Now could we combine all the good qualities of the two races in one we should certainly have a group to satisfy even the most exacting of Rosarians, and such a result is probably only a matter of time. All the varieties of this class are but hybrids of one generation only, probably, as these are again inter-crossed with other varieties, the rough points and imperfections which many of them at present possess will become toned down or entirely obliterated. For with Roses, as with animals or birds, where two distinct breeds are crossed, we must frequently wait for even the third or fourth generation for satisfactory results.

Already one or two varieties, such as Cheshunt Hybrid and Reine Marie Henriette, are taking a leading position in English rose-gardens. The great fault found, however, with most of them is that they do not open their flowers freely. This may be the case in England, but it certainly is not so in this country. For I have tried nearly all of them, and never yet saw a flower refuse to open, except occasionally in the rainy season, when we have scarcely any sun for days together. On the whole, I believe, these will eventually be found one of the most useful families of Roses for our climate. For they have these advantages : they are more hardy and vigorous than Tea Roses, and besides not only possess their free blooming qualities, but also embrace a wider range of colour. In fact they are just what is required where Roses are grown for quantity rather than for quality of bloom. They certainly do not possess the grand size and exquisite form, or the wonderfully varied shades of colour to be found in the Hybrid Perpetuals, nor can they lay claim to the delicate refined beauty found in most varieties of Tea Roses.

They should be treated in the same way as recommended for Tea Roses, pruning, however, rather more closely. The exact nature of this operation must, however, depend on the vigour and habit of each variety, points on which they differ very materially; some leaning closely to the Teas and other inclining to the habit of the Hybrid Perpetuals. The following list embraces all the best varieties in this group :-

Name	Description	Habit of Growth
Beauty of Stapleford	Outer range of petals very pale pinkish rose, gradually shaded to a deep rosy centre; flowers very large; petals well reflexed; seedling from *Alba rosea* and *Countess of Oxford*	free.
Camaeens	Bright China rose and deep yellow; almost always striped with whtie	free.
Cheshunt Hybrid	Colour cherry carmine; large, full, open flowers; very hardy and distinct	vig.
Countess of Pembroke	Flowers of the finest form, quite full, and highly scented; colour soft; satin-rose	vig.
Distinction	Flowers not very full but of good form; colour shaded peach of a tint difficult to describe; open very freely	vig.
Duchess of Connaught	Pale rose and lavender; dwarf hybrid habit; flowers large and well formed	mod.
Duchess of Westminster	Flowers exceedingly large, without being coarse, very finely formed; colour brightest cerise	rob.
Duke of Connaught	Flowers large; buds long and of very fine form; colour deep velvety crimson, edged with the brightest red; the best of this class	dwf.
Hon. George Bancroft	Flowers very large; colour bright rosy crimson, shaded purple; distinct and good	mod.
Jean Lorthois	China-rose, deeper in the centre, changing to lilac; reverse of petals whitish; large and full	mod.
Jean Sisley	Flowers very large, very full of petals; colour outside petals rosy lilac, the centre bright pink	free.

Name	Description	Habit of Growth
Lady Mary Fits William........................	Flowers exceedingly large, of globular form but scarcely full; colour bright delicate flesh, much resembling *Captain Christy*	vig.
Madame Barthelemy Levet..........................	Rich, deep clear yellow; good form	vig.
Madame Etienne Levet............................	Fine cherry red, bordered with copper yellow; large, full and good form	vig.
Mdlle. Brigitte Violette.......................	Bright rose with light violet; large, very full and of god shape	free.
Michael Saunders.......	Flowers very large, of good form; very full colour; bronzy pink; highly scented	vig.
Nancy Lee..................	Colour bright rosy pink, dwarf hybrid habit; moderate size, very free flowering	free.
Pearl............................	Pale flesh; flowers rather small, but pretty, much resembling a hybrid Noisette	mod.
Pierre Guillot.............	Bright dazzling red; petals bordered with white, very large erect flowers; well formed and a very free bloomer	vig.
Princess Imperiale Du Bresil..........................	Bright carmine rose; large, very full and well formed; very sweet scented	vig.
Reine Marie Henriette..................	A red *Gloire de Dijon;* large and full, well formed, growth very vigorous, makes a good climbing rose	vig.
Viscountess Falmoath..................	Flowers very large and of good form; colour very delicate pinkish rose; back of the petals bright pink; highly scented like the Moss rose	free.

CHAPTER XVIII
THE NOISETTE ROSES

The first species of this group was raised in America by Phillipe Noisette in 1814 and sent by him to his brother Monsieur Louis Noisette, at that time one of the leading nurserymen in Paris in 1817.

It was produced from the seed of the old Musk rose (*Rosa Moschata*), the flowers of which had been fertilised with the common China rose. In the true Noisette family the peculiar perfume of the Musk Rose is very apparent, but in a very large number of varieties belonging to or rather classed in this group, this distinctive feature has almost entirely disappeared, owing, of course, to the fact that many of them are the result of crosses between a Noisette and some variety of Tea or other Rose. This inter-crossing has been carried to such an extent that if we trace the pedigree of some of the best varieties we shall find they have not had a true Noisette as a parent for three or four generations, and in most instances one of the parents in each generation has belonged to a distinct family. All this has given rise to much confusion in the classification of many varieties. Take, for instance, the lord of the whole Rose creation – "Marechal Neil"; sometimes he is classed as a "Noisette," frequently as a "Tea Noisette," and occasionally as a "Tea" only. The attempt made by several competent authorities to form a separate class under the term of "Tea Noisettes" cannot be said to have been successful. The difficulty seems to be to know what to take from and what to retain in the original group; nor is the term "Tea Noisette" strictly applicable to this hybrid group, as many of the varieties that are sometimes placed under it have been the result of crosses with other distinct families, for instance, Triomphe de Rennes had a true Bourbon Rose as one of its parents.

This is certainly one of the most useful and valuable families of Roses in this country, as it is on them that we have mainly to depend for climbing varieties, and grown in this way they never fail to bloom profusely, that is, if treated liberally and pruned judiciously. For this purpose we must, of course, select the strong growing varieties, such as Marechal Neil, Lamarque, Solfaterre, Cloth of Gold, Triomphe de Rennes, and Celine Forestier. In pruning these all that is necessary to be done is to cut back the strong growths about one or two feet only; this will induce them to throw out side shoots freely, on which the blooms will be produced. They are apt to become crowded with weak barren wood in the centre; these should all be cut back to within one or two buds of the main stems. One thing must be borne in mind, that is, if we want these climbing varieties to grow to perfection, we must supply them with food and drink on the most liberal scale, to force the vigorous shoots essential to the production of the grand profusion of bloom they invariably bear when all their requirements are carefully attended to. In England it is no uncommon thing for plants of Marechal Neil to throw up shoots 20 or 25 feet long and produce from 1,000 to 2,000 flowers in a season. What an enormous strain this is on the plant we can easily imagine. If this subject was in the hands of that most scientific of Indian horticulturists, Lieutenant Pogson, he would probably be able to tell us the exact quantities of sulphates of iron and lime or other chemicals necessary to support the plant through such a trial.

The dwarf varieties of Noisettes, though generally producing small flowers, are extremely valuable where quantity rather than quality is a desideratum. These should be treated in the same manner as Tea Roses.

The Best Noisette Roses

Name	Description	Habit of Growth
Aimee Vibert	Pure white, blooming in large clusters; very handsome, glossy foliage	vig.
Aimee Vibert (variegated)	A variety of the above with distinct margined leaves	vig.
American Banner	Striped rose and white like the York and Lancaster; semi-double; more curious than beautiful	free.
Bouquet d' Or	Deep yellow centre, copper colour, of medium size and full	vig.

Name	Description	Habit of Growth
*Celine Forestier**	Deep canary yellow; outer petals pale yellow; flowers good sized; well formed and very fragrant	vig.
*Cloth of Gold**	Pure yellow; globular; very large and very double; a superb rose but rather sky bloomer	vig.
Eclair de Jupiter	Light crimson colour, very beautiful and attractive	vig.
Fellenberg	Crimson; very bright and beautiful; blooming very freely in clusters; semi-double only	vig.
Jaune Desprez	Fawn colour, pink and fawn centre; highly scented and very vigorous	vig.
*Lamarque**	Sulphur yellow, very large and full; blooms freely in clusters	vig.
Emily Plantier	French white, light coppery tinge; flowers small but very pretty	vig.
*Madame A. Carriere**	Flesh white, salmon yellow at the base of petals; large, full and well formed; a very vigorous climber	vig.
Madame Caroline Kuster	Centre canary yellow; outer petals pale lemon; flowers large and globular	vig.
Madame Miolan Carvalho	Deep sulphur yellow; large, full and good form; a seedling from *Cloth of Gold*	vig.
*Marechal Neil**	Rich, brilliant yellow; petals large, smooth and of good substance; flowers very large, full, deep, and of exquisite form; the most superb of all yellow roses, almost too well known now to need any description	vig.
Ophirie	Bright salmon and fawn; distinct and peculiar	vig.
Reve d'Or	Orange yellow; flowers moderate size and full; a good climber	vig.
*Solfaterre**	Fine sulphur yellow; superb, large and very full	vig.
*Triomphe de Rennes**.	Straw, centre pale yellow, highly fragrant; flowers of good size and well formed	vig.
Unique Janne	Pale fawn with flesh tint, very pretty and distinct colour; blooms in clusters	vig.
*W.A. Richardson**	Beautiful orange yellow; large full and good shape; very vigorous	vig.

Chapter XIX
The Bourbon Rose

Bourbon Roses but a few years since, comprised one of the most important groups in the Rose family, has been almost entirely superseded by the Hybrid-perpetuals, Teas, and the numerous other classes of Roses that have sprung into existence, and which by their gorgéous colours, immense size, fine form, or delicate beauty, have ensalved all the affections of nearly every Rose-grower, to the almost total extinction of old friends tried and true. Take, for instance, the parent of the whole group, Rose Edourad. This was introduced in 1822, and for very many years was the only Rose of any value or beauty in this country, and even up to the present day we have not a single variety that equals it in its profuseness of bloom. It is a strange fact that it has retained the name of Rose Edouard in this country, as in Europe it has always been known under the name given it by its French introducer, namely, Rose de l'Ile de Bourbon. Probably it may have been introduced to India direct from Bourbon, where, it is stated, it originally bore the name by which it is best known to us.

Rivers, in his Rose Amateur's Guide, gives the following interesting history of this Rose :–

"It is now, perhaps, about fifty years since that a beautiful semi-double Rose, with brilliant rose-coloured flowers, prominent buds, and nearly evergreen foliage, made its appearance in this country, under the name of l'Ile de Bourbon Rose, said to have been imported from the Mauritius in 1822 by M. Noisette. It attracted attention by its peculiar habit, but more particularly by its abundant autumnal flowering; still such was the lukewarmness of English Rose amateurs that no attempts were made to improve this pretty, imperfect Rose, by raising seedlings from it, though it bore seed in large quantities. This pleasing task has been left to our rose-loving neighbours, the French, who have been very industrious, and, as a mattter of course, have originated some very beautiful and striking varieties, and also, as is usual in such cases, have given us rather too many distinct and fine sounding names attached to flowers without distinctive characters. Many fables have been told by the French respecting the origin of this Rose. The most generally, received version of one of them is, that a French naval officer was requested by the widow of a Monsieur Edouard residing in the island, to find on his voyage to India, some rare Rose, and that, on his return to the Isle of Bourbon, he brought with him this Rose which she planted on her husband's grave; it was then called Rose Edouard, and sent to France as "Rose de l'Ile de Bourbon." This is pretty enough, but entirely devoid of truth. Monsieur Breon, a French botanist, gives the following account, for the truth of which he vouches. At the Isle of Bourbon the inhabitants generally enclose their land with hedges made of two rows of Roses – one row of the common China Rose, the other of the red four-seasons. Monsieur Perichon, a proprietor at Saint Benoist in the Isle, in planting one of these hedges, found amongst his young plants one very different from the others in its shoots and foliage. This induced him to plant it in his garden; it flowered the following year, and, as he anticipated, proved to be of quite a new race, and differing much from the above two Roses, *which at that time were the only sorts known in the island.* Monsieur Breon arrived at Bourbon in 1817 as botanical collector for the Government of France, and curator of the Botanical and Naturalisation Garden there. He propagated this Rose very largely and sent plants and seeds of it, in 1822, to France. M. Breon named it "Rose de l'Ile de Bourbon;" and is convinced that it is a hybrid from one of the above Roses and a native of the island. "Probably in this country the Bourbon are he most easily grown of all Roses, and require but little care and attention as compared with most of the other groups, though of course, like every thing else in the vegetable kingdom, the more we strive to understand and comply with their requirements the more surely will they give us an ample return for our labours. The whole of the family are free and constant bloomers, with fine foliage, bright colours and in general finely-shaped flowers. They vary very much in habit, many varities being dwarf and compact, others of moderate growth, and some very vigorous and robust. The smaller growing kinds require to be pruned closely, and the more vigorous rather sparingly, as if these are cut too hard they will produce too much wood at the sacrifice of the flowers".

List of Bourbon Roses

Name	Description	Habit of Growth
Acidalie	Blush white; in dry weather beautifully tinted; large and full	vig.
Apolline	Flowers light pink; a very fine rose	vig.
Baronne de Noirmont	Fresh rosy pink, petals of good substance; flowers large, full and well formed possessing a delicious violet scent	rob.
Barcnne Gonella	Bright cerise, with fine bronze hue; large and full	vig.
Catherine Guillot	Carmine rose; flowers large, well formed and full : a superb rose	vig.
Dr. Berthet	Brilliant cherry red, large, full, and good	rob.
George Peabody	Purplish crimson, finely cupped, large and full	vig.
Jules Jurgessen	Rose magenta, velvety carmine with slaty reflex in the centre, very large, full and well formed	vig.
Louis Margottin	Satin rose, large, and full	free.
Louise Odier	Rosy pink, full and finely formed; a good growing and beautlful rosc	vig.
Madame de Sevigne	Very bright rose in the centre; borders of the petals lighter; large and full; blooms in clusters	vig.
Madame Joseph Guyet	Rich violet crimson; petals smooth and shell shaped	free.
Madame Marechal	Flesh colour, edged with white; very distinct	vig.
Madame Scipion	Very bright rose, large, cupped and finely formed	vig.
Marie Parc	Flesh colour with deeper centre; of medium size, full and of good form and habit	vig.
Marquis Balbiano	Deep rose, tinged with silver; very full, of medium size; a good old rose	vig.
Michal Bonnet	Fresh rose; flowers large, full and well-formed; a good rose	vig.
Modele de Perfection	Pale satin pink, fading off to a beautiful carmine tint	dwf.
Perle D'Angers	Very pale rose, almost white, large and full, finely imbricated	vig.
Queen	Clear buff rose, large and full; a very free bloomer	free.
Queen of Bedders	Deep bright crimson flowers; remarkably free flowering, produced in clusters	free.

Name	Description	Habit of Growth
Reine Victoria............	Soft delicate rose of medium size	vig.
Sir J Paxton..............	Bright rose, shaded crimson; free blooming	mod.
Souvenir de la Malmaison................	Bush, centre flesh, fine foliage and habit; one of the best roses grown	free.
Souvenir de la Malmaison a fleur rouge............	A variety of the preceding, but with flowers of a clear shade of pink	free.
Victor Emmanuel........	Purple and purplish maroon, large and double, good and distinct	vig.

Bourbon and Noisette Perpetuals

The varieties comprised in this group are occasionally classed with the hybrid perpetuals. Most of them are very free bloomers; the flowers are not large, but are well formed and generally produced in clusters.

Name	Description	Habit of Growth
Boule de Niege..........	Pure white, petals of great substance, medium size, fine form; one of the best	vig.
Comtesse Barbantine.	Flesh colour, large, full and of good form	vig.
Coquettes des Alpes...	White, centre shaded with rose; full, fine form	rob.
Coquettes des Blanches..................	Pure white globular flower; very large	
Louise Darzens.........	Pure white, not large, but full and of good form	mod.
Madame Auguste Perrin.........................	Pale rose; reverse of petals whitish, of medium size; a beautiful and distinct rose	vig.
Madame Gustave Bonnet.......................	White, shaded with rose and carmine, medium size, globular form; very free bloomer	free.
Madame Scipion Cochet.......................	Beautiful bright rose; edge of petals silvery; fine imbricated flowers	vig.
Olga Marix................	White, shaded with salmon; medium size	
Perfection des Blanches..................	Pure white, of medium size, full and of good shape	mod.
Perle des Blanches....	Pure white, rather small but very free bloomer	mod.

China Roses

These are also known in Europe as Bengal Roses, the parent of the whole race being *Rosa indica,* a native of China. They are all dwarf and compact in habit, and are admirably adapted for cultivation in this country, where they thrive most vigorously, are easily propagated by cuttings, and bloom more profusely than any other class of Roses. Of course we cannot claim for them the great diversity of form and colour found in the hybrid perpetual, or the delicate shades of colour, or the delicious fragrance of the Teas, still this is to a grteat extent compensated for by their continuity of bloom, their distinct form and colors, their hardiness and immunity from all the diseases and ills that rose-flesh is heir to. This hardiness and immunity from disease is no doubt principally due to the fact that they are almost invariably descended from one original species without having been crossed and inter-crossed with other types. The following is a list of the best varieties in this class :

Name	Description	Habit of Growth
Abbe Miland	Reddish purple, often streaked with white; large and globular	
Archduke Charles	Pale rose, changing to deep crimson, very large and double (generally known in this country as *Rosa discolor*)	free.
Belle de Florence	Pale cherry, medium size, semi-double, produced in clusters	mod.
Clara Sylvian	Pure white, rather thin petals, very pretty	
Cramoise Superieure.	Flowers large, very double, rich glowing crimson; one of the most brilliant coloured roses in cultivation	mod.
Ducher	Pure white, medium size, fine form, full, very free flowering	free.
Eugene Beauharnais	Small, beautiful bright amaranth, perfect in bud, when about half expanded	dwf.
Louise Phillipe	Dark crimson, edges of centre petals almost white, of medium size, very double	mod.
Madame Breon	Brilliant rich rose, colour tinged with salmon, large and full	free.
Marjoline	Bright vivid crimson	vig.

Name	Description	Habit of Growth
Mrs. Bosanquet	Beautiful delicate waxy white, very free blooming, one of the finest roses we have (This is occasionally classed amongst the Bourbons)	free.
Napoleon	Bright pink, very fine, large and double	mod.
Sanguinea	Small, very double	dwf.
Viridiflora	Flowers bright green, more curious than beautiful	free.

Rosa Lawrenceana (Fairy Rose)

This is frequently classed with the preceding, though by most botanists it is considered to be a distinct species. It is best grown as a pot plant, and under favourable conditions produces its pretty daisy-like pink flowers in great profusion throughout the year. There seem to be two distinct varieties of this plant, the flowers of both being of the same colour, one, however, being about double the size of the other.

Rosa Microphylla

This is frequently called the Indian Moss Rose, owing to the deep-green prickly calyx that surrounds the buds, easily recognised by its distinct, dense minute foliage; flowers very double, of good shape and medium size; outer petals pale pink; centre deep carmine. There is also a single white and a single crimson variety in cultivation in Europe, but I have never met with them in this country.

Rosa Lyellii (Rose of the Doon)

A very vigorous growing species, bearing large, double, pale pink or blush flowers; grows and blooms freely in Oudh and the N.W. Provinces, but cannot be induced to do so anywhere in the vicinity of Calcutta.

Chapter XX
Summer Roses

We must now turn our attention to the many classes that are grouped together under the head of Summer Roses. I may here repeat what has already been previously stated, that very few members of this section are adapted for cultivation in the plains, or at least not in Bengal. Probably, however, amongst my readers there are a few ardent Rosarians who are blessed with a more favourable climate, and to these a short description of the various families may prove useful; for amongst them there are some of the most beautiful Roses in cultivation. By the term *beautiful* I do not wish to infer that they rival the perfect form of the best of the Hybrid Perpetuals, or the delicate tints of colour found in the Teas, but these have beauties of their own – some for their graceful habit of growth, others on the contrary for their wild, vigorous, free flowering nature, defying all attempts to keep them within bounds, and a few for their unequalled fragrance. Take, for instance, the well-known Bussorah, which, a few years since, was almost the only Rose known in our Indian gardens; and although, in most instances, it has been discarded for the more showy Hybrid Perpetuals, none of them can bear comparison with it in fragrance.

Provence Roses (*Rosa centifolia*)

This is probably the most ancient of all cultivated Roses. It is supposed to have been the hundred-leaved rose of Pliny, and the favourite flower of the Romans, and is believed to have been first introduced into English gardens about the year 1596, and even up to the present day it is, with the old double wall flower, the chief ornament in the cottage gardens in the agricultural districts. They require to be pruned very closely; every shoot must be shortened to three or four buds. If not treated in this way they soon become straggling and unsightly. The following are the most useful members of this family :–

Name	Description	Habit of Growth
Cabbage or Provence.................	Rose, globular, full, very large and fragrant.	vig.
De Meaux or Pompon.....................	Rosy, pink and lilac, very small and pretty.	dwf.
Reine de Provence......	flowers glossy black blush, large and very double, form globular.	vig.
Unique or White.........	Pure white, a beautiful old variety.	vig.

The Moss Rose (*Rosa centifolia muscosa*)

This, as the botanical name implies, is but a variety of the preceding group, though how or where it originated there is no authentic record. Some of our early writers on gardenig mention the fact that the old double Moss Rose was introduced into England from Holland about the year 1596, strange to say, about the same time as its supposed progenitor found a home there also. That it is only an accidental sport or offspring of the Provence Rose is borne out by the fact that plants raised from seed of the Moss. Rose frequently revert to the old Provence form, showing no disposition to moss at all. Even in old plants it is no uncommon occurrence to find whole branches that produce flowers without the slightest appearance of moss. Unfortunately in the plains there is no chance of cultivating this group with any success. Plants will occasionally grow with astonishing vigour and flower freely, but with no more appearance of moss than there is in our old friend Rose Edouard. A curious instance occurred to me some two or three years since with one of this family. I had a very fine plant of *Baronne-de-Wassenaer.* This had flowered for two years in sucession, but, as previously stated, without any of the gladular excrescence we term moss. Happening to mention the circumstance to a very ardent Rosarian residing in Simla, he suggested we should try what a change of air would effect in it.

It was accordingly transferred to his mountain home, and within three months the plant was in flower again, every bud on this occasion appearing in its proper form, and so it has continued to bear up in the present day. Thinking that after the plant had become well acclimatised, it would perhaps retain its proper form, I have, from time to time, had at least a dozen of its offspring brought down to the plains, but those that have survived this ordeal and produced flowers at all, have invariably been found entirely devoid of moss.

Name	Description	Habit of Growth
Alice Leroy	Flowers lilac blush, sometimes rosy pink, large and double, good mossy buds; form cupped; very vigorous habit	vig.
Baronne d Wassenaer	Flowers deep rose, globular in form, produced in large clusters; a good rose, but scarcely full enough	vig.
Celina	Flowers deep rosy crimson, shaded with dark purple occasionally streaked with white, very fine in the bud; a delicate and weak growing variety	dwf.
Common or Old Moss	Flowers pale rose, very large and full, form globular, growth vigorous, foliage fine; one of the best	vig.
Comtesse de Murinais	Flowers pale flesh when first opened, but quickly changing to white; very large and double	rob.
Crested Moss	Pale rosy pink, outer petals often assuming a deep lilac tint; the flower buds beautifully crested, the crest sometimes extending to the leaves; an extraordinary and beautiful rose first noticed growing on the walls of a convent near Berne in Switzerland in 1827	rob.
Gracilis	Deep pink, globular in form, large and full, very free blooming	vig.
Lanei	Flowers rosy crimson, occasioanlly tinged with purple; large and very full, form globular, buds broad, bold and well mossed	vig.
Little Gem	A miniature moss rose; it forms campact bushes densely covered with small double cirmson flowers, beautifully mossed	dwf.
Luxembourg	Flowers deep crimson, often shaded with purple, of medium size and double, form expanded, growth very vigorous	mod.
Pompon (*De Meaux*)	Flowers blush; centres pale pink, small and full; cupped form. A very interesting little rose, but of rather delicate habit	dwf.
White Bath	Flowers paper white, occasionally producing striped or pink petals, well mossed, equisite in bud; very large and full	mod.
Unique	Flowers pure white, occasionally tinted with lake, medium size, well mossed, beautiful cupped shape; one of the best	mod.

Hybrid or Peripetual Moss Roses

This is one of the many new sections into which the Rose family is now divided, possessing all the properties of the Moss Rose with the desirable addition of being as free blooming as the Hybrid Perpetuals. They must be grown in very rich soil and require very close pruning.

Name	Description	Habit of Growth
Blanche Moreau.........	Fine pure white, large, full, and opening well, of perfect form, blooming in clusters	vig.
Deuil de Paul Fontaine.....................	Flowers very large, but rather loosely formed, of a deep reddish purple colour	vig.
Madame Edouard Ory............................	Reddish crimson, very large and full; habit free and good; one of the best and most constant blooming	vig.
Madame Moreau........	Bright rose, veined and shaded with red; flowers large, full, and expanded, as highly scented as the old moss...........................	vig.
Soupret et Notting......	Fine bright rose, of perfect form, very large and good, highly scented; the finest variety in this group	vig.
Perpetual White..........	Pure white, blossoms in large clusters, not constant..	mod.

French Roses

The French Rose (*Rosa gallica*) is supposed to have been introduced into England towards the end of the sixteenth century and until the introduction of the Hybrid Perpetuals and Teas was the favourite Rose of our English growers. It is stated that the once famed nurseries of Messrs. Loddiges of Hackney possessed a collection of upwards of two thousand vareities, but undoubtedly it was the same then as it is now, where such an immense number of kinds are brought forward. The names are pleasing to the ear of the enthusiast searching for novelties, but the eye searches in vain for distinct characters in the flowers. Rivers, in his Rose Amateurs' Guide, gives the following interesting history of this group : "This was one of the earliest Roses introduced to our gardens, and is supposed by some to be the *Rosa Milesiana* of Pliny; it has also historical claims of much interest, for the semi-double bright Red Rose grown in Surrey for our London druggists, and still cultivated extensively in the environs of Provins, to make their celebrated conserve of Roses is, according to a French authority, the Red Rose, the ancient badge of the House of Lancaster. Somewhere about the year 1277, a son of the King of England, Count Egmond, who had taken the title of Comte de Champagne, was sent by the King of France to Provins, with troops to avenge the murder of the Mayor of the city who had been assassinated in some tumult. He remained at Provins for a considerable period, and on his return he took for his device the red rose of Provins, which Thibaut, Comte de Brie, had brought from Syria, on his return from a crusade some years before. The White Rose of the House of York was probably our very old semi-double vareity of *Rosa alba.*

Our Provins Rose is also associated with recollections of the unfortunate Hosue of Bourbon; for when Marie Antoinette came to France in 1770, to espouse Louis XVI, she passed through Nancy, a city about 160 miles to the south-east of Provins, the inhabitants of which presented her with a bed strewed with leaves of the Provins rose. Alas! her bed was twenty years afterwards more abundantly strewn with thorns by the inhabitants of Paris. Charles X also on arriving at Provins on his return from the Camp at Luneville, September 21st, 1828, was recevied in state by the authorities who deputed twelve young ladies to present him with the flowers and conserves of roses."

Out of the many thousands of varieties of this once popular group that have been introduced from time to time, there now remains scarcely more than fifty in cultivation, and even out of this small remnant of a once glorious army not more than half a dozen kinds are generally cultivated. They are well adapted for cultivation in our Hill stations; and thrive in any good garden soil. They require careful pruning; all the weakest wood should be entirely cut out, leaving only four or six strong growths, and these must be cut back to six or eight eyes from the base or to the first plump bud.

Name	Description	Habit of Growth
Boula de Nanteuil	crimson-purple centre sometimes flery	rob.
Blanchefleur	white, slightly tinted with flesh	rob.
Cynthie	pale rose, light margin, beautiful, large	mod.
D'Aguesseau	crimson, richly shaded with purple, large and full	mod.

Name	Description	Habit of Growth
Duchess of Buccleuch................	dark rose, margin blush, beautiful........................	vig.
Kean...........................	rich velvety purple, centre scarlet	vig.
Marjolin	purple, large and full	rob.
O'Eillet Parfait...........	pure white, with broad stripes of rosy crimson, beautiful, very double	dwf.
Ohl..............................	dark crimson and scarlet shaded, large	rob.
Perle des Panachees..	white, striped with rose	mod.
Rosa Mundi................	red, striped with white, sometimes all red; large and semi-double	mod.
Village Maid..............	white, striped with rose and purple, large and full, of cupped form	mod.

Hybrid China Roses

This group originated by crossing the French and other summer blooming Roses with the Chinese, Tea-scented and Noisette varieties. They are of a very hardy nature, and grow most luxuriantly in a cool climate, but are not adapted for cultivation in the plains; they must be pruned very sparingly. The following varieties can be recomended.

Name	Description	Habit of Growth
Blairri, No. 2................	rosy blush, fine large petals, very handsome foliage; fine pillar or weeping Rose	vig.
Brennus......................	deep carmine, a handsome old variety, which forms a noble standard or pillar	rob.
Chenedole...................	brilliant glowing crimson, very showy, and a superb Rose; forms a noble standard or pillar Rose	rob.
Comtesse de Lacepede................	silvery blush, vey distinct and beautiful	vig.
Double Margined Hip............................	creamy white, beautifully edged with pink; a very pretty Rose	free.
Fulgens......................	bright scarlet-crimson, colour exquisite; a fine old Rose very showy, and an exquisite pillar or weeping Rose	vig.

Name	Description	Habit of Growth
Leopold de Bauffremont................	fresh rosy pink, shape perfect, beautiful, compact, free-blooming, and a fine pillar Rose	vig.
Madame Plantier........	pure white, an abundant bloomer, and a good pillar Rose	vig.
Madame Riviere..........	very beutiful and delicate bright rose, very large, full and well formed	
Magna Rosea.............	light blush, tinted with pink, very large and showy	vig.

Hybrid Bourbon Roses

This family of Roses has been produced by crossing the French, Provence and other summer Roses with the Bourbons. They are generally of a more vigorous habit than the preceding, being readily distinguished from them by their broad stout foliage. They require the same treatment as the Hybrid China, but may perhaps be pruned rather more freely.

Name	Description	Habit of Growth
Catherine Bonnard......	cerise-crimson flowers, moderate size, full, and well formed; a good pillar Rose	
Charles Lawson..........	bright rose shaded, very large and double a fine Rose	rob.
Coupe d'Hebe............	delicate rosy flesh, large and double; one of the most beautiful of summer Roses	vig.
Juno..........................	pale rose, globular, very large and full; a handsome Rose, and good for a pillar	rob.
Madame Isaac Pereire........................	beautiful vivid carmine, full, of immense size, perfect imbricated form, blooming all the season; growth very vigorous; first-class variety	vig.
Madame Jeanne Joubert......................	fine carmine, large and imbricated, blooming late in the autumn; a good garden Rose	vig.
Paul Perras...............	pale rose, very large and handsome; makes a fine standard or pillar Rose	rob.
Paul Ricaut...............	brilliant carmine, very large, most equisitely formed, and very beautiful	mod.
Souvenir de Mons. Faivre........................	fine scarlet-red, with slaty reflex, very large, full, and well formed..................................	vig.

The Damask Rose (*Rosa Damascena*)

The only variety of this group that can be cultivated with success in the plains is the well known Bussoorah, so extensively grown in various parts of the country for the production of attar and Rose water. The Bussoorah is only valuable for its glorious perfume, for the flowers are only semi-double, with thin flimsy petals and very evanescent in colour, in fact lacking all the points that should be found in a good Rose.

Mr. W. Paul in the "Rose Garden" says : "Formerly all dark Roses were termed Damask, probably from the first dark varieties having borne this name. But there are now dark Roses belonging to every section, and there are Damask Roses of every colour. The Damask are readily distinguished from others by a robustness of growth, in conjuction with rough, spinous shoots and downy coriaceous leaves of a light green colour. Owing to this latter feature they present a striking contrast when introduced among other groups. The flowers are mostly of fair size; some are large, and all are showy."

The Damask Rose is allowed to be of great antiquity. Some suppose it to be, of this Virgil speaks in the Georgics and elsewhere. It is generally believed that it was first introduced from Syria, and brought to England in 1573. But Johnson, in "The History of Gardening," says :- "The learned Linacre, who died in 1524, first introduced the Damask Rose from Italy". Who will fight the battle? We must not pause to do so; wherever the truth may lie, it is evident that this Rose has been cultivated in England for a great length of time, and it affords a striking example of the treasure Nature's plants are capable of yielding beneath the hand of the industrious cultivator, of the power given unto man to improve by his labor the races of the vegetable world. For two hundred years this Rose underwent but little change, but modern Rose growers have improved and varied it to such an extent, producing through it first, Damask Perpetual, then Hybrid Pepetual, that the favourites of so long standing are threatened with oblivion."

Name	Description	Habit of Growth
La Ville de Bruxelles	light rose, margin blush, large and full	vig.
Leda or Painted	blush, edged with lake, full	rob.
Madame Hardy	white beautiful, large and full	vig.
Madame Stoltz	pale straw, cupped	vig.
Madame Soetmans	creamy white, shaded with buff, large and full	vig.
York and Lancaster	red and white, striped, large and full, liable to sport	vig.

Rosa Alba

Rosa Alba, or the White Rose, so named probably because the original species is white, forms a small but interesting group of old fashioned Roses none of which we believe have ever been cultivated in this country. They would probably grow vigorously in the Hills, but it is doubtful if they could be induced to thrive satisfactority in the plains.

Name	Description	Habit of Growth
Blanche Belgique	white, very florlferous	mod.
Belle de Segur	soft rosy flesh, edges blush, beautiful, of medium size, full, form cupped	rob.
Celestial or Maiden's Blush	flesh colour, beautifully tinted with the most delicate pink, of medium size, double cupped	mod.
Felicite Parmentier	rosy flesh, margin blush, large and full	rob.
Madame Audot	glossy flesh, large and full	mod.
Madame Legras	creamy white, large and full	mod.

Scotch Roses

Rosa Spinosissima, or the Scotch Rose, is as the name implies, a native of Britain; its cultivation, I believe, has never been attempted in this country, nor is it likely that it would suceed except at a high elevation.

Boursault Roses (*Rosa Alpina*)

The species of this group are entirely distinct from any other section of the Rose family. The shoots are long, very smooth and flexible, and in most instances entirely free from thorns. The plants grow vigorously enough in the plains, but can rarely, if ever, be induced to flower freely, and when produced are invariably weedy worthles things. In the Hill stations, on the contrary, they bloom very profusely, producing their flowers in large clusters, perfect in shape and of good size, but rarely double.

Austrian Roses (*R. lutea*)

Harrisonii and the *Persian Yellow* are the showiest Yellow Roses in cultivation. The latter cannot be too highly recomended; its flowers are of a deep golden yellow, and the young leaves have the fragrance of the Sweet Brair. It blooms freely under ordinary treatment, but requires care in pruning; the head should be well thinned, and the shoots that are left for flowering suffered to remain long. Suitable only for cultivation in the Hills.

Name	Description	Habit of Growth
Austrian Yellow	single	mod.
Austrian Copper	single	mod.
Harrisonii	fine golden yellow, double, flowers profusely	rob.
Persian Yellow	the deepest yellow, large and full, superb	mod.

Rosa Sulphurea

The flowers of this vareity are of the deepest and brightest yellow found among Roses, of good globular for, very large and full. Unfortunately it is notorious for refusing to expand its blooms, and this character had adhered to it for upwards of two hundred years. Parkinson, a writer of the seventeenth century, says :- "The flower is so thick and double, that very often it breaketh out on one side or another, but few of them abiding whole and fair in our country." I remember seeing several plants of this species at Mussoorie a few years since, and on making enquiries was informed that they bloomed freely year after year, but rarely produced a perfect flower. I have plants in Calcutta that are growing vigorously enough, but although planted upwards of four years, have never flowered.

Sweet Brier (*Rosa rubiginosa*)

This dear old favourite is almost too well known to need description : it is common all over India, and grows freely if left to itself, and should never be pruned. It must be propagated either by budding or grafting as cuttings cannot be induced to strike. I have only met with one variety in cultivation in India, and this is probably the wild type of our English hedgerows. The following varieties are now grown in Europe :

Name	Description
Celestial	flowers pale blush.
Double White	flowers white.
Double Scarlet	flowers rosy red.
La Belle Distinguee	flowers bright red, cupped.
Splendid	flowers light crimson.
Superb Red	flowers bright red, very sweet.

CHAPTER XXI
CLIMBING SUMMER ROSES

The various groups belonging to this section, like those described in the preceding chapter, are, with but one or two exceptions, only suitable for cultivation in the Hills.

Ayrshire Roses *(Rosa arvensis)*

These may be described as running Roses; their growth is very slender and extremely rapid. They are of a very hardy nature, and for planting in rough situations where others will not thrive, for covering old walls, trees or pillars, they have no equal. Being natives of Europe, they can only be grown successfully in this country at a high elevation.

Name	Description
Bennett's Seedling (*Thoresbyana*)	white, small and double.
Dundee Rambler	white, semi-double.
Madame Viviand Morel	carmine-rose, tinted with cerise; flowers of medium size, full, and finely formed, produced in clusters, extra fine,blooming in autumn.
Ruga	pale flesh, large and double.
Splendens	flesh colour, large and double.
Virginian Rambler	in the way of *Dundee Rambler*, but the flowers shaded with pink; admirable for weeping.

Evergreen Roses *(Rosa sempervirens)*

This species is not actually evergreen as the name would imply, although it retains its foliage in a cold climate longer than that of any other member of the Rose family. In this country however, where the majority of Roses are more or less evergreen, the peculiar characteristic of *Rosa sempervirens* is of no value. In very bleak situations, at a high altitude, it would doubtless prove exceedingly useful. The flowers are small but extremely double, and are borne in dense drooping corymbs of from twenty to fifty bloms each. In pruning all the thin wood should be removed, and the shoots left for blooming should simply have their tips pinched off.

Name	Description
Donna Maria	pure white, small and double.
Felicite Perpetuee	creamy white, beautiful, small and full.
Flora	rosy flesh, full.
Leopoldine d'Orleans	white, tipped with red, small and double.
Myrianthes Renoncule	blush, edged with rose, small and double.
Rampante	pure white, double.

Rosa Multiflora

The varieties belonging to this group, although they grow vigorously enough in the plains, produce but very insignificant flowers, and then very sparingly after being planted for several years. At an elevation of about 5000 to 6000 feet in the Himalayas they seem to find a home in every way congenial to them, blooming most profusely year after year without any attention being given them.

Polyantha Roses (*R. polyantha)*

Japanese Roses, producing white flowers, and closely allied to, if not varieties of, *R. multiflora*. They are of very rapid growth, and valuable for climbing.

Name	Description
Bijou de Lyon............................	pure white, small, full, and imbricated, produced in clusters.
Double (Duplex).......................	double white.
Single (Simplex).......................	single white.

Banksian Roses *(Rosa Banksioe)*

The Banksians are tender evergreen Roses, very vigorous in growth, with small and beautiful shining leaves. No pruning is required until they become much crowded with branches, when a portion of the strongest shoots may be removed; all the weaker ones should be left, as from these the flowers are produced.

Name	Description
Fortuniana...............................	white, large and very sweet; introduced from China.
White..	white, very fragrant, scent of the violet.
Yellow..	yellow, flowering freely in small clusters.

Rosa ternate or *Rosa loevigata,* a very common plant in Bengal, also belongs to this group; it is of very rampant growth with bright glossy foliage, its pure white single flowers being produced in dense clusters.

Rosa Gigantea

This species is described by Firminger as producing no flowers, such is not however the case; in its wild state it flowers as freely as the common Dog Rose : under cultivation it certainly blooms very rarely, except on plants that have been left entirely undisturbed for some years, and yet *Rosa gigantea* is probably the most useful Rose in our gardens in Lower Bengal, for we depend almost exclusively upon it for stocks on which to graft our Hybrid Perpetuals, Teas and Noisettes. It roots more freely than any other species with which we are acquainted, and is the most obliging foster parent in the whole Rose family.

Chapter XXII
American Roses

It is not perhaps generally known that a large number of varieties of Roses have originated in America; some of these are to be found in our gardens, but having been imported from England, their original birth-place has not been revealed. The following list compiled by the celebrated American Rosarian Mr. H.B. Ellwanger, contains much interesting information : –

A Monograph of Roses which are of American origin has, I believe, never before been attempted; not, perhaps, because there has been a want of interest in the subject, but because of the inherent difficulty in procuring reliable data. To discover the parentage of the various varieties, and the names of the raisers, has been an arduous undertaking, and I regret not being able to present a complete record; this, however, was hardly to be expected. Two classes have had their origin in America, the Prairie and Noisette Roses. These two classes give the most valuable climber which we have, though our Transatlantic brethren do not take very kindly to the former. Besides these two classes, many varieties in other groups have had their origin in this country, several of which are leading sorts in all Rose catalogues of prominence, but our chief contributions must be considered the Prairie and Noisette varieties, as introducing new and very important groups.

The Prairie Rose *(Rosa rubifolia)* is indigenous to this country. Seeds of this were sown about 1836 by Messrs. Samuel & John Feast, of Baltimore. The seedlings from this sowing were then fertilised by some of the best Roses grown at the time, and from this lot came Baltimore Belle and Queen of the Prairies. The Messrs. Feast, together with Joshua Pierce, of Washington, have raised nearly all the varieties of this class possessing any merit. Though inferior in quality to the Tea Noisettes, their hardiness and vigorous habit make them of great value when the more beautiful Noisettes are too tender to be made useful. As an indication of their popularity we may state that, next to the Remontant Roses (H.P.) more plants are annually sold of the Prairie than of any other class. Baltimore Belle when in blossom gives a display of which any one may be proud, whether the flowers are viewed individually or in the mass. It is much to be regretted that no further development of this really valuable class has been made. There is no reason why we should not succeed in obtaining a new class of hardy climbers which shall, in a great measure, combine the good qualities of the Hybrid Perpetual, Noisette, and Prairie Roses. By patient study and care this may be done. Who is there that will do it? To accomplish this desired result the Prairie varieties might be made the seed parents, and fertilised by different varieties of Remontant and Noisette Roses known to be good seed-bearers and that are otherwise desirable sorts.

A few years ago Mr. Henry Bennett, of Salisbury, England, commenced a series of experiments in the production of new Roses by artificial fecundation; selecting a number of sort among the Tea and Hybrid Perpetual groups, and seeking, as far as possible, to combine and blend the several good qualities possessed by each. He has in this way founded a new, and what will certainly prove to be a very valuable class of Roses – the Hybrid Teas. Indeed it is my opinion that this group of Hybrid Teas will, by the improvements which are certain to be made, soon constitute our most popular class of Roses. What has been accomplished by Mr. Bennett is very good evidence, to my mind of what can be done by us, in producing a class of hardy H.P. Climbing Roses.

In the list of American Roses there are several varieties with which I am unacquainted, and the descriptions, therefore, are those of the raisers, or, where in a few instances it was not possible to obtain these, they are described by reliable parties acquainted with the varieties. Whenever possible, both the name of the raiser, and the year when the variety was first sent out, are given.

Prairie Roses *(Rosa rubifolia)*

These possess great vigour of growth, bloom late in the season in large clusters, and though the individual flowers lack many of the desirable features found in other classes, none are more effective in the mass. Anna Maria (raised by Samuel Feast, of Baltimore, Md.,

1843), colour blush or pale pink, full flowers; has very few thorns. Anna Eliza (Williams), dark purplish-red. Baltimore Belle (Samuel J. Feast, 1843), white, with blush centre, of good full form. This seems to have some Noisette blood, which makes it a little tender in very severe winters; it is, however, the most beautiful of the class. Eva Corinne, pale blush. Gem of the Prairies (raised by Adolphus Burgess, of East New York, 1865), a hybrid between Queen of the Prairies and Madame Laffay (Remontant); rosy-crimson, occasionally blotched with white. Jane, rosy-blush, double and finely shaped. King of the Prairies (Samuel Feast, 1843), pale rose. Gracilis (W. Prince, 1845), rose, varying in hue. Linnaean Hill Beauty, white or pale blush. Madame Caradori Allan (S. Feast, 1843), bright pink, semi-double. Milledgeville, pale blush, tinged with flesh. Miss Gunnell, pale pink. Mrs. Hovey (Joshua Pierce, of Washington), pale blush flowers, becoming almost white; resembles Baltimore Belle, but of rather hardier habit. Mrs. Pierce (J. Pierce, 1850), blush. Pallida (S. Feast, 1843), blush, much resembling Superba. Perpetual Pink (S. Feast, 1843), rosy-purple. Pride of Washington, deep rose; small flowers, but distinct and double. Queen of the Prairies (S. Feast, 1843), bright rosy-red, frequently with white stripe; foliage large and quite deply serrated. Ranunculiflora, small, blush flowers. Superba (S. Feast, 1843), pale rose, changing to blush. Truimphant (J. Pierce, 1850), deep rose, double and compact. There have been a few other varieties in commerce, but the above constitute those which have most commonly been grown, and are the only ones now propagated. The most valuable are – Anna Maria, Baltimore Belle, Gem of Prairies, Mrs. Hovey, Queen of Prairies, and Triumphant.

Noisette or Champney Roses

Rosa Noisettiana, or Rosa Champneyana, or Rosa moschata hybrida. The Noisette Rose is a product of America, and obtains its name from Philippe Noisette, a florist of Charleston, South Carolina. John Champney, of Charleston, from the seeds of the White Musk Rose, fertilised by the Blush China, raised a variety which was called Champney's Pink Cluster. A few years after this, Philippe Noisette, from the seed of Champney's Pink Cluster, raised the Blush Noisette, and this he sent to his brother, Louis Noisette, of Paris, under the name of Noisette Rose. The true name, therefore, for this class, should be the Champney, but the change cannot now be made. This group is naturally of vigorous growth, nearly hardy, and produces large clusters of flowers; but, through hybridisation with the Tea-section, the original characteristics have in part disappeared.

The varieties now generally grown are less hardy, and have nearly lost the clustering tendency; but the flowers have much more substance, and are far more beautiful. America (Prof. C.G. Page of Washington, D.C.; sent out by Thomas G. Ward, 1859); growth vigorous; flowers large, creamy-yellow, with a salmon tinge; a cross from Solfaterre and Safrano. Beauty of Greenmount (James Pentland, of Baltimore, 1854), rosy-red. Champney's Pink Cluster (John Champney), very vigorous; flower pink, semi-double. Cinderella (C.G. Page, 1859), rosy-crimson. Dr. Kane (Pentland, 1856), growth free; flowers large, sulphur-yellow; a shy bloomer on young plants; in the South it is highly esteemed. Isabella Gray (Andrew Gray, of Charleston, South Carolina, 1854), growth free; flowers large, golden-yellow, full and fragrant; on young plants it does not flower fully, and often opens badly; a seedling from Cloth of Gold. Nasalina (A. Cook, 1872), "of vigorous growth; flowers pink, of flat form, very fragrant; a seedling from Desprez." Tuseneltea (Anthony Cook, of Baltimore, 1860), "pale yellow; a seedling from Solfaterre." Woodland Marguerite (J. Pentland, 1859), growth vigorous; flowers pure white, freely produced. There have been other American varieties of this class, but I am only certain of those above named. We hope our southern rosarians will introduce some new types and colours of Noisettes; almost the only ones of value we now have are shades of yellow and white. In the South many Noisettes seed freely, and great improvements might easily be made by resorting to manual fecundation. I see nothing to prevent the obtaining of the same shades among the Noisettes that we have among the Hybrid Perpetuals

Bourbon Roses

Charles Getz (A. Cook, 1871), a hybrid; "growth very vigorous, making a good climber; quite hardy; colour deep pink; very fragrant." George Peabody (J. Pentland, 1857), growth moderate, colour purplish-crimson; a probable seedling from Paul Joseph. Oplitz (A. Cook, 1871), " a hybrid; growth moderate, colour fieryred; a seedling from Gloirie des Rosomenes." Renno (A. Cook, 1868), named after General Renno, of Philadelphia; colour deep pink.

Setina (Peter Henderson, 1859), identical with Hermosa, from which it is a sport, except that it is of stronger growth.

Bengal Rose

James Sprunt (Rev. James M. Sprunt, 1856), sent out by Peter Henderson, 1870; like Cramoisie Superieur, but of vigorous growth, making an excellent climbing sort.

Hybrid Perpetual Roses

Belle Americaine (Daniel Boll, of New York), deep pink colour; flowers small, but of fine form. Madame Bell (Daniel Boll), sent out by M. Boyeau of Angers, France, in 1859; growth vigorous; foliage very large and handsome, of a pale green colour; spines numerous; flowers large or very large, form flat, colour carmine-rose; a free autumnal bloomer and very hardy – perhaps the most hardy in the class. One of the most superb Roses for the garden. Madame Trudeau (Daniel Boll, 1850), deep rose, double and well formed. Charles Cook (A. Cook, 1871), scarlet-crimson. Contina (A. Cook, 1871), rosy-pink. It Defense (A. Cook, 1871), shining red, Camellia form, thornless. La Brilliante (A. Cook, 1872), brilliant red; raised from Napoleon III. Rosalina (A. Cook, 1871), rose colour. Souvenir de President Lincoln (A. Cook, 1869), dark velvety crimson. These are only varieties I can name of American origin, though others have been raised. M. Boll, now deceased, who was by birth a Swiss, produced a number of seedling Hybrid Perpetuals of merit; several of these were sold to parties in France, who sent them out as their own. Among these was Madame Boll. It would be interesting to know, whether any among them besides Madame Boll are now famous.

Tea Roses

American Banner (George Cartwright, of Dedham, Mass., 1877), sent out by Peter Henderson in 1878; a sport from Bon Silene; growth moderate, foliage quite small and leathery; flowers carmine, striped with white. The form and fragrance of the flowers seem the same as in the old variety, but in habit they are entirely distinct. It will perhaps be popular as a novelty, but it has no intrinsic merit to make it valuable, and we cannot commend it. Caroline Cook (Anthony Cook, 1871), colour pink; a seedling from Safrano. Cornelia Cook (A. Cook, 1855), growth moderate, flowers white tinged with flesh, large and very full; not a free bloomer, and often does not open well, but a superb Rose when well grown; a seedling from Devoniensis. Desantres (A. Cook, 1855), "colour flesh, very disntinct, from any other Tea Rose; a better bloomer than Cornelia Cook, and a good winter flower. Raised from Devoniensis." General Washington (C.G. Page, 1860), rosy-crimson. Isabella Sprunt (Rev. James M. Sprunt, 1855), sent out by Isaac Buchanan, of New York, in 1865; sulphur-yellow, a sport from Safrano, which variety it very closely resembles in all save colour of the flower. Paradine (A. Cook, 1858), canary-yellow, small flowers; a seedling from Le Pactole. President (sent out by Mr. W. Paul, of London, in 1860), growth moderate; colour rose, with salmon shade; flowers large, moderately full, much resembling Adam. Mr. Paul, the disseminator, states that this is an American variety, but I am unable to learn by whom it was originated.

Chapter XXIII
New Roses

The French as a nation are proverbially imaginative, but this trait seems to have attained its greatest development amongst the raisers of new Roses. Varieties that, if not actually worthless, at least are not equal to hundreds of the older kinds, are sent out yearly by the dozen. The glowing descriptions given of them by their raisers not only deceives the inexperienced amateur but frequently also many a staid old hand whose experience certainly should have taught him better; but no, the incessant thirst of the ardent rosarian for novelties, like the thirst of the inebriate, must be appeased by drinking again at the same fountain that has so frequently proved fatal to his happiness. This is a subject on which I can speak feelingly. For many years past I have imported almost every variety that has been introduced, averaging perhaps fifty new names yearly. I say *new names* advisedly, for many of these supposed novelties eventually turn out to be old friends in disguise, and what has been the result of my importations? Why, at the end of ten years, out of say 500 varieties obtained, certainly not more than fifty of them belong to the first class; another fifty may be described as second class; the other four hundred varieties have proved either synonyms of older kinds, or miserable failures fit only for the rubbish heap; – in fact at least half of them have already found a place there. Year after year I cry out "hold, enough," when in the spring disappointment follows disappointment as the bloom of each new aspirant for fame unfolds itself and prove to be almost worthless. Year after year a determined resolution is formed never to import another Rose, but to leave it in the hands of others and await the result of their foolhardiness before embarking in any more new varieties. This resolution remains unshaken all through the summer. In autumn, however, the catalogues of the Pauls, Cranston, Cant, Turner and the other mighty men of Roses commence pouring in, teeming with glowing descriptions of all the new introductions of the year. What an effect these have, not only on the nerves but on the determined resolution taken some months previously. You may have seen the same glaring description given in previous years to other varieties which have eventually turned out to be a share and a delusion, but all this is remembered no more. Perhaps to complete our discomfiture, the catalogues of the French growers will come to hand; what glories are here displayed; every variety offered is superor to anything we have ever seen; it is *tres remarquable, tres grand specialite, forme parfaite, superbe variete, admirablement fail, variete distinque, tres brillant et d'un grand effect, mangifique variete,* and a thousand other glowing terms in that most insinuating of all languages. No mortal, at least not a devotee of the Rose, can withstand it, and the consequent result is that resolutions are thrown to the winds. Once more we brave fate, for surely she cannot be always unpropitious. Could we be brave enough to carry out the suggestion contained in the following lines we might be able to adhere to our resolutions never again to embark in novelties :–

> To grow? or not to grow? that is the question :
> Whether 'tis nobler in the mind to suffer
> The greatest torment of a gardener's life
> In poring yearly through "fat catalogues,"
> Or to take means by popping them, when sent,
> In the waste basket – to be looked to
> No more; and by doing so, to say we end
> The thirst for new and "special novelties"
> That flesh is heir to. 'Tis a consummation
> Devoutly to be wished. To grow ? – To sow?
> To grow? – perchance to cram our beds and borders
> With useless rubbish. Aye there's the rub?

It is refreshing to turn from these barren lists of the French raisers to those of our own country, not so redundant in quantity, or with descriptions so charged with the overflowings of an exuberant imagination, and giving promises which are never likely to be fulfilled. English Roses have to pass through an ordeal to which the French varieties are not subject; they are submitted to the consideration either of the Floral Committee of the Royal Horticultural Society, or of the judges at our great exhibitions; they are seen by most of the Rose growers in the kingdom, and, consequently, when they are put into catalogues it is easy to see whether those descriptions are justified or not. It is yet too early to give a decided opnion as to the merits of varieties introduced is 1884 and 1885, for although many of the former have flowered with us this season, the plants are not yet sufficiently acclimatised to produce first class blooms. As far, however, as we are able to judge, there are but very few amongst them that will take a postion in the front rank of Rose society. The following we consider the most promising :

Hybrid Perpetuals

Name	Description
Baronne N. De Rothschild	Silvery rose, large and double.
Belzunce	Vermilion, shaded carmine; large and full.
Climbing Pride of Waltham	Light salmon-pink, same flowers as the type, but the plant has a vigorous habit.
Climbing Hippolyte Jamain	Bright rosy carmine, good glossy foliage, rendering it very desirable as a climbing or pole Rose.
Docteur D'Or.	Shaded red; large and full, shaped like a tea-scented variety; very free.
Duke of Marlborough	Bright red, faint tinge of crimson; large and well formed; vigorous.
Ella Gordon	Bright cherry colour; large and full.
Etendard De Lyon	Bright red; large and well-formed.
Gloire Lyonnaise	Flowers large, well-formed and full, colour of a beautiful shade of chrome-yellow, a cross between *Baronne Ad. de Rothschild* and *Madame Falcot;* a grand addition.
Gipsy	Red, shaded deeper; medium size.
Lady of the Lake	Peach colour.
Laurent De Rille	Light cherry-red; imbricated; full, free.
Madame Pitaval	Bright clear red; large and full
Madame Therese Delacour	Bright carmine-pink; moderate size; full.
Mrs. C. Swailes	Beautiful flesh colour, bright and clear; petals broad; free.
Mrs. G. Dickson	New shade of satiny pink; large; vigorous
Mary Bennett	Brilliant rosy cerise; fine for forcing.

Name	Description
Marshall P. Wilder	Cherry carmine, large, semi-globular, full, and well formed. An American variety, recommended for its vigour, hardness, and freedom in blooming.
Mary Bennett	Brilliant rosy cerise, large, and of beautiful form, opening well, thoroughly perpetual; a fine exhibition Rose.
Pride of Reigate	The first striped Hybrid Perpetual Rose; it is the light crimson of *Comtesse d'Oxford* from which it sported, charmingly striped with white.
President I Crespo	Bright pink or light red; large and full.
Professor Edward Regel	Cerise-red large, full, and of perfect form; in the way of *Mdlle. Annie Wood.*
Prosper Laugier	Scarlet-red, shaded with brilliant carmine, large and full.
Princesse A. D, Orleans	Satiny flesh pink; very large and full.
Princesse De Bearn	Deep rich crimson, tinged bright vermilion; large, and of fine form.
Souvenir D' Alphonse Lavallee	Deep chestnut-red; large and full.
Victor Hugo	Rich crimson-red; shaded purple; large.

Tea-Scented

Name	Description
Charles de Legrady	Carmine, passing to Chinese pink, with a silver margin to petals; large and double.
Grace Darling	Base of petals creamy white, tinted and shaded towards edges pinkish peach; large.
Mademoiselle Alexandrine	A pure white seedling from *Gloire de Bruel Dijon;* large and full.
Souvenir de Gabriel Drevet	Light salmon, bright pink in centre; well formed.
Sunset	A really fine novelty, it is a sport (but a rich tawny shaded saffron-coloured flower) from *Perle des Jardines,* nearly the colour) of *Madame Falcot,* but double, as the parent.

Hybrid Tea-Scented

Name	Description
W.F. Bennett	Of the same colour as *not clear Jacqueminot,* and, from its size and the freedom with which the blooms are produced, it has been likened to a crimson "Niphetos".

Chapter XXIV
Roses for Exhibition

Although the culture of the Rose has for years been steadily increasing throughout India, still much remains to be done before our Queen of Beauty can attain that degree of popularity which she has secured in almost every other civilized country in the world. It has been asserted that the number of Roses grown in England has increased at least a hundred-fold during the past thirty years, and it is claimed that this increase is mainly due to the establishment of Rose or Flower Shows in almost every town or city throughout the country. There is no race of people in the world who so steadily, and frequently unknowingly, practically illustrate the truth of the good old axiom, that, "example is better than precept," as the English. Put before them, say, a prize stand of forty-eight Rose blooms, every flower in the highest stage of perfection, it will not only have thousands of admirers, but what is of far more importance such an exhibit does much to promote a spirit of emulation amongst those who had not hitherto joined in the race, and frequently also stimulates many a faint-hearted one to increased exertion to secure the success that had hitherto failed to crown his efforts. Suppose, on the other hand, that instead of seeing these magnificent Roses, each one had been compelled to read a long and carefully written dissertation on the way to grow Show Roses, with a description of their particular points and qualifications, what would have been the result? In comparison, practically nil.

In this country, unfortunately, Flower Shows are yet in their infancy, and although at those which are held the Rose invariably occupies a very prominent position, still the flowers shown are exhibited generally under such peculiar conditions (or rather we should say without any condition at all) as almost to mar the good effect they would otherwise have. We remember being present at a Mofussil Flower Show a year or two since, at which some remarkably fine Roses were exhibited, that is if individual blooms were considered; but the effect of the whole was far from pleasing. In the first place there was no fixed number of blooms in any of the classes, the schedule simply stating that the classes were for *not less than* 6, 12, and 24 blooms repectively – not even stipulating that whatever number of flowers was exhibited they must be all of distinct varieties. What was the consequence ? The exhibitors had availed themselves freely of the licence given them, and there were entries ranging from six to seventy flowers, the one containing the latter number having actually only thirteen varieties. Then as to arrangement : there were Roses in wood boxes of all shapes and sizes, from the exhausted brandy case to a half tea chest, Roses in tin boxes both round, square and flat, one or two of which still bore the brilliantly coloured luggage labels of a well known steam-ship Company; then there were Roses in baskets in a variety of shapes too numerous to mention, and last, but not least, the very best exhibit of the whole – twelve glorious blooms that would have carried all before them at any show in England – were actually arranged in a common earthen gumlah or pan half filled with water. The Rev. S. Reynolds Hole in describing a Rose show among Nottingham Mechanics, at which he officiated as judge, states that all the blooms were arranged in empty stout or ginger beer bottles; this must have been a harmonious arrangement as compared with the above.

It is much to be regretted that those who have the management of Flower Shows do not formulate a proper code of rules for exhibitors on a similar basis to those generally employed in England; this would do much to increase the popularity of such Exhibitions. One of the leading English Rosarians on the subject of Rose showing says : –

"Having secured the best flowers, the difficulties of Rose showing and conveyancing may be said only to have begun. Those who know little and care less about Rose showing are mostly loud in their condemnation of the stiffness and ugliness of the boxes in which the flowers are arranged. If these can be improved without distracting the eye or disturbing the judgment of the jurors, well and good. But those who make such complaints only show how little they really love or care for Roses. The real Rosarian sees nothing but the flowers; all the accessories are trifles light as air to him. And though anything approaching to slovenliness on carelessness is to be condemned in regard to either boxes, cushioning, &c., yet it is nevertheless true that not a few of the most dilapidated, weather-beaten stands, very imperfectly mossed, &c. take the first prize. Depend upon it the jurors will find the best flowers, be they where or how they may, and will give them their deserts. Those who can see at a glance the perfect points of Roses see nothing else. The Roses by their overmastering beauty absorb their senses, steal their sight, enchain, enrapture, and confirm their judgment.

What form, substance, color, size, sweetness, contrast may be seen in a perfect stand of Roses, and what an amount of thought, work, energy, perseverance, love, genius it represents. Thus a Rose show embodies – incarnises, as it were – many of the noblest physical qualities, mental powers, and moral characteristics of the exhibitors. It is not simply a concentration of sweetness, a display of beauty, but also to a great extent a measure and a test of men. The qualities that win success at Rose shows are exactly those that command it in any ordinary and every extraordinary sphere of life. Give exhibitors of Roses something like a fair start, that is, an equality of conditions and of material, and it will be found that he who puts the most thought, the best work, and the strongest love into his flowers, win all the chief prizes. It may be going too far to say, as is often said, that the best men will win, but assuredly the best Roses will, and he who grows these will probably also be the better man.

One of the greatest difficulties in Rose showing is to muster sufficient perfect flowers at a given time. Something may be done by semi-forcing and retarding to increase the number of our marshalled hosts on a given day. But Roses are bad keepers; hardly are some of them cut till they open their eyes as if to see what was the matter, and an open eye, or one about to open, is fatal. But the chief difficulty is with their colour; that though so deep and dense, is fugitive to a fault as soon as the Rose is cut. It is possible to keep their eyes closed, their form perfect, their substance intact ; but hardly have the Rose stems touched the water than the colour of the Rose begins to dissolve or to be dissipated into the air. Now a Rose that has lost its colour has also lost its character. It is as true of a Rose as of a horse – than a good flower cannot be of a bad colour : and jurors reckon all colours bad that are not true to character. They may be extremely beautiful, but then they are not themselves, and therefore are nigh to rejection. Roses, like virtues, should be above suspicion, and need no explanation. When the latter is needed the stand may be said to be already doomed, just as a man who is always explaining his words or actions has a blot or a blemish somewhere in his character. Each bloom should not only be strong enough to stand alone, but be able to lend support to its immediate neighbours, and to strengthen every bloom in the stand. It is difficult to explain in detail how this is done, but each exhibitor has to solve the difficult problem for himself in his own way, and the ways of arranging Roses so as to win honours seem almost innumerable; cutting, carrying, and setting up demand and receive the utmost attention. Rosarians never excite our sympathy and admiration so thoroughly as when finally disposing of their forces at the last moment before the final tug of war and test of merit in the presence of the jurors. Every power and faculty is in lively exercise to place each Rose to the most advantage. My impression is that these last touches are often overdone. The violent exertion and incessant changes indulged in by some of the largest exhibitors can hardly be favourable to the exercise of a sound judgment and cultured of correct taste; neither is a sort of St. Vitus' Dance, from place to place, or box to box, the most favourable exercise to preserve the freshness or sustain the stability of the Roses. The practice of making so many changes at the last minute also frequently leads to the accidental transference of names even by those that know Roses best.

Wise jurors can generally tell whether or not such changes are accidental or designed. Where it is obvious that a mistake has occurred, I have always advocated its correction, but, of course, a fraudulent aplication of a name merits disqualification. But most of such mistakes would be avoided were the Roses arranged carefully at first, and few or no changes made afterwards.

The lids should be kept on the boxes till the last minute, then a last look taken, and generally that look will confirm your hopes of victory, or tell you, you are beaten. Thus forearmed, you will be able to bear victory more modestly and defeat with more equanimity than if you had neither the knowledge nor the fairness to judge your own and others' Roses righteously. Either way, having done our best, let us rejoice in the beauty and perfection of the Roses, have a word of hearty praise for the victors, and one of kindly sympathy for the vanquished, and thus, whether we win or lose, Rose showing will bring us pleasure and profit."

Show Boxes

The following is the standard measurement of Show Boxes generally adopted by the principal Rose Societies in England, for Exhibits in the various classes :

Length	Breadth	Height
For 24 Roses 3 ft. 9 in.	1 foot 6 in.	Back of box 7 in. front 5 in.
For 18 Roses 2 ft. 9 in.	1 foot 6 in.	Back of box 7 in. front 5 in.
For 12 Roses 2 ft. 0 in.	1 foot 6 in.	Back of box 7 in. front 5 in.
For 6 Roses 1 ft. 3 in.	1 foot 6 in.	Back of box 7 in. front 5 in.

Mr. W. Paul, on this subject, says in the *Rose Garden :* The boxes may be made of inch deal of the simplest construction and painted green. By the laws of some Societies framed for general convenience the lids must shift off at pleasure. No boxes are allowed to be placed on the exhibition tables whose dimensions exceed three feet in length, six inches in height when the lid is removed, and eighteen inches in width from front to back. A handle at either end is desirable whihc should drop into the wood so that the ends may approach closely. The box may be filled with moss, into which zinc tubes may be sunk filled with water to contain the flowers.

The tubes may be about three and a half inches deep, an inch wide, with a rim half an inch broad. Nothing perhaps forms so agreeable a ground on which to place the flowers as green moss, which may be gathered in most hollows of woods and from shady banks. It is not indeed a bad plan to place the moss on the boxes a few days before they are wanted, keeping them in a light but shady place, sprinkling the moss with water once or twice daily.

Selection of Blooms

With regard to the choice of flowers, we may presume that the only who has formed a tolerable collection, and must consequently have acquired some taste in Roses, will enter the lists as a competitor, we would therfore say, cut such flowers as appear best at the time wanted, a good variety may be in a bad condition at the time wanted, and a second rate one unusually fine. But the exhibitor must in a certain degree conform to the tastes of others; and there are points of beauty almost universally agreed on. The *outline* of Show Roses should be circular, free from all reggedness ; the flowers should be full and the petals arranged as regularly as possible, the larger the flowers the better, provided they are not coarse; the colours should be varied with due care. In gathering the flowers, we would say, choose the morning for the purpose ere the sun has risen upon them, or before he has had time to dim their beauty. When the place of exhibition is at a distance, it is usually necessary to cut them the morning before the show. There is full occupation for two persons, beside the advantage of having a second opinion in cases where the merit of two or more flowers is doubtful. It is not always easy to determine this point satisfactorily, for we have not only to consider *what a flower is*, but *what it is* likely to become. The business of one should be to cull the flowers, that of the other to name and arrange them in the boxes. It is desirable that every stage of the flower should be presented to view; but if cut the day before the show, the forwardest should not be more than three quarters blown. Some of the stiff-petalled Roses, which remain a long time in perfection, may be made exceptions to this rule, but their number is few. When the flowers are gathered on the morning of the show some may be full blown, when less judgment and foresight are necessary in selecting.

Some little success perhaps depends on the way the flowers are arranged. This requires a little study, and we would take nature for our model. Let the exhibitor walk among his plants occasionally with an eye to this point, and he will not fail to single out certain flowers remarkable for elegance of position; this is the true source from which to copy. A few leaves should be gathered with each kind, for the grace and beauty of the flowers are materially heightened by the judicious arrangement of foliage; and this is a point by which we may judge of the habits of a variety. As to the arrangement of colours, little need be said on that point. Much will depend on the materials in hand. Contrast should, we think, be aimed at, but with regard to the exact tints fitted for each position the eye of him who arranges is usually best qualified to determine. A neat and commodious method of naming is to procure some deal sticks, about four inches long and half an inch wide, gradually tapering to a point. Let them be painted white, the names written in a ground legble hand with a good dark pencil, or small strips of card-board, the names written in ink, placed in the front of each sort, are both neat and convenient.

But the flowers are arranged, and what is to be done with them during the interval that must elapse ere they depart for the scene of competition? Shall the lids be placed on the boxes and the flowers be kept closed from the air? By no means. Seek as cool a place as possible, where there is no draught and where the light is not too strong. There place them till the time of departure. So necessary do many exhibitors consider it, that the flowers should not be wholly closed from the air, that they have several holes made in the ends of their box-lids with a small auger. This I have found by experience a capital contrivance to admit the dust; and if these holes are made use of they should be stopped with corks when travelling on a dusty road.

Exhibiting Pot Roses

But besides the flowers of Roses, the plants are exhibited grown in pots, and it remains for us to say something of them. The advantages gained by their introduction, are, that the character and habit of the varieties are shown. Cut Roses create a great display, but Pot Roses afford us more information. We may propose to ourselves, while viewing them, these questions : – What is the habit of the variety? Is it a free bloomer or otherwise? Is it a good trusser ? These questions cannot always be answered by presenting a mere flower, or bunches of flowers; but the introduction of Pot Roses offers the means of a ready solution. In cultivating these for exhibition it is necessary to grow at least double the number required to be shown. This is no overdrawn calculation, as all who have had any experience in the matter will testify. There is no difficulty in flowering *every plant,* but there is a difficulty in bringing all to perfection by a given time. Remember the Rose is one of the most ephemeral of flowers, and the day of exhibition is a fixed one. These facts, however, should deter no one from growing for exhibition, for they affect all exhibitors alike; all fight on equal ground, and the greater the difficulties to contend with the greater is the triumph when achieved.

Chapter XXV

Catalogue Descriptions

In the selection of varieties there is perhaps nothing more puzzling to the inexperienced amateur than the descriptions given in Rose Catalogues. In some instances the multiplicity of technical terms employed are frequently sufficient to confuse even our oldest veterans, not that we would imply that these descriptions are necessarily overdrawn – on the contrary, we believe that the catalogues of the leading English Rosarians are amongst the most straightforward of what may be termed "trade literature", only of course they describe each variety at its best stage and grown to the best advantage. We wish we could say as much for the descriptions given by French raisers of new Roses. From my own experience of this class, I should say on no account purchase any of their novelties until they have passed through the hands of some reliable English grower and have been favourably recommended by him.

Mr. W. Paul in "The Rose Garden" gives a very exhaustive summary of the many terms employed in describing varieties. As this valuable work is probably in the hands of but very few of my readers, I give them *in extenso* :– "The first terms which present themselves are those relating to the *size of the flowers* : they are *five*, namely:–

Very small, applied when the flowers are about 1 inch in diameter.

Small, applied when the flowers are from 1½ to 2 inch in diameter.

Of medium size, applied when the flowers are from 2 to 3 inch in diameter.

Large, applied when the flowers are from 3 to 4 inch in diameter.

Very large, applied when the flowers are from 4 to 5 inch in diameter.

These are also five terms used expressive of *the degree of fulness : – Single, Semi-Double, Very Double, and Full.*

The Single are such as possess but one row of petals.

The Semi-double have from two to five rows of petals.

The Double have more than five rows of petals, yet when full blown usually show the stamens in the centre of the flower.

Examples : - General Jacqueminot (Hybrid-Perpetual), Safrano (Tea-scented).

The Very Double have a sufficient numbe of petals to hide the central stamens.

The Full have the petals closely together. Example : - Countess de Chabrillant (Hybrid-Perpetual), Marechal Niel (Tea-scented).

It should however be stated that the flowers of some varieties vary at times and under certain conditions as to fulness.

In reference to the *form of the flowers* we have the terms *globular, cupped, compact, and expanded.*

The term *globular* is applied to such varieties as assume that form in which the outer petals encircle the flower, the latter remaining closed or almost closed until nearly full blown; thus the flower in its early stage is a perfect globe. Examples of this term : – The Cabbage Rose (Provence), La Reine (Hybrid-Perpetual), Gloire de Dijon (Tea-scented). It is worthy of remark that Roses of this form usually remain perfect for a longer period than others.

The term *cupped* is applied in cases where the outer petals of the flower stand erect or are slightly incurved, the petals within being in general of smaller size than the outer ones, the flower thus being a little hollow in the centre like a cup. Examples of this term :– Auguste Mie, Beauty of Waltham, Louise Peyronny (Hybrid-Perpetuals.)

The term *compact* is applied to those varieties whose petals are stiff and upright, the centre of the flower being almost level with its circumference, usually rising above it rather than being depressed. Examples of this term : – De. Meaux (Moss), Madame Boll (Hybrid-Perpetual).

The *expanded* differ from the *compact* in this respect – the outer petals instead of standing erect, lie almost horizontal, usually turning back upon the flower stalks in the last stage of the flower. Examples : – Barrone Prevost, Geant de Batelles, (Hybrid-Perpetuals). These are the terms which I have thought it expedient to make use of, to convey a correct idea of the size, form and fulness of the different varieties of the Rose.

With regard to the form of the flower, it may be remarked that it often varies as the flower passes through its various stages of existence. Thus Roses which are globular when young frequently pass into the cupped state as they advance in age, a Rose which is cupped when half-blown may become compact when full blown; and a Rose that is compact in the former stage, may become expanded in the latter; and the same with regard to colour, a Rose may be pink or rose-colour when first opening to the sun and fade to blush ere it decay. Now with regard to form, as it would be difficult in all cases to record such peculiarities. I have contented myself with seeking out the most perfect stage of the flower and noting the form of such. As to colour, where this changes it will be found noted in the description.

The *habit of the plant* is the next character which presents itself. The terms used are - *branching, erect, dwarf* and *pendulous.*

By *branching* I intend to point out the varieties whose shoots have a somewhat lateral tendency of growth, branching away from the centre of the plant.

Erect is applied to those whose shoots rise perpendicular, or near so.

Dwarf is applied to those of humble growth.

Pendulous is used to point out those that are of a pendulous or drooping habit.

There are four terms used illustrative of the *rate of growth* : – *vigorous, robust, moderate* and *small.*

Vigorous is used to point out such varieties as form long shoots.

Robust alludes to those which form very shoots of less length than "vigorous".

Moderate alludes to those which are of moderate growth : such usually form neat and compact bushes.

Small is applied where any variety is of small or dwarf growth.

To know the rate of growth of a plant is of the highest importance in the selection of varieties. How otherwise can they be properly adapted for particular puposes? How else arranged correctly in Rose clumps or in the formation of a Rosarium. One cannot always judge correctly of the rate of growth by a young plant, its vigour may be extraordinary, when in reality the variety is only a moderate grower. Hence it frequently happens that we find Roses in clumps and elsewhere badly placed, the guiding line when planting having been the rate of growth of the young plants, and thus a moderate grower fills a position suited only for a robust and vigorous one or *vice versâ*.

Chapter XXVI
Selection of Varieties

Although in the long list of varieties described in previous chapters, I have been careful to include only such as can be confidently recommended, still amongst such a host the inexperienced amateur may find a difficulty in choosing the kinds best suited to his requirements. I will therfore now endeavour to assist him, as far as possible, by giving selections of varieties adapted to the various purposes for which Roses are generally required. Some of my readers may exclaim, Why ! a good Rose must be good no matter for what purpose it may be required ! But such is far from being the case. A variety that would be considered a first class Exhibition Rose is rarely a good garden Rose, and a good garden Rose would certainly be out of place among Exhibition varieties, and mainly for this reason, that in the one we need quality and in the other quantity of bloom. It may be well to state a few of the leading characteristics of what most of us consider a fine Rose, whether species or variety. All varieties (excepting the Moss Rose) should possess foliage of a deep shining green, which colour to be perfect needs to permanent, although not likely to be found in many varieties, our preference being for a sort of evergreen foliage. However size, form, &c., may vary in different varieties, uniformity in the same variety is desirable. A fine Rose is one which is beautiful in all its stages of bud and blossom, up to and previous to wide and full expansion. Single and double flowers while enclosed within their calyxes, are alike beautiful up to a point where they expand to hide the calyx; but the double possess that characteristic which make them magnificent when full blown, while the singles are best shown previous to full expansion. Whatever difference there may be otherwise, the petals of all Roses should be thick, broad and smooth at the edges. The flower should be double to the centre, high on the crown, round in outline, with regularly disposed petals.

The peculiar characteristics of any and all varieties should be strongly and fully developed in each flower. The bud and blossom should possess fragrance, and the higher that fragrance the more beautiful the variety. On this point a well known writer says : – "To all who grow Roses for the beautifying of the garden and the adornment of the house, it is pleasant to hear from various sources that a growing feeling of protest is aroused against the many scentless varieties so constantly appearing at exhibitions generally. As in the tournaments of old knights contended for the sake of a smile from their chosen dame, so should we also in these modern days imitate their example; may more, raise a crusade against those who dishonour the queen of flowers by raising and showing scentless Roses that do but mock our sense by an outward show of all that is beautiful; and thus begin a war of Roses; no longer of York and Lancaster, or of red and white, but of the sweet-scented *versus* the scentless, in which all should enlist to oppose resolutely the taste that condones any defect that is not apparent at the exhibition table – a taste that values size more than scent, indeed usually ignores the latter altogether; uniformity of shape more than that variety which we are elsewhere told is so pleasing, and even encourages rankness of growth rather than freedom of flowering, and has, to make a long story as short as may be, loaded our gardens and the lists of nurserymen with many varieties that are grown merely to be discarded. It would hardly be just to accuse exhibitors as the source of all these evils, but rather confess that the love of novelty, to which all must plead guilty, has also largely contributed; and as all true lovers of the Rose must always desire to see something more beautiful than they yet possess, the most obvious way of effecting a change so desirable, is to establish prizes for Roses in which scent shall rank as an equal qualification to those already demanded, and in the case of new Roses, excluding them from the highest honours at shows if they lack the crowning grace of sweetnes. It cannot be urged that exquisite perfume and freedom of habit are incompatible with size and shape, when such a Rose as La France has been for years before our eyes and noses; and those who raise new Roses should be invited by special prizes to leave no stone unturned to bring us still nearer to perfection, and, by demanding a guarantee that their beautiful novelties are sweet-scented, throw back on their hands all that are faulty in this particular. If this were done, how often should we be spared the annoyance of finding that a Rose we had admired at a show was, when grown at home, devoid of scent and scanty in blossom.

Herbaceous borders, Alpine rockeries, and wild gardens are just now the ruling taste of the day, and in the latter place we can all find beauty in the Paeony when its brilliant petals are bathed in June sunshine there, then let us place those beautiful impostors that will, in the end, bring discredit on the Rose, and reserve for our Rosery and loving care only those that really are of highest excellence; and, if we cannot refrain from showing scentless Roses, let them have a class to themselves, and then no one can complain. A list of all the scentless Roses would be instructive, in the sense of how to avoid, if some great authority would compile such an "Index expurgatorius" for who would buy a scentless Rose?); but, , in the meanwhile, a few of the head offenders may be mentioned as a guide to the unwary. Perhaps there is no greater offender than the familiar Victor Verdier, scentless itself, and the parent of so many scentless offspring, among which are Comtesse d'Oxford, Mdlle. Eugenie Verdier, Hippolyte Jamain, and many others. Baroness Rothschild, Paul Neron, Duke of Edinburgh and his descendants, are also in the same list, and Etienne Levet and Marquise de Castellane, Mons. Noman and Anna Alexieff must be added to it.

It is curious to remark that, while Tea Roses are generally considered the most powerfully scented, the new Tea Hybrids hitherto are lacking in this quality, though they may just escape the imputation of utter scentlessness; and, still more remarkable, that Gloire de Dijon, one of the sweetest of Roses, has not transmitted that quality to its desendants. For instance, Madame Trifle, Madame Levet, and Tour Bertrand are without scent, and Belle Lyonnaise and Madame Berard are nearly so, and as an instance to the contrary, Marechal Niel, itself one of the most remarkably powerful scented Roses, is said to have Isabella Gray for its parent, a Rose that is devoid of all smell. While urging the necessity of scent to the Rose, if it is to keep its place as first and foremost among flowers, the desirability of free blooming must not be overlooked; but this is just now not likely to be forgotten when the tide is setting in favour of these Tea Hybrids, which promise so much ; and, until such a combination has been achieved, till our gardens are full of new varieties surpassing all we now possess in sweetness, size, shape, colour, and freedom of blooms, let us not rest content or turn our attention to other qualifications.

Among old Roses none is more resplendent in a garden than Eugene Appert; its glowing colour, endurance, beautiful foliage, and freedom of flower still place it in the front rank. Senateur Vaisse is too well known to need further notice. Dr. Andry is a Rose that no garden should be without, a sure physician to heal all disappointment; his complexion is an index of his vigour, which defies all ordinary trials. Madame Victor Verdier is also a model Rose in every respect, brilliant in colour, deliciously sweet and free-flowering, handsome in growth and leaf. This Rose, I fancy, is not yet appreciated fully; perhaps from its resemblance to Senateur Vaisse, which, to my thinking, it surpasses. Duke of Edinburgh would be second to none if it were not scentless; and Paul Neron, were it not for the same grave defect, would be as necessary to a garden as La France is, for its huge size and coarse appearance vanish when treated with judicious neglect; and its flowering powers are indeed great when fully established and clothing some pillar. Baroness Rothschild and Countess of Oxford are, alas! also scentless, but who could leave such beauty in the lurch ? Of less strongly growing Roses, Maurice Bernardin, Louis Van Houtte, and Xavier Olibo are remarkable for their excellence in every way; and the twin Roses – Alfred Colomb and Marie Baumann – make it an impossibility for anyone to choose between them. Charles Lefebvre and Jules Margottin must not be left out of our "garden party," though it is hardly neceassary to mention them and other favourites whose fame is as great as their deserts."

As a full description of all the varieties mentioned in the following groups has already been given in previous chapters, it is unnecessary for us to give anything more than their names.

The Best One Hundred Hybrid Perpetuals
for general culture

Abel Carriere
Abel Grand
Alfred Colomb
Alfred K. Williams
Annie Laxton
Annie Wood
Antoine Ducher
Auguste Neumann
Auguste Rigotard
Beauty of Waltham

Crimson Bedder
Devienne Lamy
Dingee Conard
Docteur Andry
Duc de Rohan
Duc de Wellington
Duchess of Bedford
Duke of Albany
Duke of Connaught
Duke of Edinburgh

Camille Bernardin
Captain Christy
Centrifolia rosea
Charles Lefebvre
Charles Rouillard
Comtesse de Chabrillant
Comtesse de Serenyi
Countess of Oxford
Countess of Roseberry
Francois Louvat
Geant des Batelles
General Jacqueminot
Harrison Weir
Hippolyte Jamain
Horace Vernet
John Hopper
Jules Margottin
La France
La Rosiere
Le Havre
Lord Bacon
Lord Beaconsfield
Lord Macaulay
Louis Van Houtte
Madame Charles Wood
Madame Clemence Joigneaux
Madame Gabriel Luizet
Madame Hippolyte Jamain
Madame *la Barrone de Rothschild*
Madame *Lacharme*
Madame *Noman*
Madame Victor Verdier
Madame Vidot
Mdlle. Julia Dymonier
Mdlle. *Marie Cointet*
Mdlle. *Marie Rady*
Magna Charta
Marechal Vaillant
Vicomte de Vigier
Victor Verdier.
Dupuy Jamain
Earl of Pembroke
Edward Morren
Elie Morel
Emilie Hansberg
Emily Laxton
Eugene Appert
Exposition de Brie
Fisher Holmes
Marguerite de St. Amand
Marie Baumann
Marquis de Castellane
Masterpiece
Maurice Bernardin
Mervielle de Lyon
Miss Hassard
Monsieur Boncenne
Monsieur Etienne Levet
Monsieur *E.Y.Teas*
Monsieur *Noman*
Monsieur Paul Neron
Mrs. Baker
Mrs. Laxton
Nardy Freres
Peach Blossom
Pierre Notting
Pride of Waltham
Prince Arthur
Prince Camile de Rohan
Princess Beatrice
Princess Louise Victoria
Reynolds Hole
Senateur Vaisse
Sir Garnet Wolseley
Star of Waltham
Sultan of Zanzibar
Thomas Mills
Ulrich Brunner Fils
White Baroness.
Xavier Olibo.

The best Fifty Varieties are printed in italics.

A Selection of the Best 60 Varieties for Exhibition

Alfred Colomb	Harrison Weir
Alfred K. Williams	Horace Vernet
Annie Wood	John Hopper
Baroness Rothschild	La Boule d'Or, T.
Beauty of Waltham	Lady Mary Fitz William, H.T.
Camille Bernardin	La France
Captain Christy	Le Havre
Catherine Mermet, T.	Louise Van Houtte
Charles Lefebvre	Madame Bravy, T.
Comtesse de Nadaillac, T.	Madame Clemence Joigneaux
Countess of Oxford	Madame Gabriel Luizet
Devienne Lamy	Madame Lambard, T.
Devoniensis, T.	Madame Margottin, T.
Dr. Andry	Madame Victor Verdier
Duc de Rohan	Mdlle. Marie Rady
Duchess de Caylus	Marechal Niel, N.
Duchess of Bedford	Marechal Vaillant
Duke of Edinburgh	Marguerite de St. Amand
Duke of Wellington	Marie Baumann
Dupuy Jamain	Marie Van Houtte, T.
Elie Morel	Marquis de Castellane
Emilie Hansberg	Mervielle de Lyon
Etienne Levet	Mrs. Baker
Francois Michelon	Monsieur E. Y. Teas
Monsieur Noman	Senateur Vaisse
Niphetos, T.	Souvenir d'Elise, T.
Perle dos Jardins, T.	Souvenir d'un Ami
Pierre Notting	Sultan of Zanzibar
Reynolds Hole	Victor Verdier
Rubens, T.	Xavier Olibo

The names with no letter attached are Hybrid Perpetuals.

T. signifies Tea-scented, H.T. Hybrid Teas, N. Noisettes.

The Best Forty Varieties of Tea-scented Roses

Adam	Madame Angele Jacquier
Adrienne Christophle	Madame Berard
Alba rosea	Madame Lambard
Aline Sisley	Madame Levet
Beauty of Stapleford, H.T.	Madame Trifle
Catherine Mermet	Madame Welche
Cheshunt Hybrid, H.T.	Marcelin Roda

Climbing Devoniensis	Marie Ducher
Comte de Paris	Marie Van Houtte
Comtesse de Nadaillac	Niphetos
Countess of Pembroke, H.T.	Pearl, H.T.
Devoniensis	Perfection de Montplaisir
Duchess of Connaught	Perle de Lyon
Duchess of Westminster	Perle des Jardins
Etoile de Lyon	Pierre Guillot, H.T.
Gloire de Dijon	Reine Marie Henriette, H.T.
Jean Sisley, H.T.	Safrano
La Boulé d'Or	Souvenir d'Elise
Lady Mary Fitz William, H.T.	Souvenir d'un Ami
Vicomtesse de Cazes	Viscountess Falmouth

The varieties to which the letters H.T. are attached belong to the Hybrid Tea class.

The Best Varieties of Climbing Roses

Cheshunt Hybrid, H.T.	Gloire de Dijon, T.
Climbing Captain Christy, H.P.	Lamarque, N.
Climbing Charles Lefebvre, H.P.	Marechal Niel, T.
Climbing Countess of Oxford, H.P.	Reine Marie Henriette, H.T.
Climbing Victor Verdier, H.P.	Solfaterre, N.
Climbing Devoniensis, T.	Triomphe de Rennes, N.
Celine Forestierl; N.	W.A. Richardson, N.
Cloth of Gold, N.	

H. P. Hybrid Perpetual, T. Tea-scented, H.T. Hybrid Tea, N. Noisette.

Chapter XXVII
Rose Synonyms

In the preceding chapters frequent allusion has been made to varieties of Roses possessing one or more synonyms, or which so closely resemble each other as to render it almost impossible to distinguish them. A brief list of the most prominent of these, compiled by some of our leading authorities on the subject, will probably prove interesting.

M. Schwartz, of Lyons, contributes the following list of Roses and their synonyms to the *Journal des Roses :*

Tea-scented

Alba rosea	Same as	Madame Bravy
Adèle Pradel	Same as	Madame Morin
Boiron	Same as	Guillot
Clothilde	Same as	Bougere
Duchesse de Brabant	Same as	Comtesse de Labarthe
Gloire de Bordeaux	Same as	Belle de Bordeaux
L'Enfant Trouvé	Same as	Elisa Sauvage
Lady Warrender	Same as	Clara Sylvain
Madame Denis	Same as	Madame Morin
Madame Plantier	Same as	Albion
Madame Roussel	Same as	Eugénie Jovain
Madame Sertot	Same as	Madame Bravy
Madame William	Same as	Elise Sauvage
Mathilde	Same as	Niphetos
President	Same as	Adam
Queen Victoria	Same as	Souvenir d'un Ami
Smith's Yellow	Same as	Smithy
Surabondant	Same as	Guillot
Triomphe de Orléans	Same as	Fafait

Bengal

Agrippina	Same as	Cramoisie Supérièure
Comte de la Gloire	Same as	Gros Charles
Marguerite Lartay (Bourbon)	Same as	Impératrice Eugènie
Madame Lacharme (Tea-scented)	Same as	Virginale

Noisettes

Adélaïde Pavie	Same as	Madame des Longchamps
Beauty of Glazenwood	Same as	Fortune's Yellow
Cloth of Gold	Same as	Chromatella
Comtese de Beaumetz	Same as	Chromatella
Enfant de Lyon	Same as	Narcisse
Liésis	Same as	Celine Forestier
Madame de Challonge	Same as	Le Pactole
Marechal (Tea-scented)	Same as	Lamarque

Bourbon

Alice Fontaine	Same as	Emotion
Beauté de Versailles	Same as	Georges Cuvier
Celine Gonod	Same as	Modele de Perfection
Duc d'Estrees	Same as	Henri Lecoq
Eugénie Breon	Same as	Virginie Bréon
Gloire de Brotteau	Same as	Edouard Desfosses
Isabelle Latour	Same as	Duc de Richmond
Madame Neumann	Same as	Hermosa
Madame de Stella	Same as	Louise Odier
Margat Jeune	Same as	Charles Souchet
Mélanie Lamarie	Same as	Hermosa
Michel Bonnet	Same as	Catherine Guillot
Sappho (Tea-scented)	Same as	Mrs. Bosanquet
Sou. de la Malmaison a fleurs Rouge	Same as	Leveson Gower

Portland

Rose du Roi à fleur blanches	Same as	Céline Dubos
Rose du Roi à fleurs pourpres	Same as	Mogador

Rosa Rugosa

Himalayensis	Same as	rugosa rubra fl.-pl.
Regeliana	Same as	rugosa rubra. fl.-simplex
Taicoun	Same as	rugosa rubra fl.-simplex

Centifolia

Madame d'Hébray	Same as	Unique Panachee

Hybrid Perpetuals

Alexander Dickson	Same as	Madame Pulliat
Avocat Duvivier	Same as	Maréchal Vaillant
Beauté Francaise	Same as	Le Lion des Combats
Belle Egarée	Same as	Madame Damet
Duc d'Elchigen	Same as	Poupre Royal
Enfant d'Ajaccio	Same as	Souv.d'Anselme
Francois Fontaine	Same as	Senateur Favre
Froissard	Same as	Mrs. Standish
Empereur des Francais	Same as	Prince Albert
Général Hudelet	Same as	Comte de Paris
Général Lamoriciére	Same as	Gervais Rouillard
Gloire de Châtillon	Same as	Madame Masson
Isoline	Same as	Paul Dupuy
Julie de Saint-Aignaut	Same as	Sophie Coquerel
Laelia	Same as	Louise Peyronny
Mme. Eugénie Cavaignac	Same as	Baron Heckeren de Vassenaer
Madame Hérivaux	Same as	Madame Charles Crapelet
Madame Liabaud	Same as	Virginal
Madame Rival	Same as	Auguste Mie
Mdlle. Henriette	Same as	Auberon
Marguerite Brassac	Same as	Charles Lefebvre
Marquis d'Ailsa	Same as	Dr. Marx
Miss Hassard	Same as	Madame Renard
Mrs. Wood	Same as	Clementine Seringe
Pauline Plantier	Same as	Clement Seringe
Puebla	Same as	Senateur Favre
Reine du Midi	Same as	La Reine
Rose la Reine à fleurs blanches	Same as	Queen Victoria
Souv. du Petit Roi de Rome	Same as	Conseiller Jourdeuil
Triomphe de la Terre des Roses	Same as	Henderson
Triomphe de Valenciennes	Same as	Madame Campbell d'Islay

An interesting paper on this subject appeared in the Rosarians' Year Book from the pen of Mr. George Paul. His extensive culture and his experience as a successful exhibitor gave him great advantages in dealing with it or indeed any subject connected with

Rose culture, still, as he himself urges in the paper, he is but. one; and strongly appeals to the National Rose Society to take up the subject, and by pronouncing authoritatively on it set the matter at rest. The following is the list of synonyms given by Mr. Paul :–

Hybrid Perpetuals

1. Maurice Bernardin, Exposition de Brie, and Ferdinand de Lesseps.
2. Charles Lefebvre and Marguerite Brassac.
3. Mdlle. Eugénie Verdier and Marie Finger.
4. Reine du Midi and Madame Alice Dureau.
5. Madame Boutin and Christine Niellson.
6. Maréchal Vaillant and Avocat Duvivier.
7. Mons. Boncenne and Baron de Bonstettin.
8. Louise Peyronny and Laelia.
9. Mad. Clemence Joigneaux and La Souveraine.
10. Prince Camille de Rohan and La Rosière.
11. Francois Fontaine and Senateur Favre.

Teas

12. Adam and President.
13. Alba Rosea and Mad. Bravy.
14. Belle de Bordeaux and Gloire de Bordeaux.
15. Elise Sauvage and L'Enfant Trouvè.
16. Madame Denis and Madame Maurin.
17. Niphetos and Mathilde.
18. Fortune's Yellow and Beauty of Glazenwood.

Following the publication of this list an attempt was made through the medium of the *Journal of Horticulture* to obtain the collective opinion of all the most prominent Amateurs and Nurserymen on the subject, and with the following results:–

General Returns – *Hybrid Perpetuals*

1. Mrs. Baker and Villaret de Joyeuse.
2. Baronne de Maynard and Boule de Neige.

3. Madam Hunnebelle and Mrs. Veitch.
4. Mrs. Bellenden Kerr and Mdlle. Bonnaire.
5. Lord Beaconsfield (Bennett) and Leopold Premier.
6. Duchesse de Caylus and Penelope Mayo.
7. Princess Christian and Virgil.
8. Dupuy Jamain and Auguste Rigotard.
9. Antoine Ducher, Marie Louise Pernet, and Mad. Ed. Pynaert.
10. Senateur Vaisse Avocat Duvivier.
11. La Reine and Alice Durean.
12. President Thiers and Souvenir d'Adolphe Thiers.
13. Sultan of Zanzibar and Duke of Edinburgh.
14. Madame C. Crapelet and Beauty of Waltham.
15. Jules Margottin and Madame Louise Levêque.
16. Comte de Nanteuil and Marquise de Lignières.
17. Camille de Rohan and Edouard Dufour.
18. Pierre Notting and Velours Pourpré.
19. Madame C. Crapelet and Madame Hugard.
20. Prince Arthur and Triomphe de Caen.
21. Reynolds Hole and Sultan of Zanzibar.
22. Marguerite de St. Amand and Duchess of Edinburgh (Bennett).
23. Marie Baumann and Alfred Colomb.
24. Fisher Holmes and Duke of Wellington.
25. Comtesse d'Oxford and Hippolyte Jamain.
26. Black Prince and Pierre Notting.
27. Princess Mary of Cambridge and Margerite de St. Amand.
28. Fisher Holmes and Duke of Wellington.

Teas

1. Perle de Lyon and Perle des Jardins.
2. Bougère and Clothilde.
3. Devoniensis and Climbing Devoniensis.

4. Madame Trifle, Gloire de Dijon, and Madame Levet.
5. Alba Rosea, Madame Sertot, and Josephine Malton.
6. Niphetos and Mathilde.

It would thus appear that there are in the opinion of some Rose-growers, besides the eighteen given by Mr. Paul, twenty-eight cases of duplicates amongst Hybrid Perpetuals, and five cases of Tea Roses.

It is instructive to note how little these three lists are in accord; in only two or three instances are they unanimous. Nor is this surprising when we consider how vastly Roses vary in appearance according to the soil and treatment they receive, for instance, in Lower Bengal Antoine Mouton and Paul Neron are thoroughly distinct in every point, but grown in the richer soil of the North-West Provinces, they can scarcely be distinguished from each other.

Chapter XXVIII
Roses in Towns

Cultivators of Roses in large towns have difficulties to contend with, of which those resident in rural districts know little or nothing. It is to the growers in such towns, and under such adverse circumstances, that we now tender a little advice. The first and most important thing is to make a selection of such varieties as resist to a great extent smoke and impure air, and these will be found to be kinds having hardy constitutions and glossy foliage such as the following :–

Paul Neron	Climbing Devoniensis
Dupuy Jamain	Belle Lyonnaise
Cheshunt Hybrid	Dr. Andry
Gloire de Dijon	Alfred Colomb
Auguste Rigotard	Baronne Maynard
John Hopper	Boule de Niege
Madame Victor Verdier	La France
______ Berard	Charles Lefebvre
______ Clemence Joigneaux	Countess of Roseberry
______ Hippolyte Jamain	______ of Oxford
Mdlle. Marie Finger	John Stuart Mill
Mdlle. Annie wood	Marquis de Castellane
Etienne Levet	Victor Verdier
Jules Margottin	Senateur Vaisse
Francois Michelon	Star of Waltham
Reynolds Hole	General Jacqueminot
Duke of Edibnburgh	Celine Forestier

Many more names may of course be added to this list, but those given will be sufficient to indicate the class of Roses most likely to succeed under the circumstances named. With such good town Roses as these to choose from why select delicate growers, which require all the care and attention which a more open country affords, to be satisfactory, and which if planted in towns only too frequently lead to disappointment ? Amongst those which will not thrive in towns are Horace Vernet, Madame Furtado, Hippolyte Flandrin, Mdlle. Eugénie Verdier, Duc de Rohan, Thorin, Lord Macaulay, Madame Nomen, Xavier Olibo, Monsieur E. Y. Teas and Marie Baumann. From this it will be seen that some fine acquisitions in the way of Roses are unfit for town growers; indeed, Roses with rough leaves and delicate constitutions cannot thrive in the atmosphere of our large towns. Thick non-porous leaves are not easily injured by smoke and dust, which they throw off more readily when washed by rain than those just named. We should however in all cases recommend syringing or sponging frequently during the growing season, for we need scarcely say that plants cannot thrive when covered with dust and dirt.

Rose Growers' Calendar

According to time honored custom all Calendars are presumed to begin with the New Year, but I think, in the present instance, we may break through this rule and commence with the month of September which may be considered as the commencement of the Rosarian's year, for it is on the preliminary work now taken in hand that future success depends.

New Plantations

Where it is intended to make fresh plantations of Roses, advantage should be taken of the first favourable break in the weather to get the ground in order. When the soil is naturally adapted for Roses, little preparation will be necessary except to trench it to a depth of at least two feet, adding a good layer of old cow manure, or, better still, horse and cow manure in equal proportions, and incorporating it thoroughly with the soil. Roses more than most deciduous plants are affected by the nature of the soil in which they grow, and to those - and there are many – who think more of Roses than all other flowers put together, it is a matter of extreme disappointment, after having procured a collection, to find that they gradually dwindle away. Light sandy soils do not grow Roses in anything like the way in which they grow in strong heavy loam, and on such it is simply a waste of time and expense to attempt their cultivation, unless means be taken to add to the natural soil in sufficient quantities that in which it is deficient. A few words on what may be done to render such soils as I have mentioned suitable for them, may not be out of place. First I must observe that in this, as in other gardening operations, it is much better to do all that is attempted thoroughly than to hazard the result by half measures; consequently it will in all cases be better to limit the extent of ground that is to be prepared, than to extend the space further than the available material will render suitable. Wher good heavy loam, almost approaching a clayey nature, (that is containing little or no sand) can be had in quantities so as to lay it on to the light soil to the extent of one foot in thickness, this will be the best addition, digging it in with about an equal depth of the land to which it has been added. Put on six inches of good rotten manure, digging the whole over so as not only to incorporate the manure with the soil, but, as far as possible, to mix the heavy land with the light. It may then be left to lay for about a couple of months, say till the end of October, when it should be turned over two or three times at intervals of a few days to render it in a good condition for planting. On the other hand, should the ground selected be of a very tenacious character, the first thing to be done is to drain it well, four feet deep, with a good fall. When water stagnates round the roots of plants they cannot receive the air which is essential to their health. Trench the ground and make it as porous and friable as possible. Burnt clay, lime, or vegetable matter, will considerably alter its texture and improve its quality. We have found burnt clay to be most advantageous. The application of this renders the soil less compact, less tenacious, and less retentive of moisture.

Soil for Pot Roses

Where Pot Roses are grown, no time should now be lost in preparing suitable compost for them, into which they may be shifted at the end of October or early in November. Composts prepared a considerable time before they are required for use are always better than those that are mixed just before being used.

Pruning

Firminger and many other Indian authorities recommended this month as the best time for a general pruning of Rose-trees. With all due respect for their opinions, I, certainly advise my readers to defer the operation till much later on in the season : my reasons for doing so are given in Chapter Eight.

October

To most Rosarians this is an interesting and yet an anxious time – interesting because it brings us once more into active work among our Roses – and an anxious time, because, no matter how carefully we lay our plans, unpropitious weather may overtake us and cause sad havoc among our plants, that is if we have commenced the more important work of the year. I remember a few years since having opened out the roots of a fine bed of hybrid perpetuals, and after they had been exposed for nearly a week, we had a night's continuous rain, how I longed then for an umbrella large enough to protect that unfortunate bed, but it was of no avail, and I had to patiently await the break of day before I could visit the scene of slaughter, and a slaughter it was with a vengeance. Out of nearly 400 plants less than 50 of them retained a perpendicular position; the rest lay in heaps around, most of them just hanging to the soil by a few roots. At first sight it appeared that the only remedy for the disaster would to remove the old trees and plant the ground afresh with young stock as soon as it was sufficiently dry; this, however, would be such a terrible sacrifice, that I determined to see what could be done to prevent it. We set to work and staked all the plants as firmly as possible, and by nightfall every one had been got into an upright position again. Rainy weather continued for nearly a week, but the plants bore it without flinching, although for the greater part of that time they had almost a foot of water covering their roots. As soon as the weather became more settled, our hot October sun soon told on them, and in less than a week almost every tree was as leafless as in an English winter. This looked serious certainly, but still I persevered, and allowed the plants to remain with their roots uncovered for nearly six weeks; they were then liberally manured, purned back as closely as possible and flooded.

The result of the rough treatment they had received astonished everyone; they broke into growth with surprising vigour, and produced such blooms as I have never possessed before or since, carrying off the highest honours for the best stands of 24 and 12 varieties at our local show the following February.

Artificial Hibernating

In this country, or at least in the plains, where the temperature does not sink sufficiently low to insure for the Rose a natural season of rest, and thereby secure a thorough ripening of the previous seasons' growth, we are obliged to adopt artificial means to attain this end, and it is for this object that we remove soil from the roots and expose them for a lengthened period, heat and drought being made to answer the puıpose that cold naturally effects under other circumstances. The time for commencing this operation will of course depend upon the season selected for pruning. It may be taken in hand immediately on the cessation of the rains, continued all through October, and occasionally even up to the middle of November. Plants opened immediately after the rains require longer exposure than those operated on later, – for this reason, that the soil then contains more moisture and the plants more sap; for these, 20 to 30 days will genereally be sufficient, and later on 12 to 15 days will be ample. After exposing for the time mentioned, pruning must be taken in hand, and immediately after pruning manure must be applied, the roots properly closed up, copiously watered, and the whole surface of the beds dug over.

Pruning

As regards the best time to prune Roses, there are many things to be considered. In low, damp situations it is a mistake to prune too early, as the wood that the plants make will always be weak and result in a poor display of flowers. Those who have a considerable number will do well to prune a portion at different times – say some at the middle of October, another portion ten days later, and another at a similar interval. Not only are the chances of fine flowers much increased by this, but there will be a longer succession of bloom.

The time being fixed, the question arises how shall we best perform the operation? Not, as I have frequently noticed – by cutting all sorts down alike. No, pruning must be done in accordance with the forms of growth and the flowering habits of each variety. For Marie Baumaun, Louis Van Houtte, Lord Macaulay, Xavier Olibo,

Senateur Vaisse, La France, Monsieur E.Y. Teas, Alfred Colomb, A.K. Williams, Duke of Welling on, Dr. Andry, Beauty of Waltham, Baroness Rothschild and Marquis de Castellane severe pruning is necessary to insure free, well built blooms; and for those who prefer this class of flowers to those of an inferior type, but in greater quantity, I should recommend that they be pruned back to say five or six eyes from the base of the young shoots, never forgetting to cut away all thin and weakly wood.

To prune the following varieties in the same way would be to court failure. Being of stronger growth, and not so floriferous, I would suggest that they be left with from eight to ten eyes from the base of the shoots. Among Roses of this class are to be founa the following : – Mme. Clemence Joigneaux, Madame Lacharme, Madame Hippolyte Jamain, Paul Neron, Paul Verdier, Auguste Rigotard, Madame Gabriel Luizet, Francois Michelon, Duke of Edinburgh, Baron de Bonstetin, Edouard Morel, Abel Carriere, Madame Sophie Fropot, John Hopper, John Stuart Mill, and Mdlle. Annie Wood. Some of the above, and indeed many of the stronger growing varieties of the Hybrid-Perpetual class, are not unfrequently used as pillar Roses with success. When they are used as such, they may be treated the same as climbers properly so called, pruning sparingly, taking out worthless shoots, shortening those left only at the extremities.

A celebrated English Rosarian says that the highest art in pruning Roses may be said to be reached when we cut them at the best time to ensure the development of the best flowering and best placed shoots. But, alas these are by no means always, nor often, found together. The best flowers might often be produced from the buds on the extremities of the shoots; but were these chosen the symmetry of the tree and a succession of good flowers within a reasonable space might both be rendered impossible. Thus we must prune, not only for the immediate future, but for succeeding years as well.

The mode and extent of pruning must vary widely with the Rose pruned and the objects of the cultivator. In general terms Roses may be said to be pruned to keep them within bounds, to improve the quality of their flowers, to preserve the form or vigour of the trees, and to remove weak, useless, or dead wood.

Keeping Roses within Bounds

Many of these would grow themselves almost out of the garden were they not pruned, for not a few Roses are giants. These would overrun others, and speedily grow out of all resonable bounds were they not restrained by the knife. Even more moderate-growing Roses may make several feet of wood a year, and need restraint unless only a few are to be grown in any one garden. No doubt there is a strong tendency to plant Roses too closely together, and not a few gardens would look richer and better with fewer Roses allowed to grow larger than with a crowd of smaller Roses always threatening each other. But while the present modes of growing Roses continue, a considerable amount of pruning will be needed to keep each in its place, and in due proportion to others.

Pruning to Improve the Quality of Rose Blooms

On most Rose shoots there are probably from six to a dozen in embryo. Were all these allowed to grow, the blooms must necessarily be smaller than if only one or two of them were allowed to develop into flowers. Pruning, in so far as it reduces the number of flowers, concentrates the force of the plant, and thus heightens the colour and enlarges the size of the Roses. This is so obvious as to need no proof. In Europe the shoots of summer Roses, such as the Cabbage and Moss, are spurred back to two or three buds, or even less. Each of these produce one or more flowers of higher quality than if the entire shoot were left intack. The same principle is kept in view in the pruning of other Roses though in some varieties feet or even yards of young wood may be left instead of eights or quarters of an inch.

Pruning for Form and Vigour

This is absolutely necessary in gardens, shrubberies, and in the case of isolated Roses on turf; the more the trees or bushes are left to themselves to wander freely as they list, the more artistic and beautiful the effect. But generally in gardens, Roses must be pruned into form and kept in shape afterwards by the knife. No doubt many of them are over-pruned, all the grace and not a little of the beauty is cut out of them. Still, it need not be so. Pruning may be made to heighten beauty as well as to mar it. And then we prune for vigour as well as form. By cutting out exhausted branches we cause young and more vigorous ones to spring forth from their base, and thus force the Rose to renew its youth at the point of the knife.

Removal of Weakly, Worthless, Unsightly and Dead Wood

No one can object to this sort of pruning, as it at once improves the appearance and the health of our Roses. Few things are more unsightly than weakly, worthless, or dying branches among Roses, and all such should be carefully removed at the annual pruning. The plants being almost leafless, every imperfect part can be the better seen. In fact, Roses carefully pruned every year should never show such imperfections. As soon as a branch fails it should be pruned out before it becomes diseased. Treated thus the very weaknesses of Roses become tributary to their strength, for though new Roses do not spring from the ashes of dead ones, yet will fresh strong shoots leap forth from the base of weakly ones promptly removed at the annual pruning.

Pot Roses

Towards the end of this month these will require attention, for full particulars regarding their treatment in Chapter Nine.

November

Planting Roses

Where ground has been prepared select as early as possible plants to form new beds and to make up blanks in last season's plantations. In the case of worn-out beds remove their contents, trench the ground, working into it some good loam and rotten manure, and start afresh with young plants. In planting, thoroughly spread out the roots, well working the soil in between their fibres and where the soil is naturally heavy, use budded or grafted plants which always do best in such soils, and especially if the ground be wet, place some friable garden soil over the roots.

When planting, all tap-roots should be removed, and any roots of great length shortened. Roses are frequently planted much deeper than is necessary – in many cases to save the trouble of staking. They should be planted just deep enough to be firm in the soil. After planting cover the surface over with a stratum of manure; this serves to retain a greater degree of moisture in the soil by preventing evaporation, and also acts as a reserve store of food for the plants. Liquid manure is also very beneficial, but let the reader remember the true rule of application, namely, weak and often. Bones are largely used by cultivators, and we have a very high admiration of bones as a manure. Nevertheless bones are not the manure for Roses, and the same may be said of Guano; its influence is quickly evident in size, brightness of foliage, but the flowers, so far as our experience goes, derive no advantage, and even on the leaf the effect is transitory. After careful experiments with various manures, such as Bones, Guano, Blood, Poudrette, Linseed cake, Mustard cake, (*khüllee*), and several artificial preparations, we have found nothing so effectual in promoting the Roses' health and beauty as a liberal dressing of very old cow manure and horse manure mixed in equal proportion.

Avoid if possible all fantastic forms in the designs for Rose beds as they are difficult to fill in with plants, that is, to produce a good effect; perhaps the most effective means of arranging Roses so as to bring the largest number under the eye at once, is to plant a broad border on either side of a walk, with tall growing varieties such as Noisettes at the back followed by strong growing Hybrid. Perpetuals, next dwarfs, and those nearest the margin of the walks pegged down. One of the finest effects I have ever seen produced by Roses was the result of planting in this way. It was in the case of a walk some 9ft. or 10ft. wide, and about 350ft. in length, with 3-ft. Grass margins, flanked right and left by borders that admitted five rows of plants in each. The front rows were planted 3ft. from the Grass, and 3ft. 6in. asunder; the kinds used in these front rows consisted mostly of Teas, with some Noisettes and a few Moss varieties, all on their own roots, and they are kept pegged down close to the ground each year when pruned. A space of 4ft. intervened between these and the next row, which consisted one-half of Teas and Noisettes; the other half were Hybrid Perpetuals. These, also, were all on their own roots, and were allowed to grow in bush fashion sufficiently limited in size so as to rise gradually higher than the inner rows; in this second row the plants stood 4ft. apart. The third row, which consisted of half-standards, were one-half Hybrid Perpetuals, the other half Noisette and Bourbon Hybrids. The fourth row on each side was composed of full-sized standards, mostly dark-coloured Hybrid Perpetuals, with some strong growing, light-coloured Noisettes and a few Gloire de Dijon. These stood 5 ft. behind the preceding row, and the same distance apart in the row. At 6 ft. behind these was a row of pillar plants trained to strong iron supports 9 ft. high, with a stout wire attached to the top of each, and allowd to dip in the middle between the uprights in the usual festoon fashion. The kinds employed in this row were such as are generally used for similar purposes, and comprised the strongest-growing. Hybrid Perpetuals with a climbing habit, Noisettes, Boursaults, and Ayrshire. These were not kept trained any closer than was necessary to prevent their being blown loose from the ironwork that upheld them. At a distance of some 9 ft. on the north side was a dense bank of shrubs sufficiently high to act as a background to the whole in a way that brought out the full effect of the blooms when in perfection, and served as a protection without too much confinement, a matter of such importance in the case of Roses that it should never be lost sight of. On the southern side at the bank was a row of Hollies.

Arrangement of Rose Borders

To avoid the too even formal descent from back to front in the case of the Roses that would otherwise have occurred, there were introduced into each of the three front rows on both sides at intervals a few taller plants that broke up the surface without any appreciable interference with a sight of the whole when in flower. The walk and borders slightly diverged from a direct line which still further tended to prevent the formality inseparable from straight lines of plants running parallel with each other. The colours were so arranged so as to secure much the greater proportion of light kinds on the front rows with a preponderance of darker shades at the back, but the rows furthest from the eye were sufficiently broken up by light kinds to do away with the objectionable effect often produced by continuous straight lines of any particular colour, as seen in ordinary modern floral arrangements. The walk was spanned at each end by a light broad arch of wire-work, and three others of similar character were placed at intervals between these, covered with Roses, which still further helped to break up any appearance of formality. The whole arrangement was very much superior to that of the Rose gardens often introduced in too much exposed places, where the plants on pillars and arches are too frequently seen struggling for existence against the adverse influences of wind, unbroken by any surrounding objects, yet, as is well known to all who have had only limited experience in Rose growing, they cannot bear to be much confined; still, on the other hand, they do not succeed when trained to any height if too much exposed.

Pruning Roses

Where Roses are yet unpruned the work should be done at once; those who have acted on the wise plan of deferring the pruning of a considerable portion of their plants until a later than that chosen by the generality of growers, will reap the advantage of their delay in seeing their plants break right off into growth, and bloom frequently before those that had been pruned perhaps a month earlier.

December

Examine all Roses and pick off any insects that may be damaging the young shoots; caterpillars will frequently be found to be very destructive at this season, and if we are favoured with changeable weather this will frequently bring on blight, which in many parts is very destructive to Roses. The foliage of many of the tender leaved varieties is frequently much injured by this disease, therefore every means should be used to restore it to health and vigour, such as administering liquid manure, to which soot has been added, to the plants. Soot used in this way is one of the best manures we have for Roses; where blight has set in, syringe the plants well with a weak solution of soap-suds, or soot and sulphur, in order to stop it. I have found soot used with soap-suds syringed on the trees on the evening, and washed off in the morning, to have restored trees to health, that have shown themselves to be much blighted and the leaves all crumpled up. Train in young growths of climbing Roses, pyramids &c., so as to keep them in shape; if the young wood be allowed to ramble too much it hides the bloom and thus impairs the effect that the plants would otherwise have.

Staking Roses

If not already done all climbing and pillar Roses should be gone over, and where any broken or doubtful stakes exist they should be removed. The whole stock ought to be retied every season, and for this there is nothing better than good tar twine, not low priced inferior material that will give way on the first strain. The larger the heads the stoouter the supports should be, as will be obvious from the greater hold the wind has on them.

Labelling

Rose growers generally know most of the varieties they grow by the wood and leaves even when not in flower, nevertheless in every well appointed garden each plant should be named, or half the pleasure derivable from seeing them when in flower is lost by those who are equally fond of Roses but who do not know so much about them; consequently all that require it should have fresh labels attached to them. For ordinary cultivators I have found nothing better or neater in appearance than zinc labels written on with indelible ink.

Grafting

Where grafting on the *Rosa gigantea* stock is adopted as the method for propagating, no time should now be lost in commencing opeations : select strong half ripened wood and secure the stocks as nearly as possible of the same size and age as the shoots to be grafted.

January

Watering

Roses should now be growing freely, and to induce the production of vigorous flowering wood the plants must be kept liberally supplied with water. Rich manures are of no value to the plants without a sufficient supply of moisture to render it in a fit state to be absorbed by the plants. By liberal watering I do not mean a daily sprinkling with a watering can; this frequently does more harm than good, rendering the soil so hard as to make the admission of air to the roots of the plants, which is so essential to their existence, almost impossible. A drenching of half a dozen gallons applied once a week to each plant, will do ten times as much good as if it were supplied at the rate of a gallon a day.

Insects

The Rose maggot is very active at this season, and where there is a large collection it must be looked over every day. Destroy the maggots with as little injury as possible to the Roses. Suckers are now making vigorous growth to the sad detriment of the trees; work underground and cut the sucker where it unites with the roots or underground stem. Destroy green-fly as soon as it appears.

Pot Roses

The plants at this season must be carefully watered, never letting them get too dry, as the roots under this system of culture are continually at work, but still so much must not be given as will produce anything like a saturated condition of the soil, – a result which will follow if water be applied in nearly the same quantity necessary in the hot season when independent of what the plants absorb, the drying powers of the sun and air are so much greater. Under this system of Rose growing, with a number of plants, many that make more vigorous progress than the others will require potting at times apart from those at which the general collection are thus attended to, and at whatever time in the year a plant gives evidence of needing more root room I should recommend a shift being given. It will usually be found that these specimens that are thus treated apart from the rest are the ones that do the most to keep up a succession of flowers. Roses that are kept on growing in this way will from time to time, as they gain strength, throw up stout sucker shoots from the bottom. It is from these that the largest number and finest flowers are produced, and to make room for them, the weak small shoots that do not appear inclined for further development should by degrees be cut away, not going through the whole collection at once but a few at a time. This treatment will be found to favour the having always some in flower, better than subjecting all the plants to similar treatment at stated intervals. Again, where flowers are thus continuously wanted from a somewhat limited space, the plants must not be allowed to get too large, for though such will afford an abundance for a time, still they will not keep on like a larger number of smaller plants. Plants may be kept within bounds without actually heading them down at any one time but by progressive reduction of the weakest shoots, for, as will easily be understood, the result required under this system of cultivation are of a continuous character and quite different from that which aims at a blaze of bloom during any given time.

Grafting

If not taken in hand last month should now be pushed ahead as fast as possible; if the wood is fully matured before being worked, the union is rarely so satisfactory as when the growth is in a more succulent state.

February

We now come to the month for Roses in India when we may hope to receive the reward of our arduous and anxious labours of the previous season, labours which at times seem never ending, and according to the ideas of those possessing no knowledge of a true Rosarian's love, always apparently ill required. And yet how fully are we repaid when on some January or February morning we stroll among our Roses and behold them a thing of beauty and a joy for ever. A well built bloom of A.K. Williams, Marie Baumann or it may be the equally fine form of Senateur Vaise or Xavier Olibo at once banishes all our murmurings and inspires us with further and fuller zeal. Being the time of Roses it is also the time of

Rose Shows

And I trust that among my readers will be many aspirants for fame who are anxious to enter the list and fight once more the "Wars of the Roses." The following instructions as to the way in which Roses should be shown will probably prove useful to those who are exhibiting for the first time. The blooms should be exhibited in boxes, the stem of the blooms being placed in tubes filled with water, the tubes being imbedded in moss, the smoothest and freshest of which should form an emerald surface to display the blooms to the greatest advantage. Each bloom should be cut with as much foliage attached to the stems as possible, but no leaves must be added. If the blooms are cut on the morning of the show, they should be secured early and before the dew has evaporated from their petals. The moss in the box must be moist, and the blooms should be arranged so as to stand a few inches above it. Many new beginners spoil their boxes by pressing the blooms close down on the moss. The boxes should have lids which, especially on a sunny morning, must be kept over the blooms until the last possible moment before the judges enter the show. We have known many prizes lost and Roses spoiled by the blooms being exposed too early and too long. The boxes should be 18 inches wide, 6 inches high at the back, and 4 inches in the front. The length of the boxes should be, for twenty four Roses, 4 feet; eighteen Roses 3 feet; twelve Roses, 2 feet 2 inches; and six Roses, 1 foot 6 inches; the covers being 7 ½ inches in depth at the back, and 5 inches in front, 4 feet 1 inch in length, 1 foot 7 inches in breadth, and having a narrow beading within the four sides, half an inch from the bottom of the lid, overlap the boxes, having ample room for the Roses, and are secured for travelling by stout leather straps. So much for showing the Roses to the best advantage, let me now add a few words of advice to exhibitors from the pen of that excellent Rosarian, Mr. D.T. Fish. "I have carefully read all that Canon Hole says of the delights of Rose showing. But in the effort to keep the Roses cool and fresh not a few of their growers get hot and excited; and Rosarians seldom show to less advantage than in the show tents after the awards. On the entrance to every Rose tent it might be wise to write,"Greater is he that ruleth his spirit than he that taketh a city" or any number of firsts. The self-command and self-possession are as much needed by the victor as the vanquished. Silence best becomes both for a season, until success can be enjoyed with meekness, and defeat with patient continuance in well-doing. Prepared for either defeat or victory, their only anxiety being that the best Roses should win, of which there is really little doubt; and it is for this purpose that Rose shows are held. The more the Roses are seen and the less the Rosarians are seen and heard of, the better. Occasionally we see exhibitors so proud of their own products that they post themselves in front of them, thus hindering the public from seeing and admiring their merits. Could the Rose speak they would address their owners in the sense of the philosopher who, pestered by the offer of service from his sovereign, replied, "Yes, sir, you can render me a great service; stand aside that I may see the light." Would also that our Rose tents could be less crowded and more silent. The crowd is unavoidable; it is the highest complement that can be paid to the popularity and beauty of the Rose; but the talking might be subdued by good taste. A Rose show is an exhibition of the highest art of which Nature is capable. The effect of art is to inspire silence in those who can appreciate it. We have only to visit the National Gallery, Louvre, or any other great collection of paintings to feel this. The sight of such exquisite art inspire silent, reverend absorption and admiration. Nothing is so annoying in the presence of the grand or the beautiful as the irrepressible chatter of thoughtless ignorance. It is just so in Rose show. Absorbed in such matchless displays of many formed, many coloured beauty, one passes their most intimate friends unnoticed; and they ought to be allowed to do so. Thus absorbed and enraptured, the beauty and sweetness of the Rose sink as it were into our very souls. Some Rose shows I have seen live for ever not only as sunny picutres in the memory, but as sources of wisdom, strength, comfort, gladsomeness to my head and heart. Amid the Roses that thus live for ever, there also spring up visions of faces, hands, and hearts, gentle, firm, true, that once met among the Roses, are forgotten never. But what of the blank. Only this, that the true Rosarian never despairs. Roses, however, like all else, come and go past recovery; and the new though sometimes better, never really can fill the places of the old, but yet the new are welcome, and the oldest stagers genrally give the new Roses and exhibitors the heartiest welcome.

Budding

Where budding is the favourite method of propagation it may be successfully carried on during the present month. The cuttings of Rose Edouard that are used as stocks should be well rooted, and the buds should be inserted as near the ground line as possible.

March

Roses in Pots

These will now require careful attention, especially in being regularly supplied with water; large plants that have done flowering, should be cut slightly back, removing entirely all weak and exhausted wood; small plants are however best left unpruned, and should be encouraged to make a good growth and therby lay a good foundation for next season's success.

Budding

This may still be carried on in the North-West, but in Lower Bengal the weather will have become too warm for the bark to rise freely. Buds inserted last month should now have their ligatures loosened.

Layering

The present is a good time to layer Roses; select for this purpose strong, half ripened wood. Full instructions regarding this method of propagation are given at page 40.

Grafting

Plants grafted on the *gigantea* stock should now be ready for removal; they should be planted at once into their permanent quarters if the ground has been previously prepared for them; care must be taken that the point of union is placed well below the ground level after seeing that the stock has been carefully disbudded. Plantations of Roses made during this month grow almost as freely as those planted in November, provided proper attention is given to their being liberally supplied with water till well established.

April, May and June

During this season little can be done in our Rose gardens beyond keeping them in good order, turning the surface over at regular intervals and giving liberal supplies of water; this is a point that is frequently neglected in many gardens at this period, some people seem to imagine that it is necessary to treat the Rose with proper respect or care only up to its blooming period, and that, when this is over, the plants may be left to take care of themselves. I do not know a more fallacious idea, from my own experience I should say that the success or failure of the next season's operations depend mainly on the treatment the plants receive at this season. It is no uncommon case for plants to remain during these three months without receiving a drop of water : what must be the result of such treatment? Simply this, that the wood produced is weak and stunted, and by the time the rainy season sets in, the plants are so debilitated as to be unable to absorb such a superabundant supply of moisture, and as a consequence frequently succumb entirely, or else the young unripened shoots die back to the previous season's growth. We frequently hear complaints of Rose plants dying off during the rainy season, and in nine cases out of ten this has been casued by neglect similar to that described above. On the other hand plants treated rationally, that is encouraged to make a free vigorous growth at this season, are rarely if ever affected by climatic influences.

July

Our rainy season should new be in full swing and care should be taken to disturb the surface of our Rose beds as little as possible, the firmer the surface the better will the excess water be carried off; weeds however must be kept in check, but this is easily done by hand, that is where proper attention has been given previously to the careful cleaning of the soil.

Layers

Layers put down in February and March should now be ready for removal; take up with a good ball of earth attached, and either plant in pots or place in their permanent quarters at once.

Budding

May be taken in hand any time during this month in the North-West Provinces.

August

Budding

Budding on Rose Edouard as a stock may now be carried on successfully in Lower Bengal, as the bark rises more freely than at any other season of the year. Full instructions on this subject are given in Chapter III.

Cuttings

Of most varieties of Tea Roses strike freely if put down during this month, they do best in a mixture of three parts sand and one part charcoal, and should be kept in a close frame or under shelter.

Index

F

G

H

I

L

M

N